Oracle E-Business Suite R12.x HRMS – A Functionality Guide

Design, implement, and build an entire end-to-end HR management infrastructure with Oracle E-Business Suite

Pravin S. Ingawale

[PACKT] PUBLISHING enterprise professional expertise distilled

BIRMINGHAM - MUMBAI

Oracle E-Business Suite R12.x HRMS – A Functionality Guide

First published: June 2015

Production reference: 1180615

Published by Packt Publishing Ltd.
Livery Place
35 Livery Street
Birmingham B3 2PB, UK.

ISBN 978-1-78217-738-8

www.packtpub.com

Credits

Author
Pravin S. Ingawale

Reviewers
Brian R. Bouchard
Wei Chung, Low
Hendrik Voges
Paul Graeme Wilkinson
Mitchell Wrobel

Commissioning Editor
Vinay Argekar

Acquisition Editor
Vinay Argekar

Content Development Editor
Parita Khedekar

Technical Editor
Vivek Arora

Copy Editor
Merilyn Pereira

Project Coordinator
Milton Dsouza

Proofreader
Safis Editing

Indexer
Tejal Soni

Graphics
Abhinash Sahu

Production Coordinator
Manu Joseph

Cover Work
Manu Joseph

About the Author

Pravin S. Ingawale is currently working as an Oracle apps HR/Payroll techno-functional consultant and has more than 8 years of experience. He has been involved in end-to-end implementations, more than two of which involved modules such as Core HRMS, Self Service, Payroll, and so on.

His role included conducting CRP with end users, gathering requirements, building the best solution, demonstrating the solution to end users, conducting UAT, and performing a successful Go Live. He is also engaged in post Go Live support, if required.

About the Reviewers

Brian R. Bouchard is a passionate person who enjoys helping others understand the complexities of Oracle Financials applications. He was introduced to Oracle applications back in the '90s when he served as the fixed assets manager at Motorola. Playing an integral role in the implementation and rollout of the application, he decided to change career paths from accountant to consultant. In his consulting career, he has designed, developed, and implemented over 50 full life cycles of Oracle EBS Applications ranging from Release 9 to Release 12.1.3. He has always strived to help others, to find the most efficient ways to perform tasks and utilize the system; these characteristics lead him to develop bolt-on products for Oracle Assets and he opened the doors of his own company in 2006. As President and CEO of Chi-Star Technology SM, he strives to improve the utilization of Oracle Assets and streamline manual efforts by automating some of the most tedious processes of Oracle Assets. Due to his passion to educate people on the complexities of Oracle applications, he has conducted well over 200 training sessions on various applications and releases. In the summer of 2009, he founded the CST Education Network, which was started to offer low-cost education on Oracle Applications via webinars and video training.

He realized the areas of opportunity in Oracle Assets—Asset Transfers and Reconciliation. In April 2006, the introduction of AssetCross® came to the market as a solution to the manual asset transfer procedure. The AssetCross® software will transfer single or multiple assets between corporate depreciation books, transfer full or partial (cost or units) assets, translate transferred amounts to the receiving depreciation book's currency, and maintain an audit trail with the original asset. In June 2008, the introduction of AssetTie® came to the market as a solution to the reconciling Oracle Assets procedure. The AssetTie® software will capture balances from Oracle General Leger and compare them to balances in Oracle Assets and identify variances. The same technology is used to compare the transactions copied from corporate books to the associated tax books. Within seconds of posting a journal entry from Oracle Assets, the user can determine if there are any reconciling differences.

The introduction of AssetCross® and AssetTie® to the business world has revolutionized the asset transfer and reconciling processes. Fortune 500 corporations, as well as mid-sized family-owned companies, can all benefit from this software.

Visit Chi-Star Technology at `http://www.chistartech.com` to learn more about the bolt-on products and the education sessions/training offered.

I would like to acknowledge my family, who have been with me at every step and who have endured the schedule of a business traveler.

Wei Chung, Low is the chief data officer of one of the most remarkable big data programs in Kuala Lumpur, Malaysia. He is also a member of PMI, and has held a PMP certification since 2007. Since then, he has been an MCT Alumni, where he started teaching the Microsoft .NET, SharePoint, SQL Server, and BizTalk technologies.

In the last few years, he has been very focused on platform data integration, big data, mobile development, and cloud hosting. He strongly believes that great system implementation delivers precious value to businesses, and that the integration of various systems across different platforms shall always be a part of it, just like people from different cultures are used to living together nowadays in most major cities, with respect and in harmony.

Hendrik Voges is a seasoned professional with more than 35 years of experience in business and industry to build on. He has gathered a vast amount of experience in business management, management consulting, information systems implementation, human resources management, and development, as well as project management.

In the field of Oracle HRMS, he has a successful track record of project management and as a subject matter expert consulting a number of major Oracle HRMS implementations for large international corporations. In addition to this, he has extensive client-facing experience with other smaller ERP and HRMS applications, some with a client base of over 400 active clients.

His areas of expertise further include organization and people development initiatives and transformation consulting, labor relations negotiations and conflict resolution, project management, and human resources information systems implementation.

He was a key player in a wide range of engagements focusing on organization restructuring, business function transformation, organization redesign and organization strategic planning, and information systems implementation. He has consulted for clients in the United Arab Emirates, Kuwait, Mozambique, Kenya, Namibia, Sudan, South Africa, Egypt, and India.

His industry sector experience includes manufacturing, public sector, utilities, finance and investment, banking, life insurance, building and construction, agriculture, healthcare, oil and gas exploration, automotive, telecommunications, and defense industries.

Paul Graeme Wilkinson, born in New Zealand, is a chartered accountant. He is a former employee of Price Waterhouse, The Hertz Corporation, and Oracle Corporation. In 1999, he became an independent Oracle consultant specializing in the training manager and delivery roles. He is currently employed at the Ricoh Corporation Plc. as the UPK administrator, configuring the UPK Professional LCMS across 14 European OpCo's and assisting with the creation of over 1,200 e-learning topics across the APRO, Click, Cognos, Dashboard, Docuware, Esparto, Hyperion, Oracle, and Siebel applications. This includes translation into Dutch, Finnish, French, German, Italian, Polish, Spanish, Turkish, and Russian.

He has thoroughly enjoyed reviewing this book. The market needs a book of this nature to link processes to the application.

Mitchell Wrobel is an Oracle certified master DBA and developer. Over his 20-year career as a consultant, he has developed thousands of objects within the many modules that comprise the Oracle E-Business Suite.

Through his company, Application Everything, Inc., he provides one solid solution after another for top companies, governments, and universities across the globe.

I'd like to give special thanks to Jerry King of Biscon Consulting, he is the best mentor and professional big brother a guy could have; my children, Michael and Elizabeth, who are the two reasons that I work so hard at my chosen profession; and Carol Waldron, the most gifted developer I've ever met. For inspiration and guidance, I'd like to thank Andy Blanco, Mark Davison, Kevin McCarthy and John Dean.

Table of Contents

Preface

This book is a functional guide for Oracle Application HRMS R12. This guide will help implementers to design, implement, and deliver an Oracle apps HRMS system for customers.

What this book covers

Chapter 1, Introduction to Oracle Applications E-Business Suite, introduces Oracle EBS and describes the architecture of Oracle apps. Along with the architecture, it will cover various modules that are part of the Oracle HRMS family. In addition to this, it will cover the Multi Org Concept in Oracle Application and an overview of multiple organization structure in HRMS, along with practical examples.

Chapter 2, Oracle Application System Administration, shows you how to create application users, responsibilities, custom menus, request groups, and data groups. You will also learn to create concurrent programs and to attach them to responsibility.

Chapter 3, Fundamentals of Flexfields / Value Sets, explains the basics of flexfields. You will learn to define values sets, key flexfields, and descriptive flexfields.

Chapter 4, Business Group, Locations, and Organizations, covers the concept of work structures in HRMS. You will learn the basics of business groups, organizations, and locations in HRMS.

Chapter 5, Job, Position, Pay Grade, and Payroll, deals with the concept of jobs and positions. It defines a job, position and position hierarchy. It explains the concept of people group and payroll terminologies, such as payment methods, salary basis, and payroll definition.

Chapter 6, Entering People Information, talks about creating a new employee and entering employee data and additional data using DFF and KFF. You will also learn the concept of person type.

Chapter 7, Entering Assignment Information, teaches you about entering assignment information, in which you will study various components of assignments. You will also learn about entering assignment-related information. Then, you will also learn about assignment statuses in Oracle HRMS and entering salary for employees.

Chapter 8, Terminations, teaches you about terminating an employee. You will also learn how to reverse terminate an employee. We will also see how to terminate an assignment rather than an employee.

Chapter 9, Absence Management, covers the basics of absence management in Oracle. You will study the configuration of absences in which you will learn about defining absence types, elements, and so on. You will also learn about entering absences by HR and employees. We will see the important concept of calculation of absence duration.

What you need for this book

The list of software required is as follows:

- Internet Explorer, which can be downloaded from `http://www.microsoft.com`
- Oracle EBS R12 Instance
- Jinitiator 1.3.1.26

Who this book is for

This book is for Oracle Apps HRMS Functional Consultants.

Conventions

In this book, you will find a number of text styles that distinguish between different kinds of information. Here are some examples of these styles and an explanation of their meaning.

Code words in text, database table names, folder names, filenames, file extensions, pathnames, dummy URLs, user input, and Twitter handles are shown as follows: "We had entered value `TEST_1` for the country `SWEDEN` in the value set."

New terms and **important words** are shown in bold. Words that you see on the screen, for example, in menus or dialog boxes, appear in the text like this: "Click on **Segments** to create the segments to be used."

[Warnings or important notes appear in a box like this.]

[Tips and tricks appear like this.]

Reader feedback

Feedback from our readers is always welcome. Let us know what you think about this book—what you liked or disliked. Reader feedback is important for us as it helps us develop titles that you will really get the most out of.

To send us general feedback, simply e-mail `feedback@packtpub.com`, and mention the book's title in the subject of your message.

If there is a topic that you have expertise in and you are interested in either writing or contributing to a book, see our author guide at `www.packtpub.com/authors`.

Customer support

Now that you are the proud owner of a Packt book, we have a number of things to help you to get the most from your purchase.

Downloading the color images of this book

We also provide you with a PDF file that has color images of the screenshots/diagrams used in this book. The color images will help you better understand the changes in the output. You can download this file from `https://www.packtpub.com/sites/default/files/downloads/7388EN_ColoredImages.pdf`.

Errata

Although we have taken every care to ensure the accuracy of our content, mistakes do happen. If you find a mistake in one of our books—maybe a mistake in the text or the code—we would be grateful if you could report this to us. By doing so, you can save other readers from frustration and help us improve subsequent versions of this book. If you find any errata, please report them by visiting `http://www.packtpub.com/submit-errata`, selecting your book, clicking on the **Errata Submission Form** link, and entering the details of your errata. Once your errata are verified, your submission will be accepted and the errata will be uploaded to our website or added to any list of existing errata under the Errata section of that title.

To view the previously submitted errata, go to `https://www.packtpub.com/books/content/support` and enter the name of the book in the search field. The required information will appear under the **Errata** section.

Piracy

Piracy of copyrighted material on the Internet is an ongoing problem across all media. At Packt, we take the protection of our copyright and licenses very seriously. If you come across any illegal copies of our works in any form on the Internet, please provide us with the location address or website name immediately so that we can pursue a remedy.

Please contact us at `copyright@packtpub.com` with a link to the suspected pirated material.

We appreciate your help in protecting our authors and our ability to bring you valuable content.

Questions

If you have a problem with any aspect of this book, you can contact us at `questions@packtpub.com`, and we will do our best to address the problem.

1
Introduction to Oracle Applications E-Business Suite

Oracle E-Business Suite is an Enterprise Resource Planning, which is also abbreviated as ERP. What exactly do we mean by an ERP? The three words themselves describe the meaning of this. You have an Enterprise that is a company, an organization, or even a small start-up. You need manpower to run this enterprise. Hence the word resource. In order to function effectively and efficiently, you need to manage and plan these resources.

In short, you need to plan your resources in your enterprise to meet the objective of your enterprise. Hence, you need an ERP. There are numerous benefits of Oracle E-Business Suite in today's world. Each business today has various aspects, and managing those aspects is, in its own way, very challenging. Almost every enterprise today is dependent on software technology and applications to perform their day-to-day operations.

So in order to provide an integrated solution, Oracle has come up with a unified solution that helps in managing all facets of running a business on a single platform. Oracle E-Business Suite provides this capability. This helps businesses to make better decisions. In addition, it also reduces cost and in turn increases productivity and profits, which is the bottom line for all businesses.

Oracle E-Business Suite has a wide chain of applications as follows:

- Oracle Customer Relationship Management (CRM)
- Oracle Financials
- Oracle Human Resource Management System (HRMS)

- Oracle Logistics
- Oracle Supply Chain Applications
- Oracle Order Management
- Oracle Transportation Management
- Oracle Warehouse Management System

The following diagram is a pictorial representation of the Oracle EBS. In the following diagram, we have various applications across Oracle EBS such as CRM and Human Resource and modules such as self-service, which are used across all the applications of Oracle EBS.

Business Intelligence (**BI**) is the set of techniques and tools for the transformation of raw data into meaningful and useful information for business analysis purposes.

Local and vertical extensions are used in order to integrate, orchestrate, access, and analyze data and processes across applications. Local is within particular applications such as Human Resource, and vertical might be across other applications such as BPEL or other ERPs.

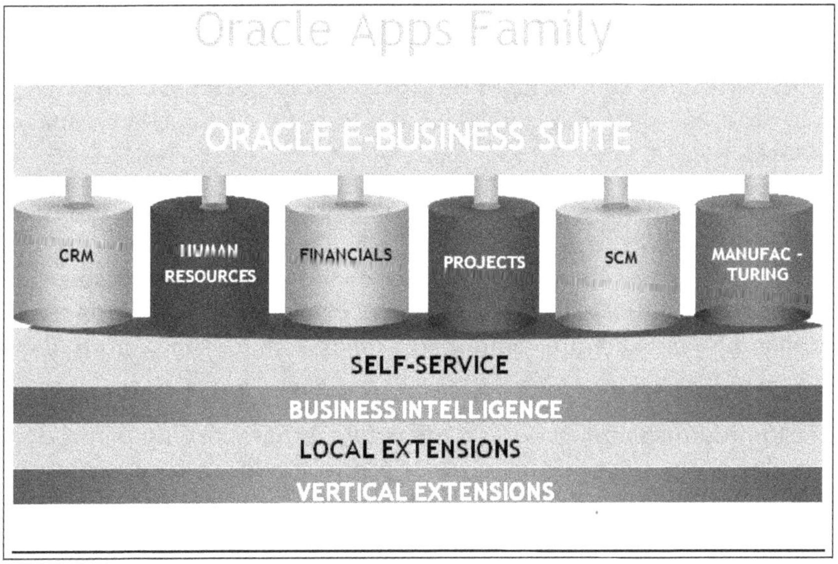

In addition to the preceding applications of E-Business Suites, there are a few other ERPs such as Oracle JD Edwards, Oracle People Soft, and so on, which are provided by Oracle. These also work on similar lines as E-Business Suite and each has their own architecture, as explained in later sections.

Architecture

The following diagram shows the basic architecture of Oracle E-Business Suite:

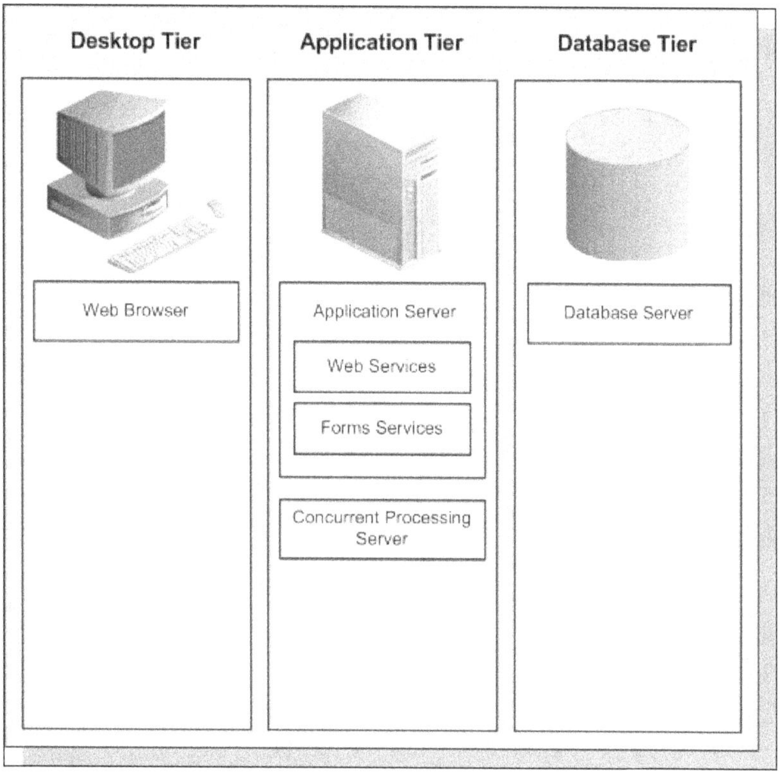

There are basically three tiers in the architecture:

- The desktop tier
- The application tier
- The database tier

The desktop tier

For HTML-based applications, the client interface is provided via HTML. The traditional form-based application used a Java applet in a web browser for client interface. Thus, it supports form-based as well as web-based client interfaces.

There is also an emerging trend of using the Oracle EBS application on mobile phones and hence, various mobile interfaces to use Oracle EBS are coming up in the market which offer an interactive platform for end users.

The following diagram is a form-based desktop tier architecture:

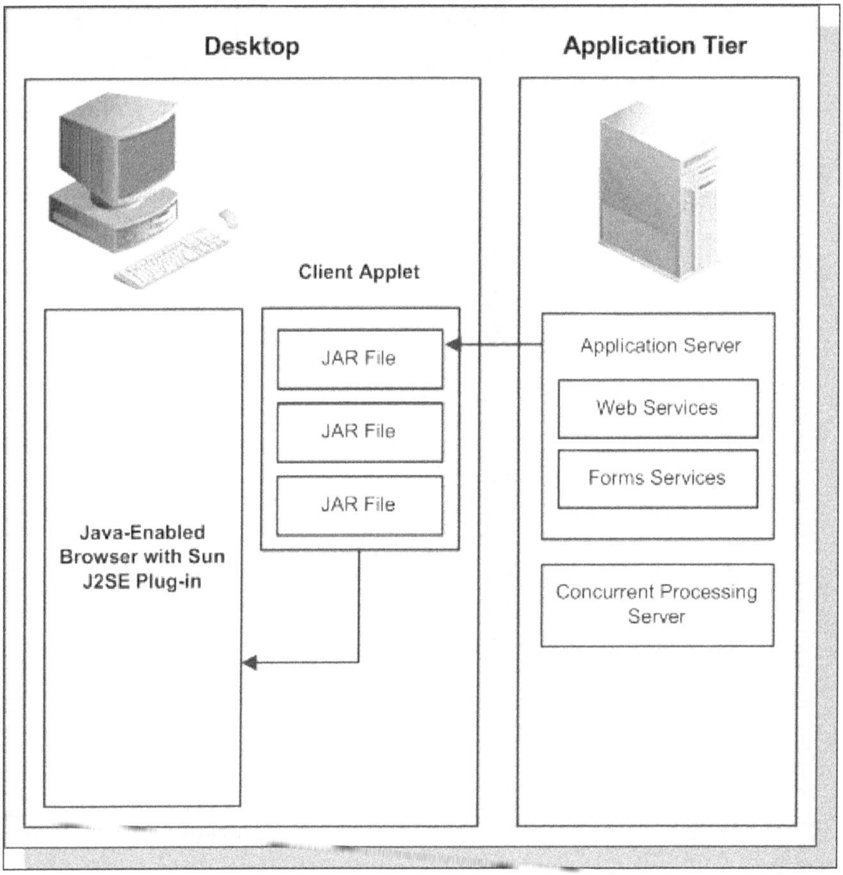

The desktop tier is actually the starting point of accessing the application as seen in the preceding diagram. The Oracle E-Business suite home page is used to log in to the system. This home page can be opened on a desktop client web browser. For all applications, whether web-based, form-based or BI, this home page acts as a single point of access. The following screenshot shows the login page for Oracle applications.

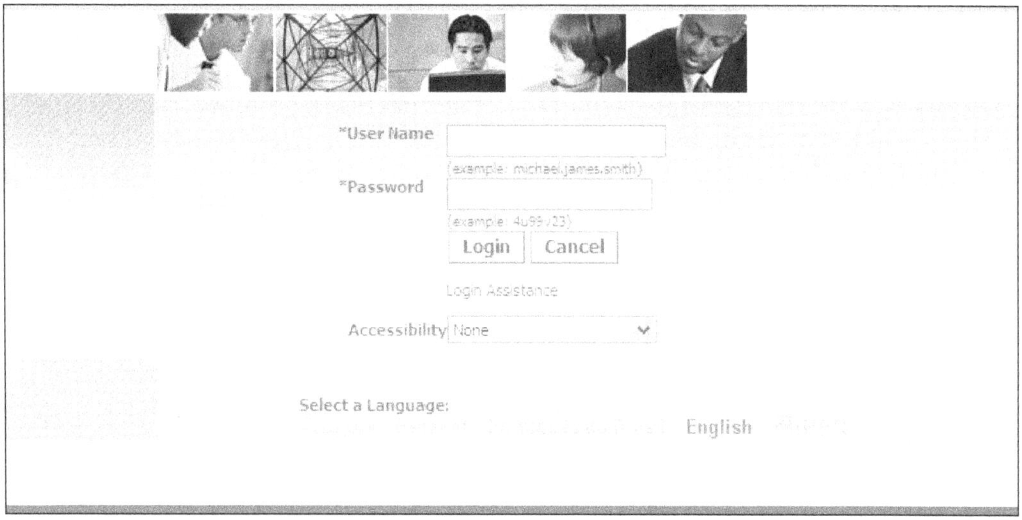

Once you open the home page, it will ask you to enter your username and password. On the login page, there will also be an option to select the preferred language in which you want to use the system. Once you select a language, Oracle will retain this preference as you navigate through the system. This language is set for all the applications you use in the system, whether form-based or web-based.

The application tier

The application tier performs two jobs:

- It acts as a host for servers/service groups. These are used to process business logic.
- Also, it manages the communication between the desktop and the database tier. This tier is also known as the middle tier.

Three servers which form the basic application tier for Oracle E-Business Suite are as follows:

- Web services
- Form services
- Concurrent processing server

The database tier

The Oracle database servers are part of the database tier. It stores all the Oracle E-Business Suite data. The data includes various objects of different types. This file format includes tables, indexes, and other database objects. The database server communicates with the services on the application tier, which in turn acts as mediator between the database and the clients. There is no direct link between the database and clients.

Thus, in the preceding section, you learned the architecture of Oracle apps.

In the next section, we will go into the basics of individual modules that are part of the Oracle EBS HRMS application.

The modules that are part of the Oracle HRMS suite are as follows:

- iRecruitment
- Core HR
- Learning Management
- Performance Management
- Compensation and Benefits
- Payroll
- Time and Labor

iRecruitment

The iRecruitment module deals with the recruiting process in an enterprise. It gives its stakeholders, that is hiring managers, recruitment HRs, and candidates, the ability to manage every phase of searching, recruiting, hiring, and tracking new applicants. These processes are entirely managed via a self-service interface.

The following diagram depicts the recruitment cycle usually followed in an organization. The most important entities in the recruitment process are a vacancy and an applicant. The meaning of vacancy in generic, layman terms is an opening for a job. This opening can be a new position that needs to be filled by the company, or it might be an already existing position that might have become vacant due to a person leaving that position.

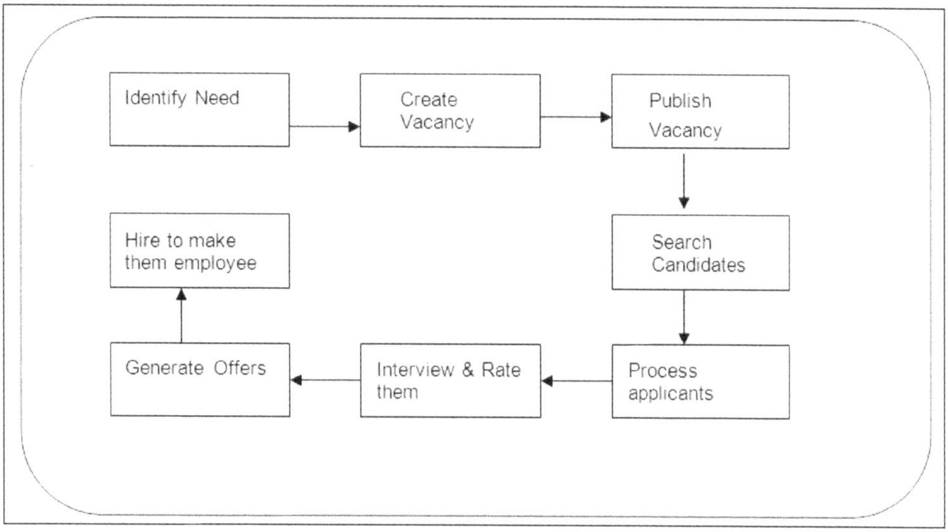

Core HR

The core HR module helps to manage the enterprise's work structures, that is, organization, grades, jobs, positions, and so on. This module is the most important of all the other submodules in HRMS, and also holds true for any other applications in E-Business such as Finance and CRM, as Core HR can be a source of data for other applications.

The work structure represents the different ways in which an employee can work in an organization. This is the framework for defining assignment for an employee. Work structure includes internal organizations (department, divisions, and business entity), payroll, jobs, grade, position, and so on.

The employee data is the most important entity that is captured using core HRMS. Core HRMS has the ability to hold data about current employees, ex-employees, applicants, contacts, and contingent workers.

When I say employee data, it holds information about the employee's organization, grade, position, job, payroll, location, and so on. Thus, we can conclude that core HRMS forms the basis of the Oracle HRMS application.

Unless we have core HR implemented, we will not be in a position to implement other modules of the Oracle HRMS suite.

Learning Management

The Learning Management module helps enterprises manage, deliver, and track training needs in online or classroom-based environments. Employees (learners) can search for the training they need, and take the training in the most appropriate mode. The mode of training can be classroom-based or online-based.

Managers can automate key business processes—from training to training delivery; from performance appraisals to training assessments—and keep tabs on their team's learning and development. Instructors can manage their own classes.

Executives can measure the effectiveness of learning and ensure alignment with organizational objectives. Learning Administrators can manage all the catalog objects, learners, and related resources. The basic process flow is depicted in the following diagram:

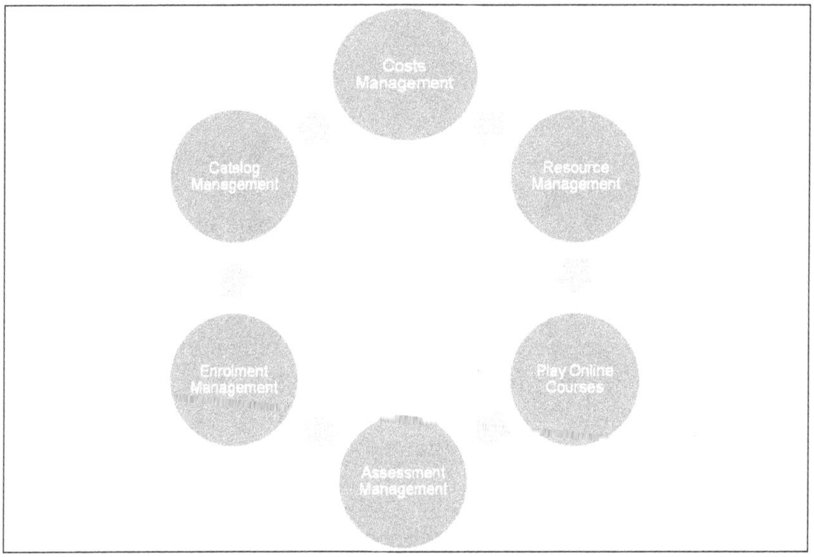

Performance Management

The Performance Management module helps the enterprise manage the performance of employees in an organization. Basically, it deals with the appraisal process in an enterprise. It enables managers as well as employees to manage various appraisal functions such as setting goals, objectives, and so on.

In addition, they can also set up questionnaires for eligible participants. The basic flow for performance management is as shown here:

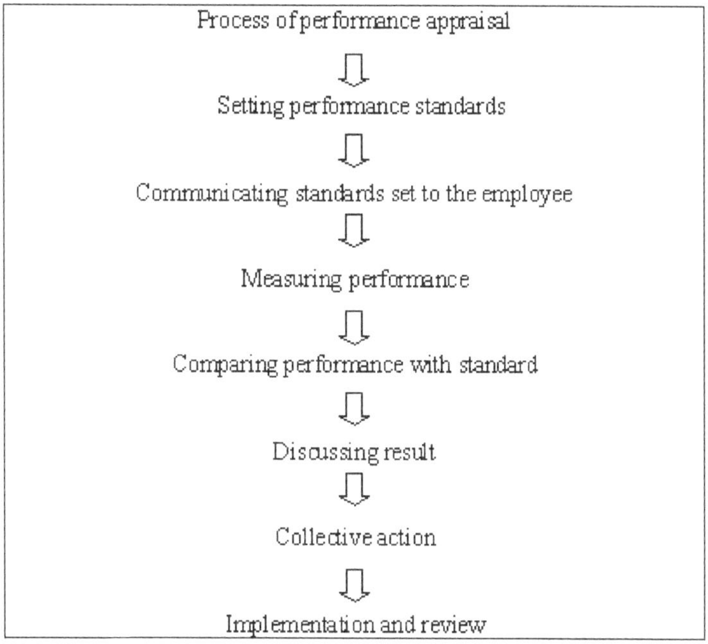

- **Setup performance standards**: This is the first step in performance appraisal; the HR department sets the standard for each employee. Basically, the expectations are set for from employees. A ranking scheme is an example. A score of 5 indicates excellent performance, a score of 4 indicates above average, and so on.
- **Communication standard set to the employee**: After the standard is set, it is communicated to the employee. Hence, the employee knows what is expected from him/her during the appraisal cycle.
- **Measuring performance**: The most important step is to measure the performance of the employee. Here, the employee is rated by his/her appraisal by the agreed suitable method.
- **Comparing performance with standard**: The performance of the employee is now evaluated against the set standard. By this, we come to know which category of performance the employee fits into that is Excellent, Above Average, Average, and so on.
- **Discussing result**: The results obtained are shared with the employee as a feedback. The employee in turn reviews the feedback and might also request for a personal review.

Compensation and Benefits

The Compensation and Benefits module deals with the compensation process followed within the organization. The stakeholders who use this module are managers, compensation professionals, administrators, and so on. This also includes defining the basic compensation structure along with advance benefits.

The advance benefit functionality is mainly used in association with the U.S. legislation for handling insurance-related processes. This module is one of the largest in the Oracle apps HRMS suite.

Payroll

Payroll is one of the fundamental modules in any enterprise that assists in managing employee costs to ensure all employees are paid in a timely manner and in accordance with the rules and regulations of the enterprise or legislation of the country.

Oracle Payroll integrates with most of the modules of the HRMS suite. Oracle Payroll involves payments, and hence is fully integrated with Oracle Financials and also with Procurement and receivable managements. Payroll Administrators are basic business users in the enterprise. Their role is to manage employee payroll and ensure that payments are made accurately and all payroll processes are managed within set timelines.

Payroll also deals with postpayroll processes such as transferring details in finance and in turn to the employee's account. The details that can be transferred to finance are the employee's bank account information (required to pay the employee) and employee costing information, which is used to cost the employee to particular cost center in the organization.

Time and Labor

Once known as **Oracle Internet Time** (**OIT**), this HR module, now known as **Oracle Time and Labor** (**OTL**), is a single source of time entry in the HRMS system. It is a web-based timecard solution, which helps to reduce cost by automating time record keeping. The following diagram describes time and labor:

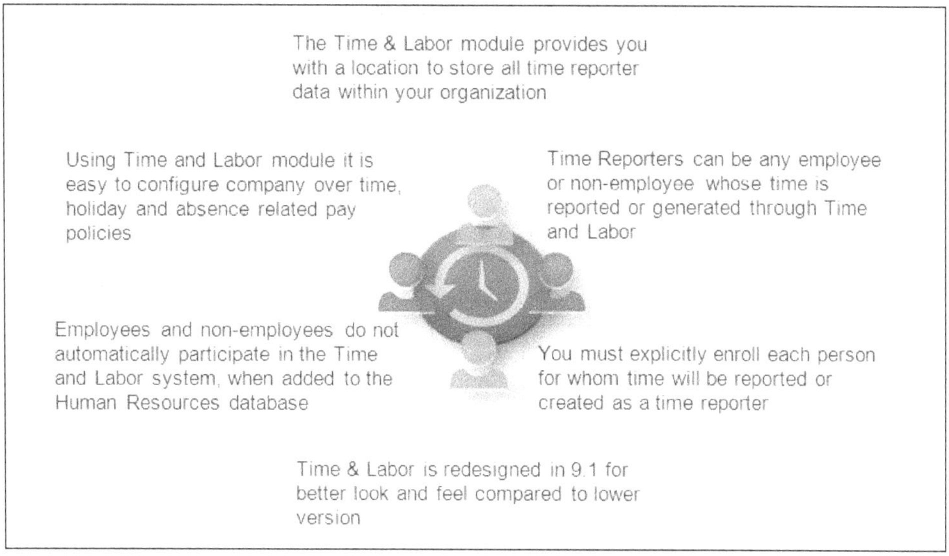

The following are the functionalities of OTL:

- Track hours worked by elapsed employees
- Clock time worked by punch employees
- Track time to pay for employees working on an hourly basis
- Track exception-time only for salaried employees
- Integrate with HR, payroll, and absence management
- Track time allocations for GL and project allocations
- Integrate with separate clock hardware devices
- In-built reports on payable status, time card, schedule hours, and so on

In terms of the employee, it offers a simple way to submit, review, track, and approve timecards.

OTL is also integrated with Oracle Payroll. The time entered by the employee is captured in OTL module and is then sent to payroll for processing. Absence management, which manages employee absences, also be used with time and labor.

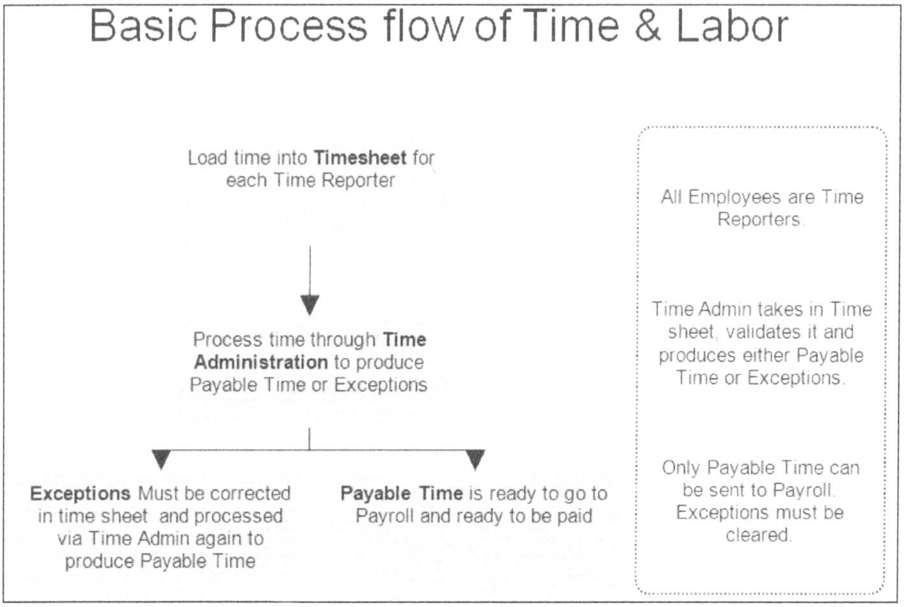

We have just covered the basic details about various modules that are part of the Oracle apps HRMS suite.

Let's now see a new concept that is used in Oracle HRMS. This is called the multi-org concept.

The multi-org concept in Oracle apps

Let's understand the multi-org concept with an example.

Suppose your company is operating in multiple countries. Working in different countries indicates multiple organizations across multiple countries. If the company wants to implement multiple organizations such as multiple ledgers (sets of books), or legal entities, which is a legal employer in that country, or business groups within a single Oracle applications, then we can say that the enterprise is going to implement a multi-org setup. Needless to say, there are certain advantages of using multiple organizations:

- Secure access to application. Security of data. Operating unit security by responsibility.
- Multiple organization reporting.

Let's see this through the following diagram:

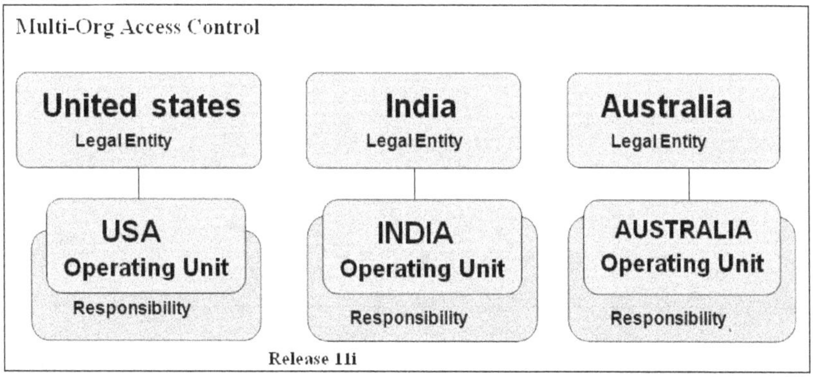

The preceding diagram shows the structure of multiple organizations in release 11i. In 11i, there are individual responsibilities within each operating unit. However, in R12, as in the following diagram, you can create a single responsibility, which can access data from all operating units.

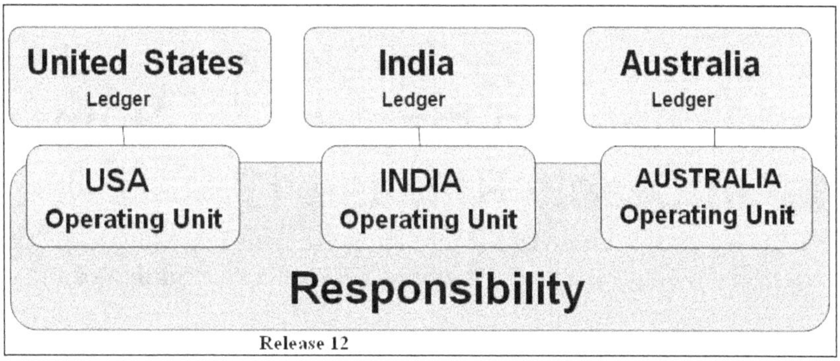

As you can see, from the preceding two diagrams, that in R12, you will need to create just a single responsibility to access data across multiple countries, whereas, in older versions, you had to create multiple responsibilities for each operating unit, which resulted in more time and maintenance.

The following diagram depicts an example implementation structure for businesses operating in India only:

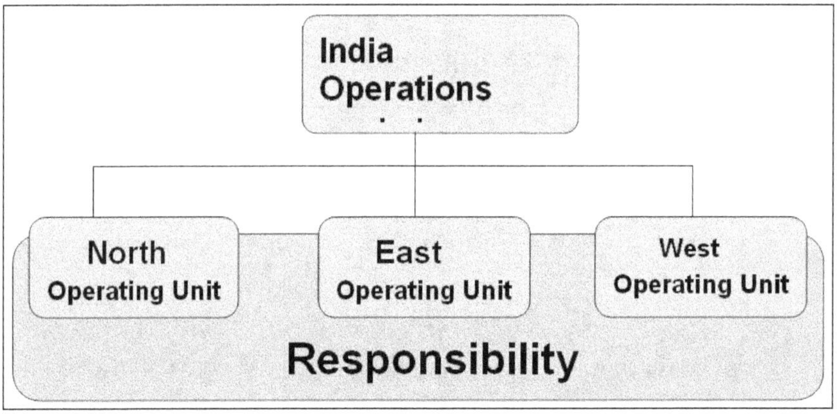

Thus, using the multi-org concept, you can access multiple operating units within a single application responsibility. This enables you to:

- Perform the tasks of viewing information
- Enter transactions
- Process application data
- Run reports for and across multiple operating units

New and changed features for Human Capital in Oracle Release 12.1

In Core HR, the legislative changes for reporting are in ethnic categories. There are statutory changes and compliance with the social security administration.

The new functionality of delete Pending for Approval transactions has been introduced. In this, before the approval of the transaction, the initiator can delete the transaction.

The pay rate functionality has been changed. It will allow multiple pay actions as part of one transaction, propose/update/delete future salary changes and it has also introduced a salary basis change functionality.

Offline appraisals can be managed in performance management. We can now download in-progress appraisals, update in the required Excel format without logging into the application; then, the updated appraisal can be uploaded to the application.

In succession plans, the Web ADI spreadsheet is used to retrieve and update succession information. This functionality is delivered in manager self-service.

In compensation workbench, being CWB administrator, you can view all employees. The compensation detail report has been modified and now employee information is grouped by tabs and the plan selection page, and parameters is replaced by filters.

Administrators have been provided with responsibility-based access. The parameter of person selection rule has been added to the compensation workbench post process. You can now perform dynamic calculations in multiple columns in which you can define dynamic calculations on worksheet amount rates, separately from custom columns, define conditions and condition results using column names, and define custom errors and warnings based on requirements.

In iRecruitment, create enrollment process has been enhanced so you can automatically enroll new hires in compensation plans included in their offer letter.

In Time and Labor:

- Days-to-Hours Conversion has been automated.
- Users can now enter Hours and Days within a single timecard, and Days into Hours conversion will be done by application for Oracle Projects.
- A user can enter a mixed format for certain time elements based on certain conditions. For example, Regular could be start and end, such as 08:00-12:00; Lunch could be entered as number of hours, such as 2—in the same timecard.

Summary

In this chapter, we provided an introduction to the Oracle Application E-Business Suite. We also discussed the architecture of the Oracle application.

Then we discussed the various modules of the Oracle applications in detail, along with new features introduced in R12.

In the next chapter, we will cover the System Administrator functionality in the Oracle Application. This will include defining users and responsibilities. It will also cover the concepts of Menu, Functions, and so on. We will also look into requests and data groups. We will also cover the creation of concurrent programs, request sets, and scheduling concurrent programs.

2

Oracle Application System Administration

This chapter will describe the role of a system administrator in Oracle applications. The main responsibility of the system administrator is to control access to the application and to ensure that operations are secure and efficient.

This chapter specifically covers the following topics:

- Creation of users. Registering these users in the application.
- Controlling access for these users through various methods, such as security profiles.
- Auditing user activities.
- Creating and managing concurrent programs, request groups, responsibilities setup, and program scheduling.

This starts with defining the application's users and assigning responsibilities to them. The responsibility used for this activity is system administrator.

Each system administrator has this responsibility assigned to them.

The system administrator uses the SYSADMIN user to log in to the application using the password they already have with them.

In the previous chapter, we looked into the Oracle apps home page, which is used to log in to the application.

The home page of the Oracle application is displayed in the following screenshot:

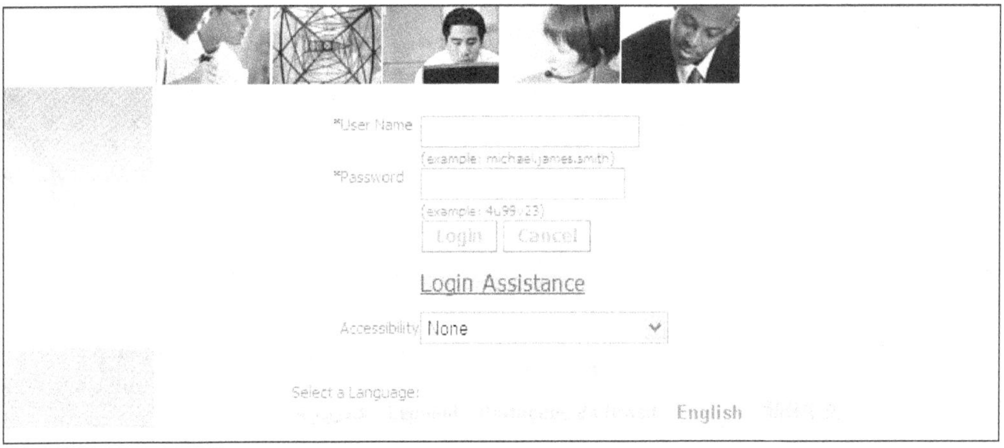

The system administrator will enter the user name as `SYSADMIN` and the required password to log in to the application:

Creating users

The first step of the system administrator is to create users. To do so, the following responsibility and navigation is used. Responsibility is a system administrator. Navigate to **System Administrator** | **Security** | **User** | **Define**.

After clicking on **Define**, a new form to create a user will be loaded, as shown in the following screenshot:

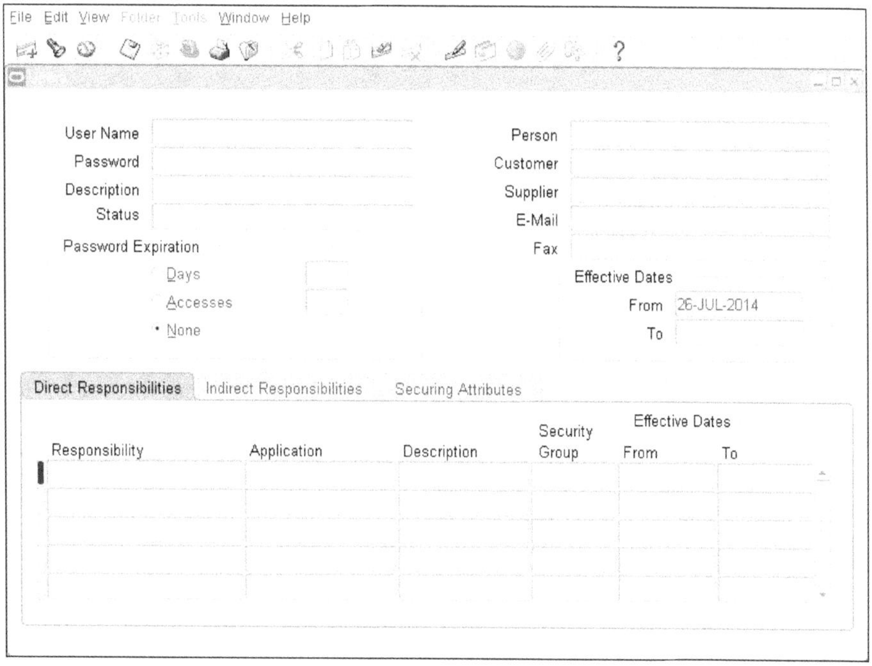

We need to enter the information in the preceding form to create a user. The fields that are marked in yellow are mandatory fields in the form. In this case, the username, password, and effective start date are mandatory. In the following form, we have entered the details that are mandatory.

In addition to mandatory fields, we have assigned a responsibility system administrator to the user.

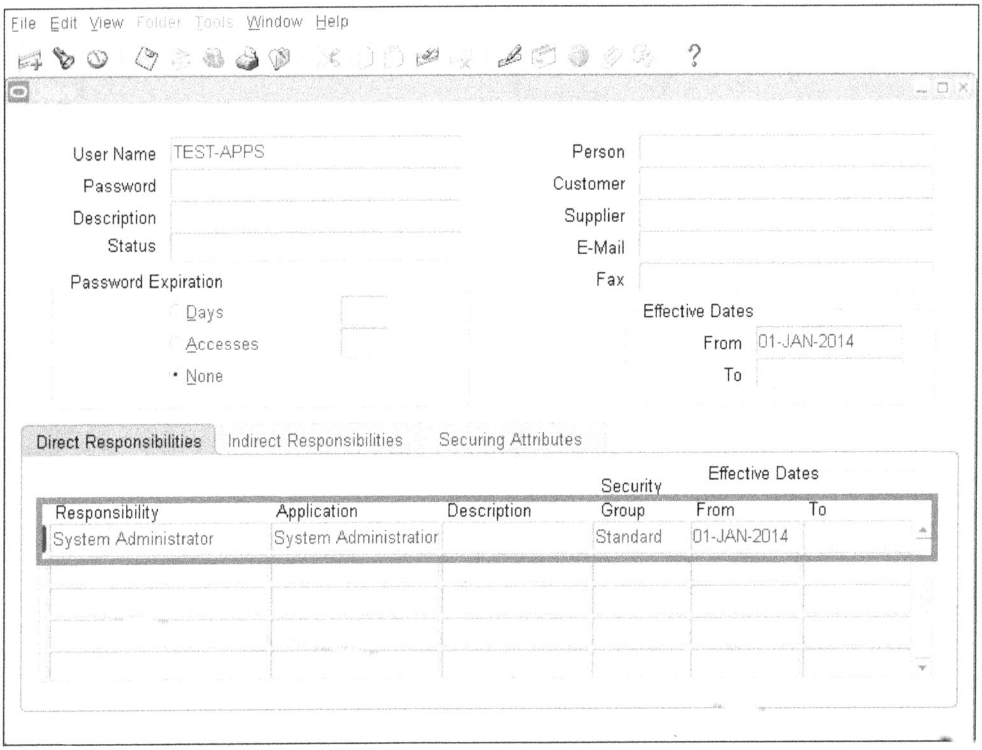

The points to define a new user are:

1. Enter the username of your choice following your company's naming convention.
2. Enter the effective date from when you want this user to be created.
3. Enter the name of the responsibility under the **Direct Responsibilities** tab. This responsibility will be available for the `TEST-APPS` user, which we are creating as per the preceding screenshot.

4. Enter the password. The password needs to be entered twice.
5. To save the new user, either use *Ctrl + S*, the **Save** option in **File** menu, or click on the Save icon (the fourth icon with the floppy disk sign) on the task bar.
6. So, as in the preceding screenshot, we have created a `TEST-APPS` user with a password and assigned the responsibility of system administrator to it.
7. The effective date to create a new user and an effective start date of responsibility is kept as `01-Jan-2014`.
8. In addition, you can also assign a person, e-mail address, and other entities to it.
9. You can also set the **Password Expiration** option as **None** or **Days**. If you set some value in days, then the password will expire in the number of days that are set in that field.
10. The end date in **Effective Dates** for responsibility will close the access to responsibility after that date. This means, you can give the responsibility to a user even for a particular duration. We should assign them all the responsibilities as in the next screenshot.

Let's now log in to the application using `TEST-APPS`:

Once you click on **Login**, it will ask you to change the password for the first time only:

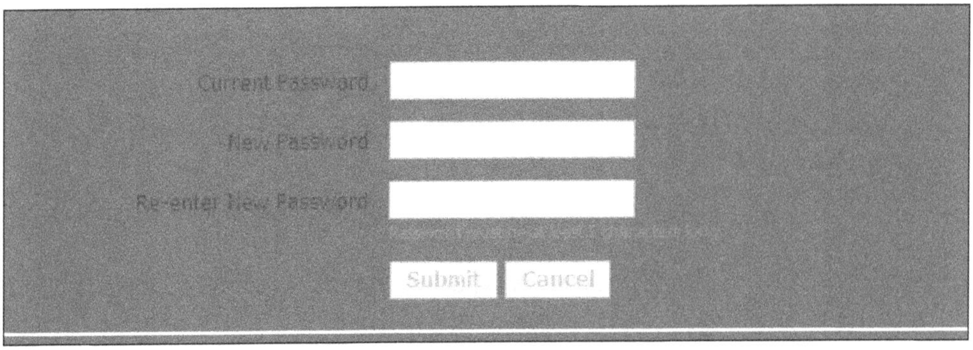

As you can see in the following screenshot, the user has been assigned three responsibilities, which are **Application Diagnostics**, **Functional Administrator**, and **System Administrator**. Thus, you learned how to create users and assign them responsibilities.

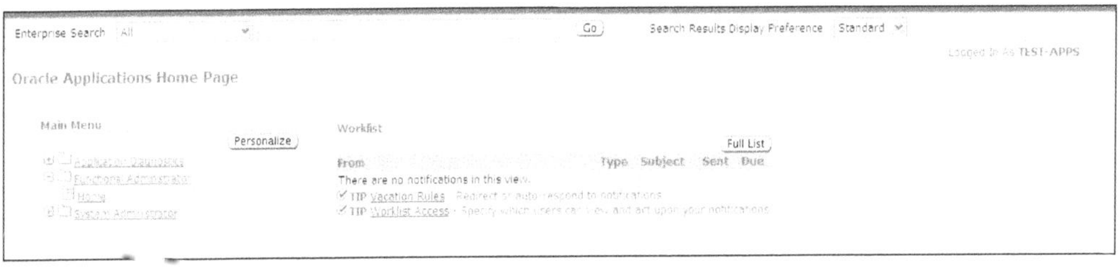

We will now cover creating responsibilities.

A responsibility determines whether the user accesses the Oracle form based application or the Oracle Self Service Web application. It also determines which application's functions a user can use and the reports and programs the user can run.

The steps to create responsibility are as follows:

1. Log in to the Oracle application.
2. Select the responsibility as **System Administrator**.

Navigate to **Security** | **Responsibility** | **Define**. Enter the **Responsibility name**, **Application Name**, **Responsibility Key**, **Menu**, and **Data group** details. **Application Name** is the application you want this responsibility for; for example Human Resource, Payroll, and so on. **Responsibility Key** is any short code you want to give to your responsibility. The menu will contain functions and submenus. This will decide which functions will be available to the user using this responsibility.

Then, click on the **Save** button. The responsibility will be saved in the system. The responsibility shown in the preceding screenshot is the responsibility for the United States (US) legislation.

This is used by HR managers. Once the responsibility is saved successfully, assign the user to the responsibility.

Switch the menu to the user (**Security** | **User** | **Define**). Query the username to which you want to add the responsibility. Then add the responsibility to the user as shown in the next screenshot.

In order to query any record in the Oracle apps form you need to follow the following steps:

1. Navigate to the required form.
2. Press *F11*. The form will be enterable.
3. Enter the required field to be queried (you can enter an entire string, or if you are not sure, then you can enter the string in `%`. For example, you need to query `TEST-APPS`, then you can enter `%TEST%`.
4. Press *Ctrl* + *F11*.

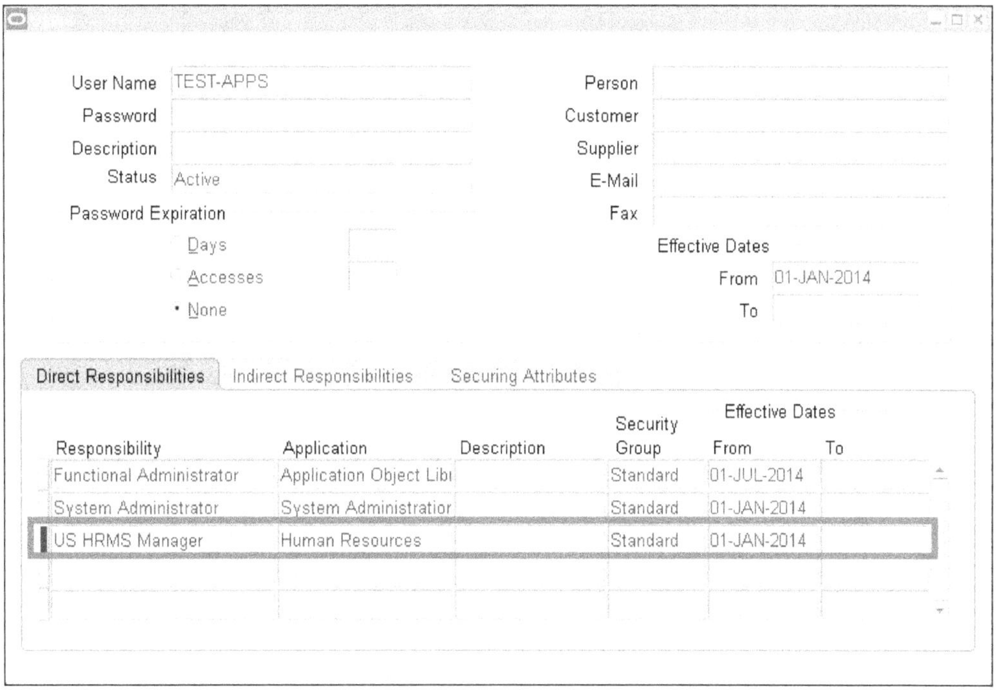

On the home page, you can see the added responsibility US HRMS Manager.

Menu in Oracle apps

Menu is a list of the functions as well as submenus that are attached to a responsibility. Every responsibility will have a menu attached to it.

As we can see in the following screenshot, `US HRMS Manager` has a `US HRMS Navigator` menu attached to it.

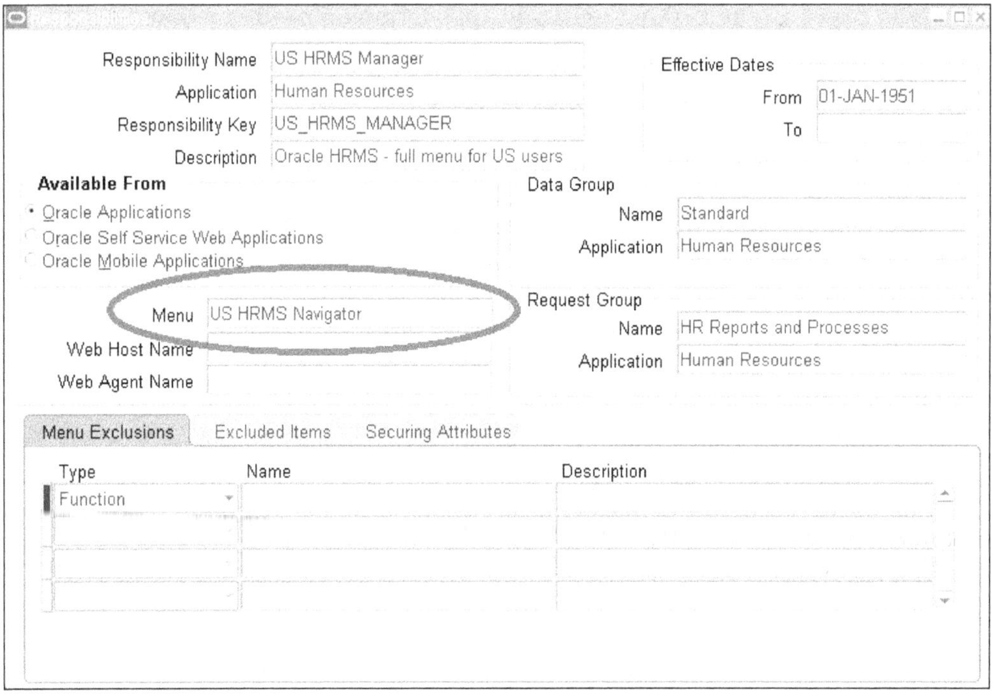

The `US HRMS Navigator` menu can be assigned to more than one responsibility. We will create multiple responsibilities and attach the same menu to each of them. Let's see how can we do this. Navigate to **System Administrator** | **Security** | **Responsibility** | **Define**.

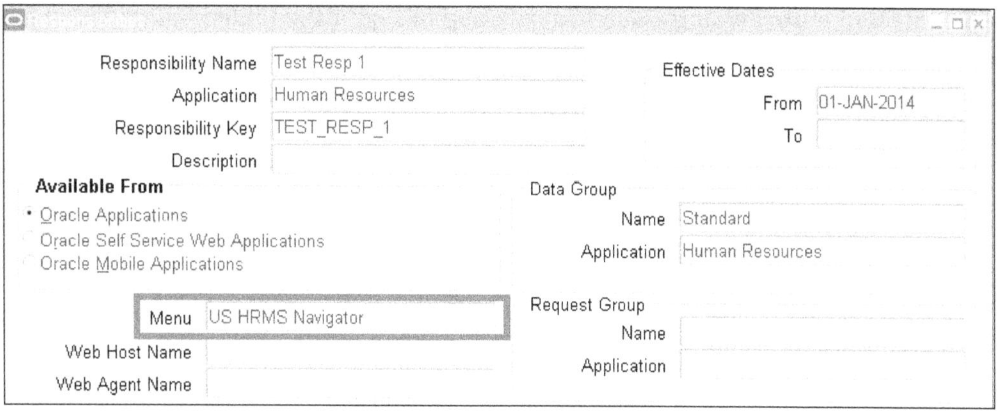

In the preceding screenshot, we have created a new responsibility name `Test Resp 1` and have assigned the same menu, `US HRMS Navigator` to it.

Similarly, we can create one more responsibility, say `Test Resp 2`, and assign the same menu `US HRMS Navigator` to it. The same is shown in the next screenshot.

The scenario for this type of setup is explained here. Suppose there are two end users, one is HR and the other is the payroll administrator. They both require the same set of functions. Hence, we can create two different responsibilities, one as `US HR Administrator` and another as `US Payroll Administrator`.

You can also restrict data based on responsibility using the profile option. There might be a requirement that both the HR and Payroll Administrator must see data specific to particular organizations only. This can be accomplished using profile options.

You will learn more about this later in the chapter under the *Profile Options in Oracle apps* section.

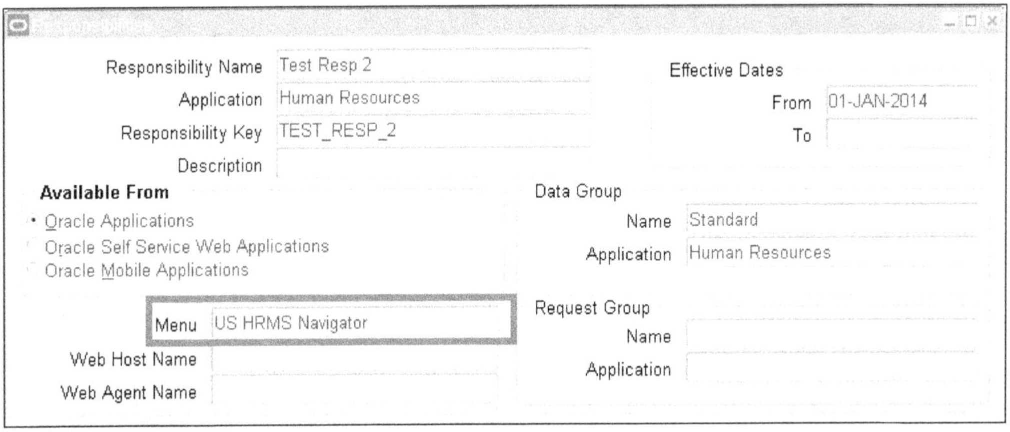

To view the menu, navigate to **System Administrator** | **Application** | **Menu**.

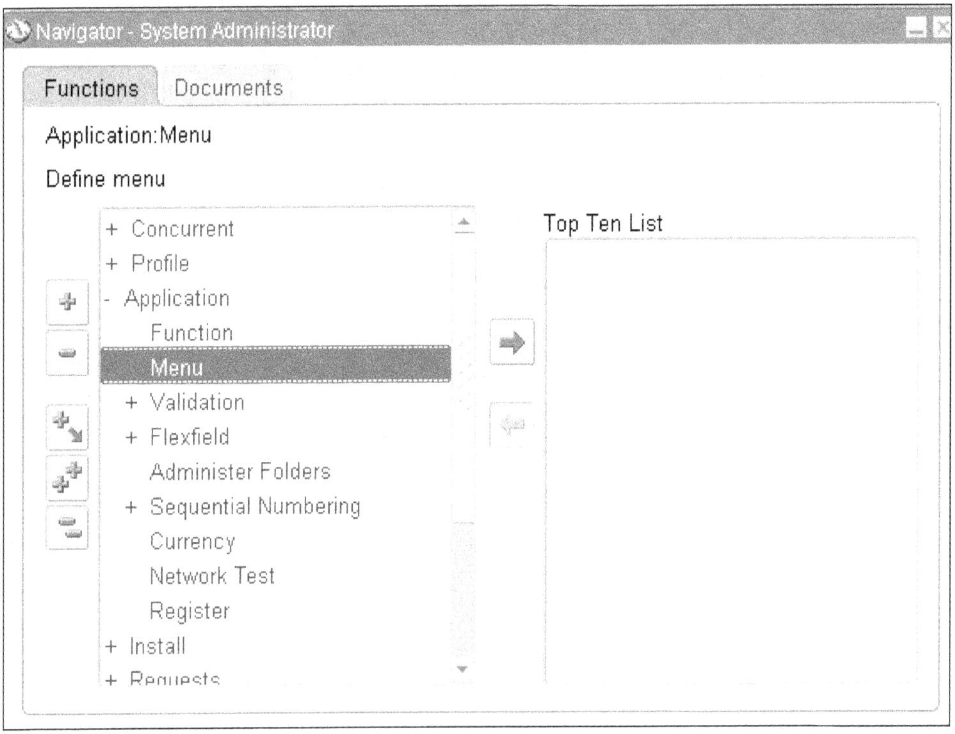

Double-click on **Menu**, and the following form will open:

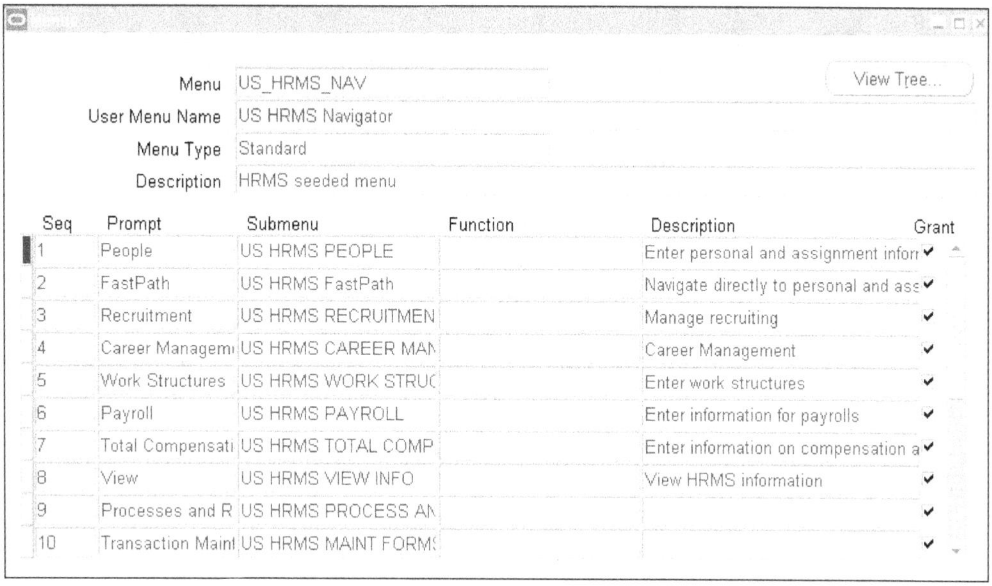

In the preceding screenshot, you can see the definition of menu. It has **Prompt**, **Submenu**, **Function**, and **Description**. **Prompt** is the name that a user can see when he logs in to the US HRMS Manager responsibility.

In order to switch to other responsibilities, you will need to use the Switch Responsibility feature, which is available from the toolbar as marked in the following screenshot:

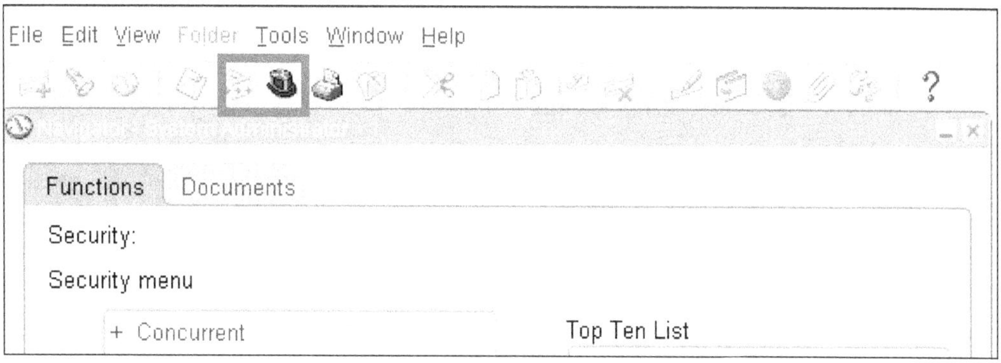

When you click on the hat icon, it will give you the option to move onto the responsibility to which you want to navigate, as shown in the following screenshot:

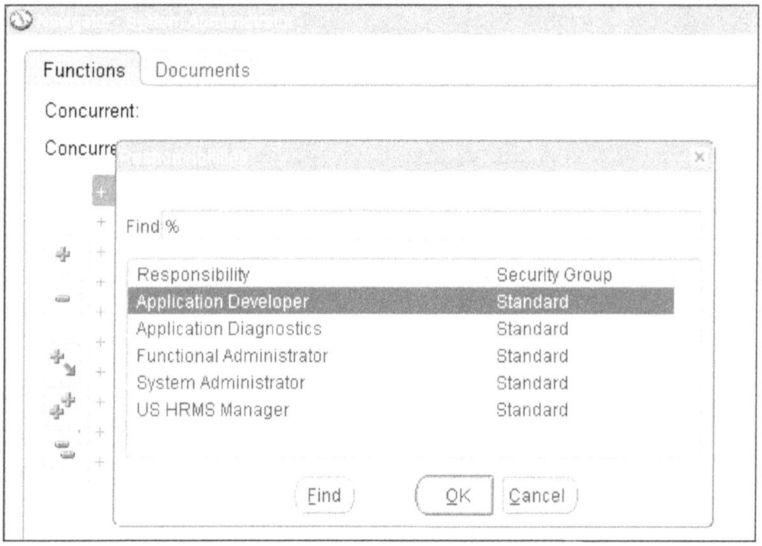

In our case, click on the **US HRMS Manager** responsibility. Once you select the responsibility, then you can see the following form.

All the preceding prompts can be seen in the US HRMS Manager responsibility.

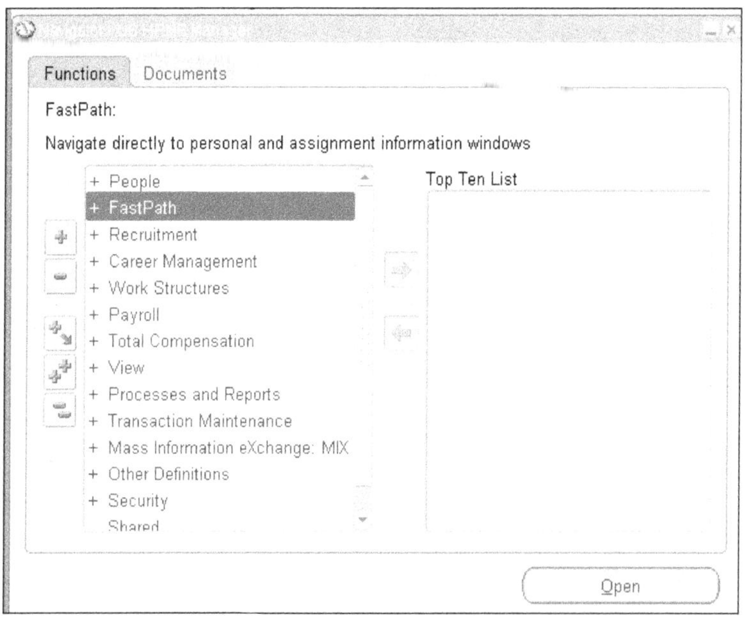

Double clicking on the **People** prompt will open that menu as displayed:

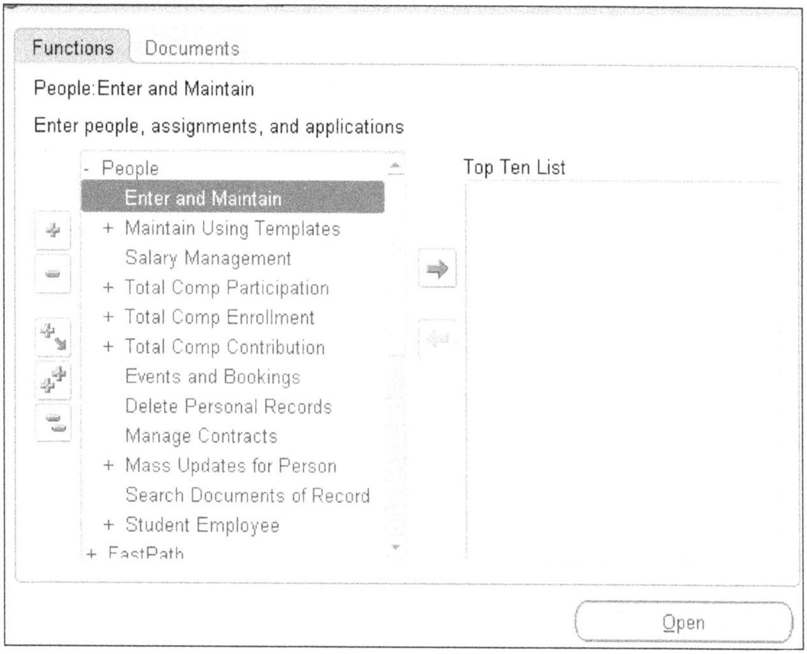

In the preceding screenshot, the **People** prompt is attached to the **US HRMS PEOPLE** submenu. When we query **US HRMS PEOPLE** in the menu you can see **Enter and Maintain** as the prompt of the submenu.

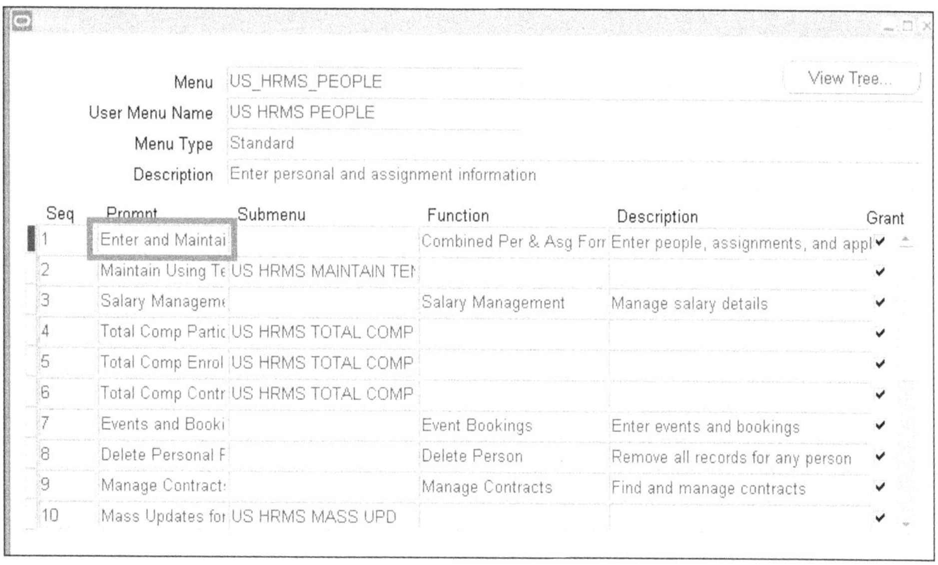

In the following screenshot, you can see that the **Enter and Maintain** prompt does not have a submenu attached.

A function `Combined Per & Asg Form WKFLW_NAME="US HRMS PERSON TASKFLOW` is attached to this prompt. This means that when you open the **Enter and Maintain** prompt, Oracle will execute this function internally and the appropriate form will open. In this case, the standard **Find Person** form will be opened, when you click on **Enter and Maintain**:

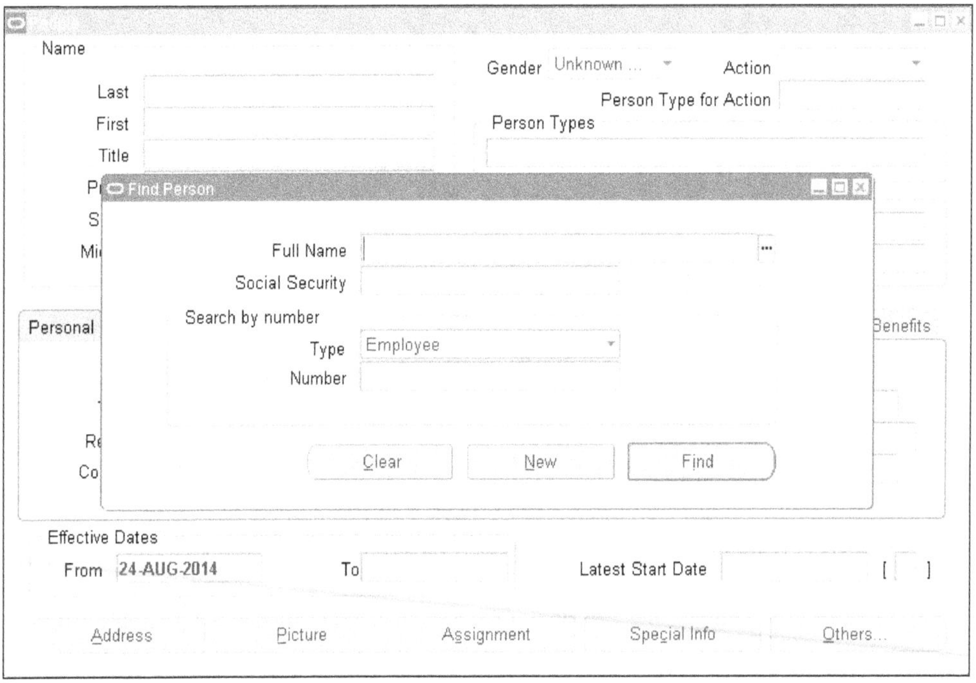

This is the standard Oracle person screen/form. In this form, you can look for a person and then make the necessary changes to his data.

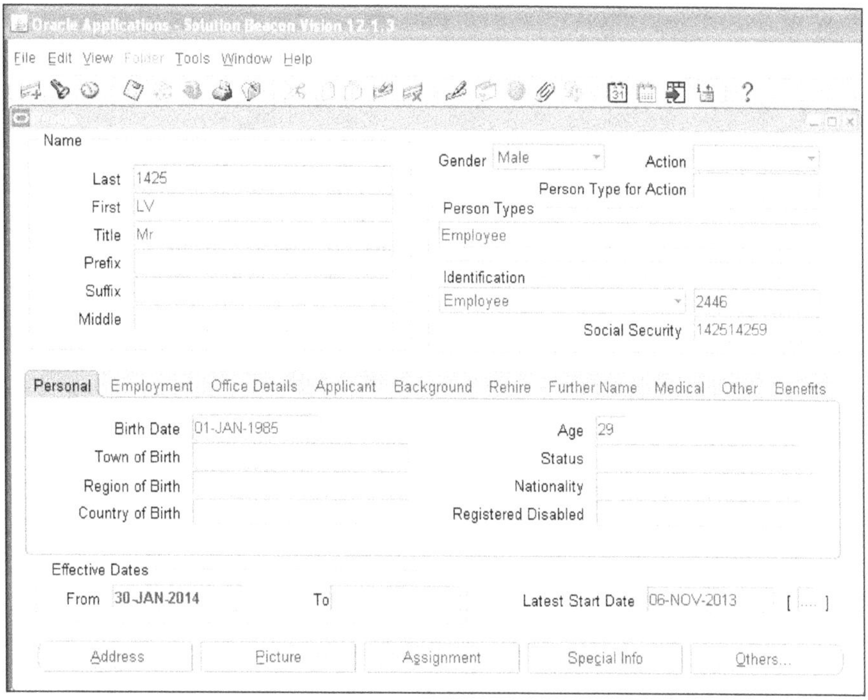

Request and data group

Now let's see the concept of request and data groups. Request group and data group are used while defining a responsibility in Oracle apps.

A request group is attached to a responsibility. It defines the concurrent programs you can execute using the responsibility to which this request group is attached.

The following screenshot shows the data and request group attached to a responsibility:

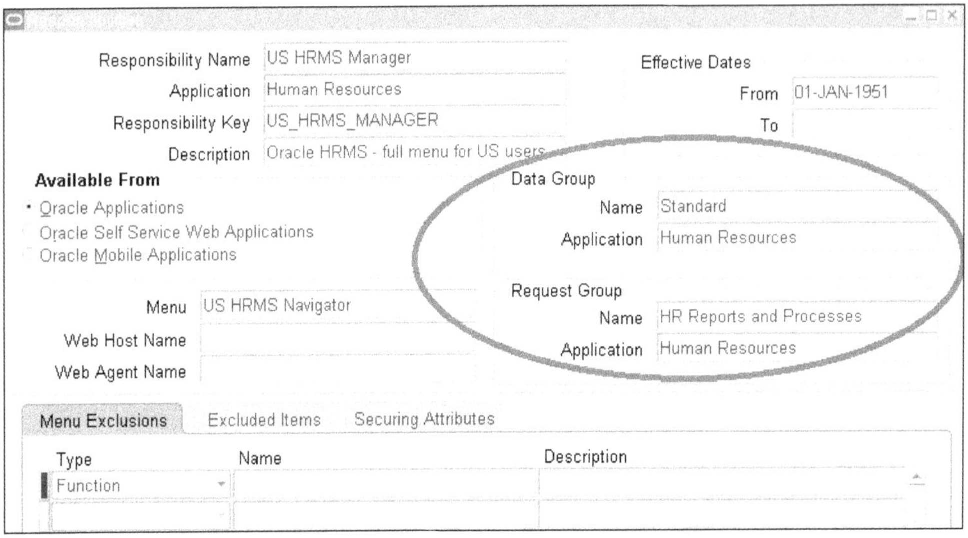

A request group can be queried; to do this, navigate to **System Administrator** | **Security** | **Responsibility** | **Request**.

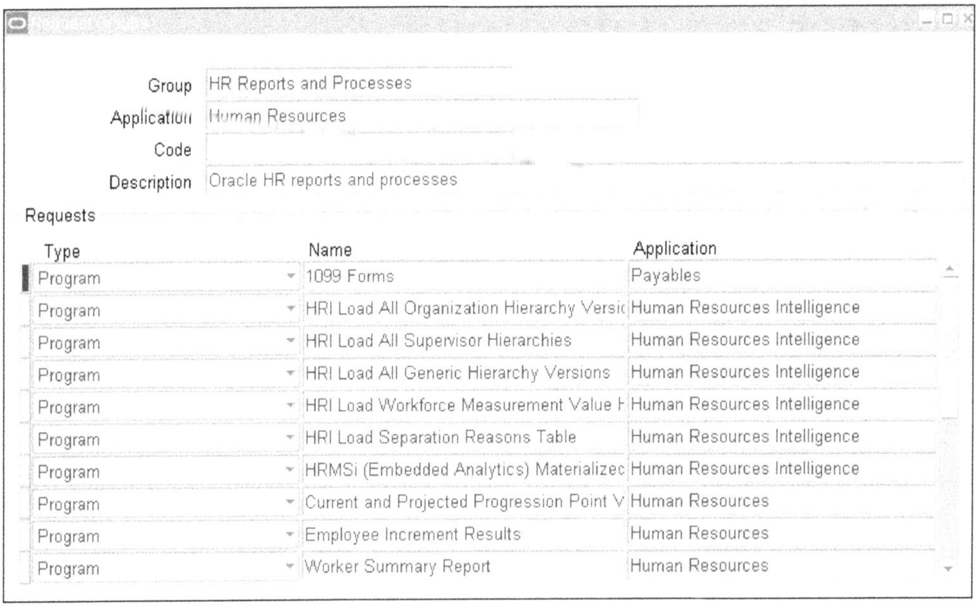

Data groups

A data group is a list of Oracle Applications (Human Resource, Advanced Benefits, Payables, Payroll, and so on) and the Oracle username (HR, AP, AR, and so on) assigned to each application. Each application in a data group must have an Oracle username assigned to it. An application may be listed in a data group only once.

Usage of a data group

Each responsibility has a data group associated with it. A data group has two basic uses, as follows:

- It determines the Oracle username that forms will connect to when you use the responsibility
- Concurrent managers use a data group to match the application that owns a report or concurrent program (submitted by a user of the responsibility) with an Oracle username

The data group attached to our responsibility is standard. To view a data group, navigate to **System Administrator** | **Security** | **ORACLE** | **DataGroup**.

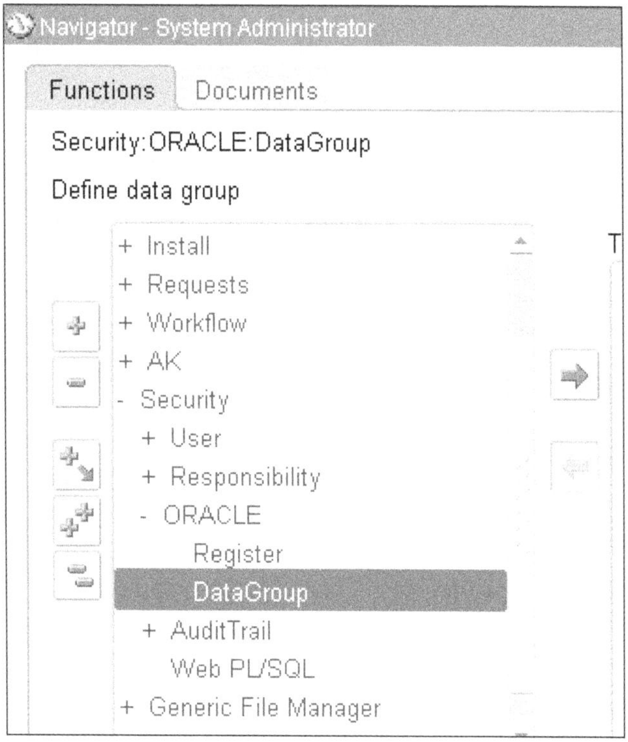

When you click on **DataGroup**, the following form will open:

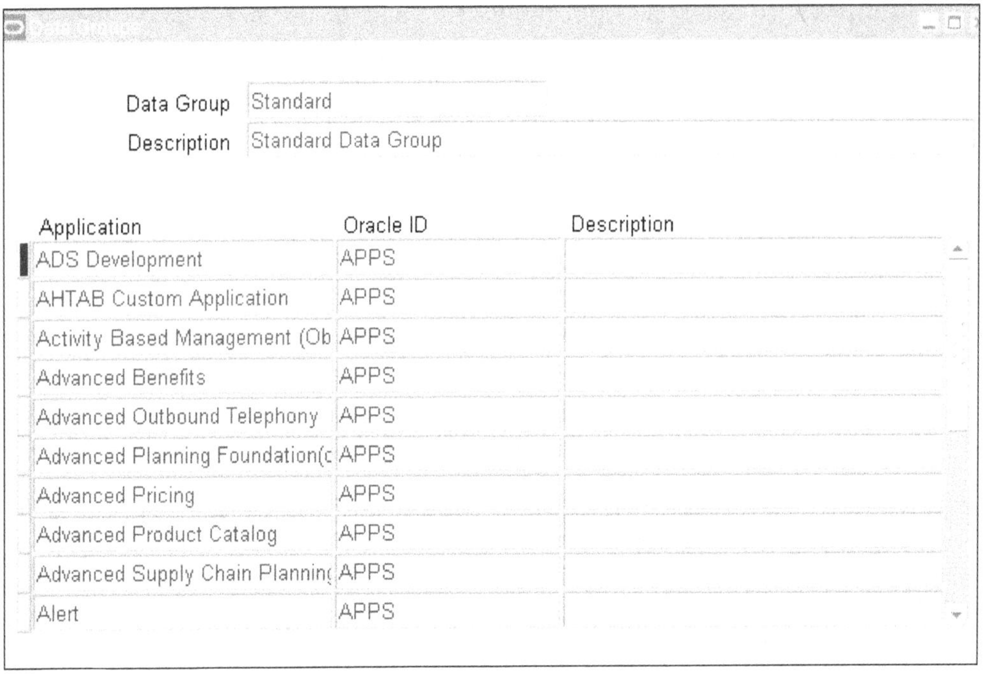

Data Group: Standard
Description: Standard Data Group

Application	Oracle ID	Description
ADS Development	APPS	
AHTAB Custom Application	APPS	
Activity Based Management (Ob	APPS	
Advanced Benefits	APPS	
Advanced Outbound Telephony	APPS	
Advanced Planning Foundation(c	APPS	
Advanced Pricing	APPS	
Advanced Product Catalog	APPS	
Advanced Supply Chain Plannin(	APPS	
Alert	APPS	

Profile options in Oracle apps

The profile option is one of the most important functionalities of Oracle apps. This will basically control the behavior of Oracle apps. You can change the value of the profile option at any time. An example of the profile option is HR, Business group will determine which business group the data user will be able to view when he uses a particular responsibility.

There are two types of profile options, as follows:

- **The system profile option**: This is used by the system administrator. These can be viewed and updated by the system administrator only. These are mainly supplied only by Oracle, which means most of them are seeded profile options.
- **The user profile option**: This is used by the Oracle apps end users. It can be viewed and updated by the Oracle apps end users.

Navigate to **System Administrator** | **Profile** | **System**.

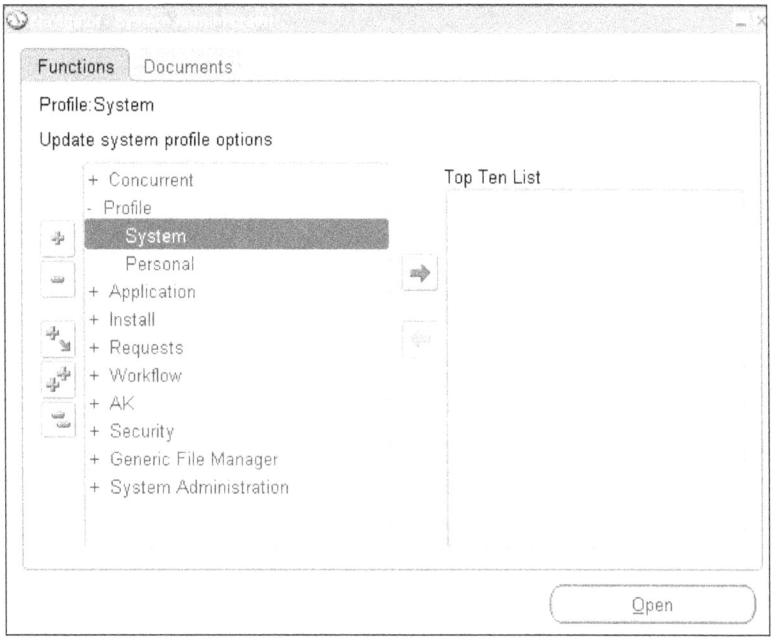

When you double-click on **System** or highlight **System** and click on the **Open** button, the following form will open:

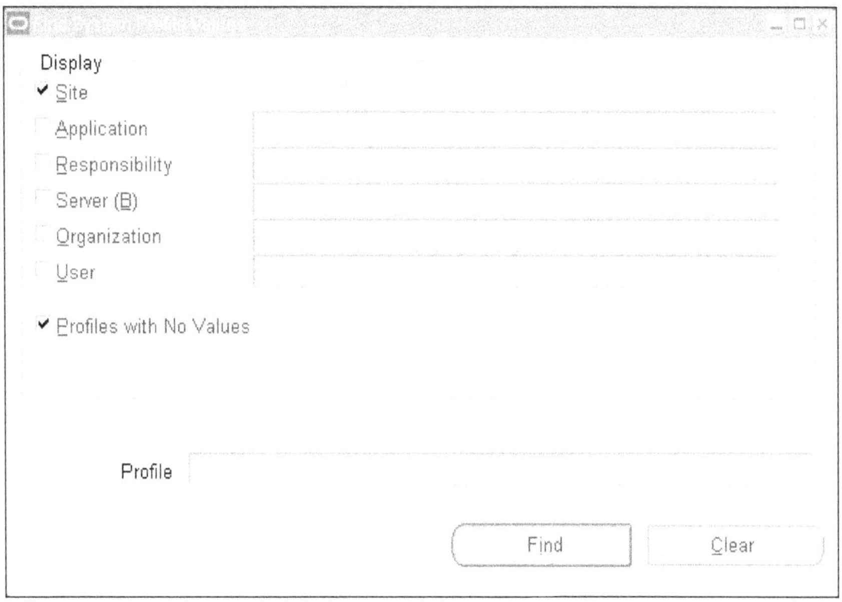

The preceding screenshot shows the various levels to which you can set the profile options. The various levels are:

- **Site**: This is restricted to the entire Oracle Apps
- **Application**: This is restricted to a particular application such as Human Resource, Payroll and Payables, and so on
- **Responsibility**: This is restricted to a particular responsibility, for example, US HRMS Manager
- **Organization**: This is restricted to a particular organization
- **User**: This is restricted to a user, for example, `TEST-APPS`

Site is the highest level and **User** is the lowest level. If you set profile options at both levels, then the lower level will take precedence.

You need to select the level and profile option value and click on **Find** to set the value for that profile option:

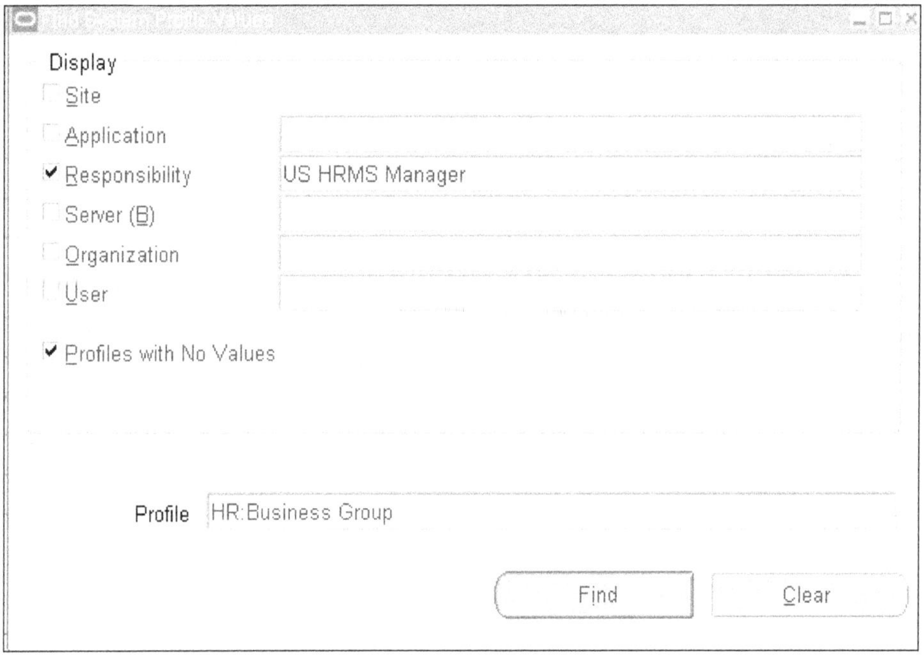

Whenever you create a new responsibility for a particular enterprise, then you need to set three basic seeded profile options, as follows:

- **HR: Business Group**: This will define the business group that is linked to the security profile for a responsibility.

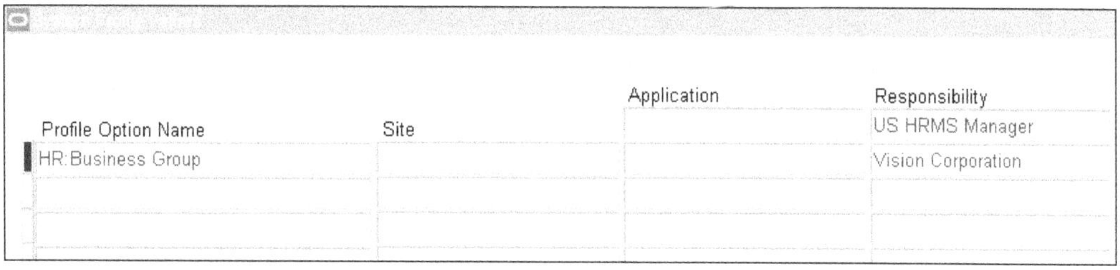

- **HR: Security Profile**: This is used to restrict the data in human resources according to the business group or whatever criteria you define in this security profile. It restricts access to the organizations, positions, and payrolls defined in the security profile.
- **HR: User Type**: This will define the type of data visible. There are three options, as follows:
    - **HR User** will show the user only HR-related data
    - **HR with Payroll User** will show HR and payroll data
    - **Payroll User** will show only payroll-related data

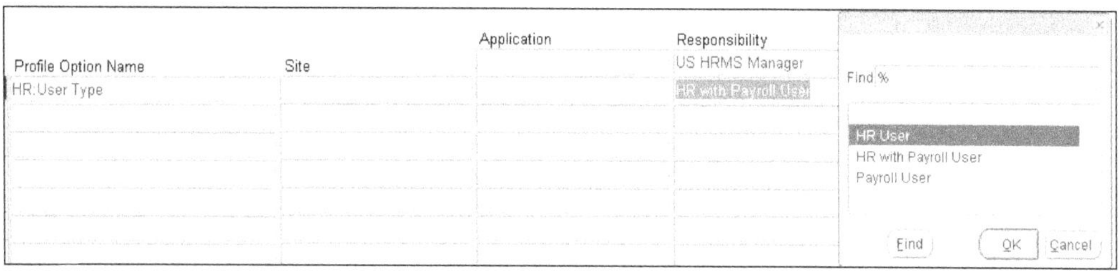

Apart from these, there is one more option that can be used, which restricts the user from updating any data. The user will have read only access to data and hence cannot modify/update any data for employees. The name of this profile is **HR: Query Only Mode**.

You can set the value as `Yes` or `No`.

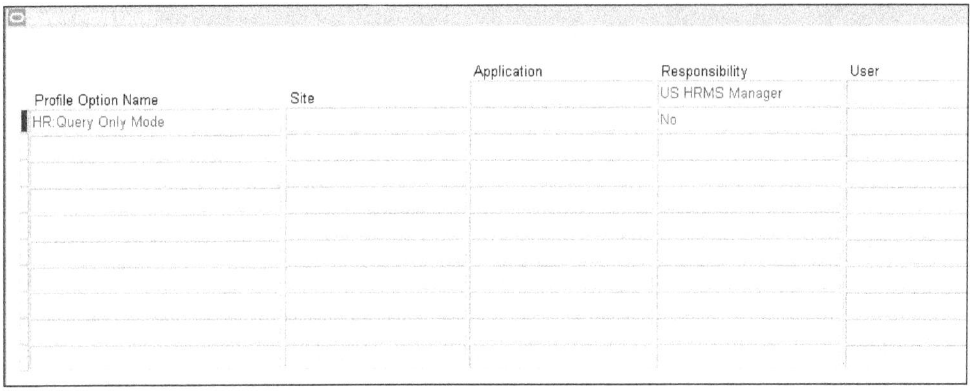

All the profile options used earlier are seeded options. Apart from these, the user can create his/her own profile and use it appropriately. Navigate to **US HRMS Manager | Security | Profile**.

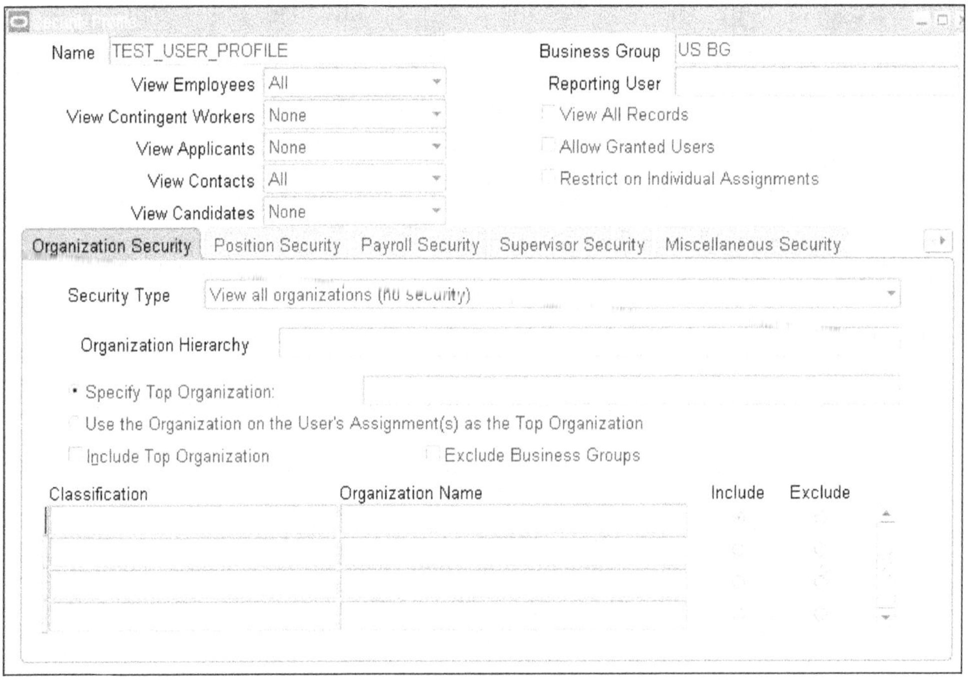

In the preceding screenshot, we have created a new profile option `TEST_USER_PROFILE`. In it, **View Contingent Workers**, **View Applicants**, and **View Candidates** are set as **None**.

If we attach this profile option to any responsibility then, we cannot view contingent workers, applicants, and candidates using that responsibility; apart from this, we can also set other parameters such as organization, position, payroll, miscellaneous, and so on.

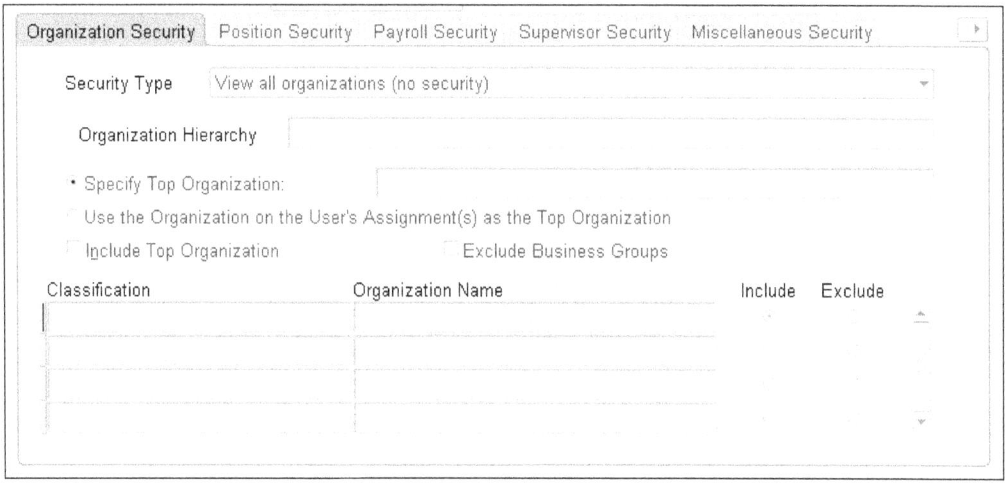

You can also use custom security where you can write your own logic using an SQL query.

Standard Request Submission

Standard Request Submission (**SRS**) gives you control over how you run your requests and request sets in an application. The following are the steps involved in SRS:

1. Creating an executable.
2. Creating a concurrent program.
3. Attaching parameters to concurrent programs if needed.
4. Attaching concurrent programs to a request group.
5. Running a program.
6. Viewing the output and log.
7. Scheduling a program if needed.

Creating an executable

An executable actually holds the location of the logic of the concurrent program.

Navigate to **System Administrator** | **Concurrent** | **Program** | **Executable**:

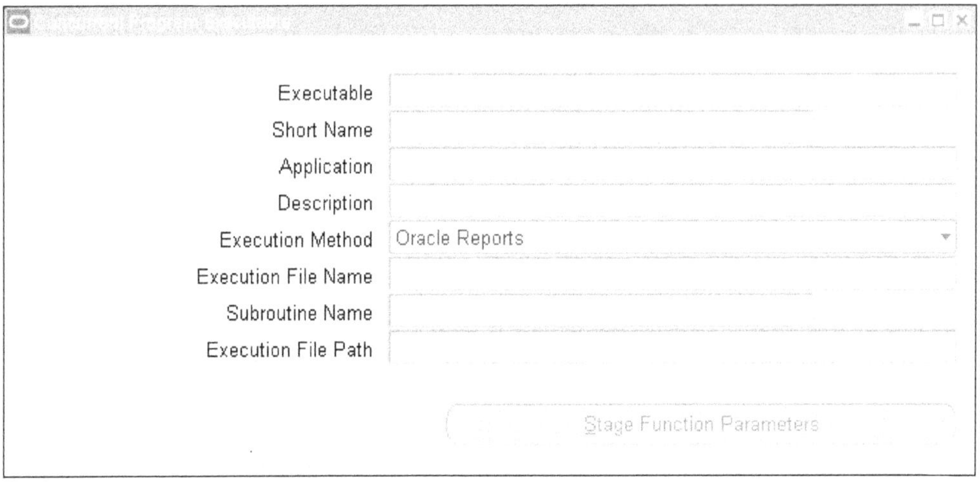

The important field is **Execution Method**, which describes the type of method used in a concurrent program. The various methods used are as shown in the screenshot:

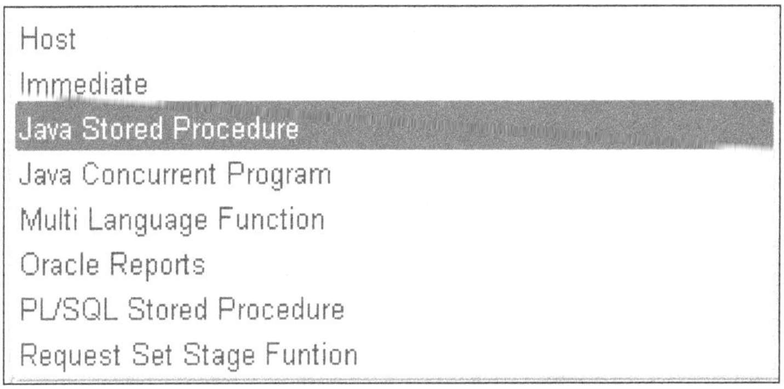

If you want your concurrent program to run the PL/SQL block, then select **PL/SQL Stored Procedure** as the execution method.

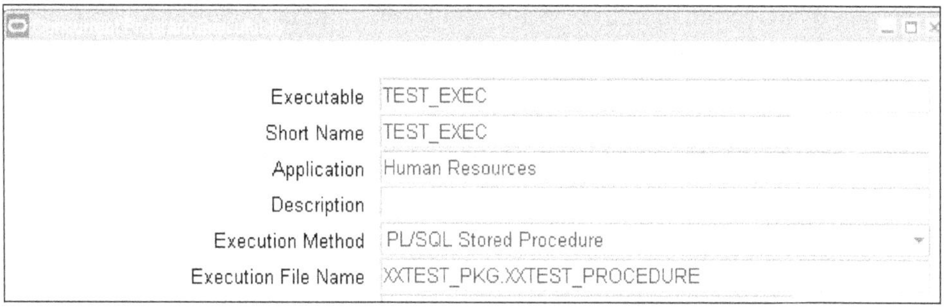

The format of the execution filename I have used is `package.procedure`. When you submit the concurrent program, the application will execute `XXTEST_PROCEDURE` defined in the `XXTEST_PKG` package.

Creating a concurrent program

In this section, we will create a concurrent program; to do so, navigate to **System Administrator** | **Concurrent** | **Program** | **Define**.

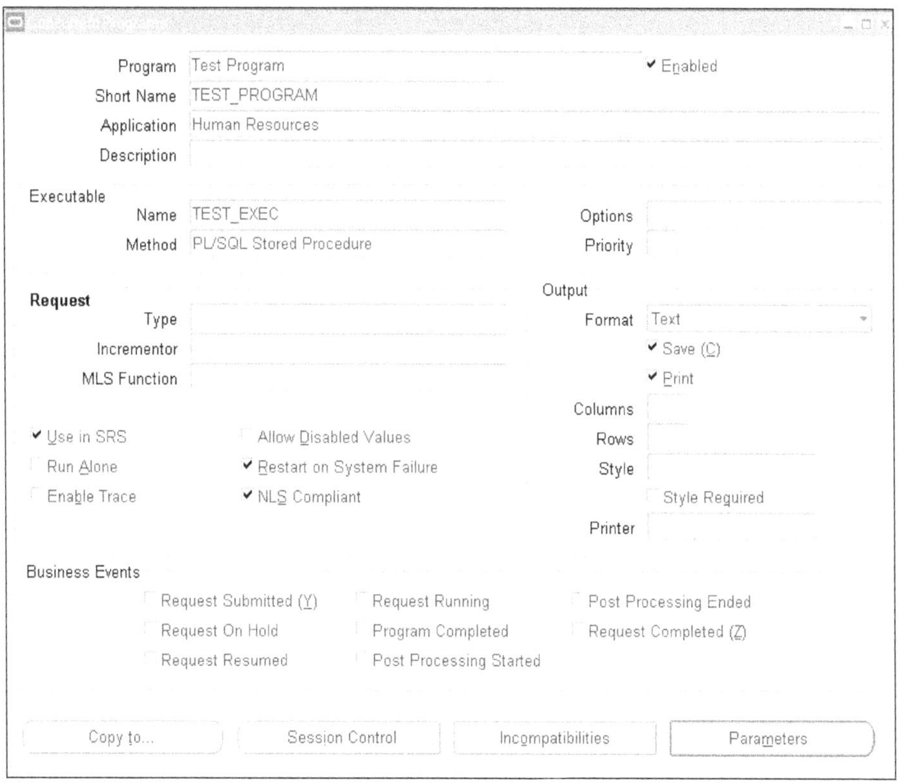

Attach the executable created in step 1 in the **Name** field of **Executable**. The method will populate automatically.

Attaching parameters to a concurrent program

You can also set parameters for the concurrent program you have defined. Use the **Parameters** button in the preceding screenshot to do so.

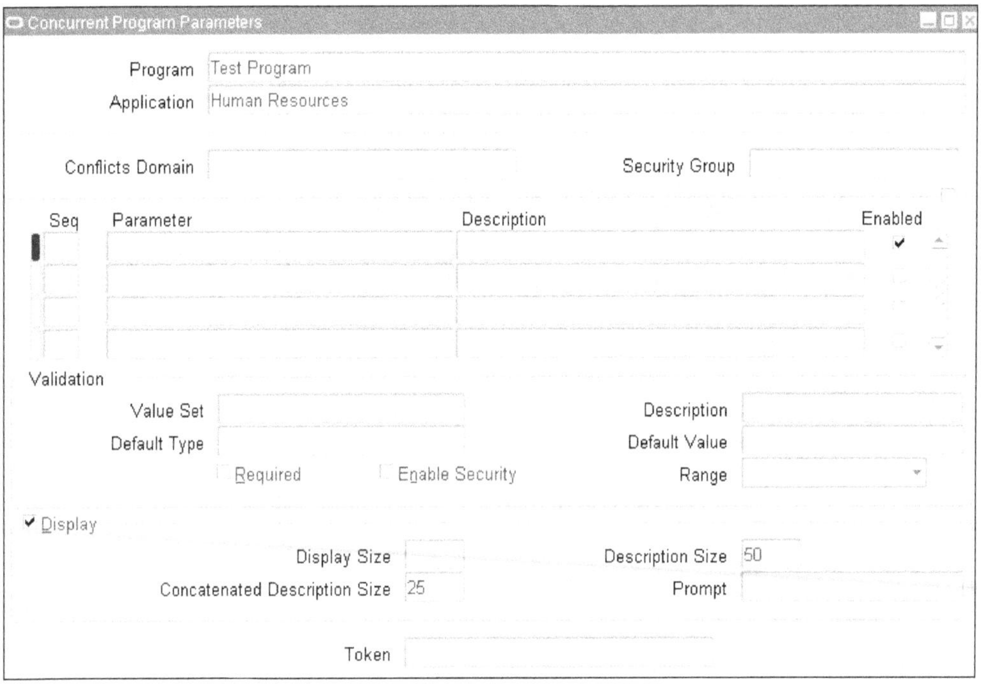

Enter the value in the **Parameter** field along with the sequence number. In this example, we will keep one parameter, that is, `Effective Date` and attach a value set. You can also set a default value for the parameter. A value set is a set of values you can define for this parameter.

The standard practice is to increment the sequence number by 10, if we want to add a new parameter.

Check the **Enabled** checkbox to view the parameter in the concurrent program.

You can set the **Required** checkbox as marked in the following screenshot if you want this parameter to be mandatory in your program.

Save the record once you have entered the details.

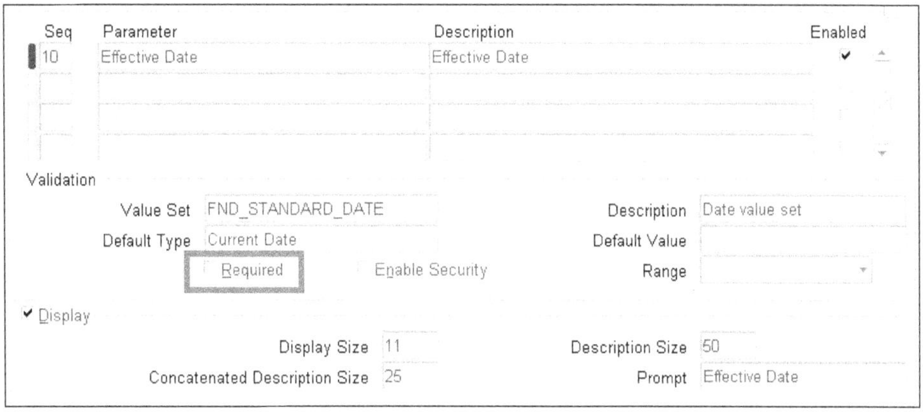

The prompt visible to the user while submitting a request is entered in the **Prompt** field. The **Display** checkbox with make it visible for the user. If you uncheck it, then it will be invisible but will still be used in the program.

This checkbox is used when the user wants to have some parameter passed to the program by default. It is not seen by the end user.

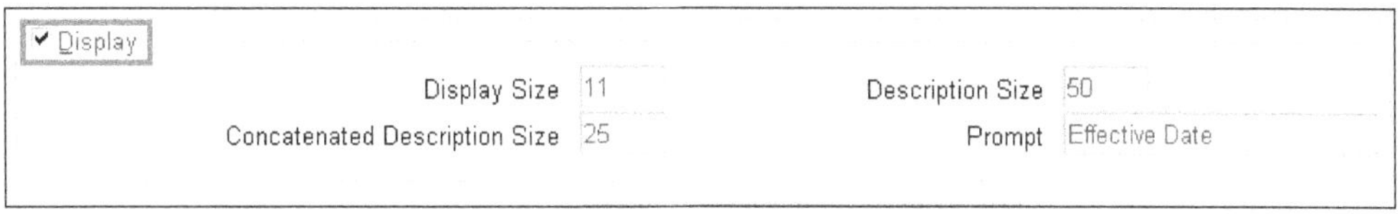

Attaching a concurrent program to a request group

Once you have defined the program, you need to specify the responsibility through which you want to run this program. For this, you need to add the program to a request group that is attached to a responsibility.

In our case, the responsibility is `US HRMS Manager` and the request group attached to it is `HR Reports and Processes`:

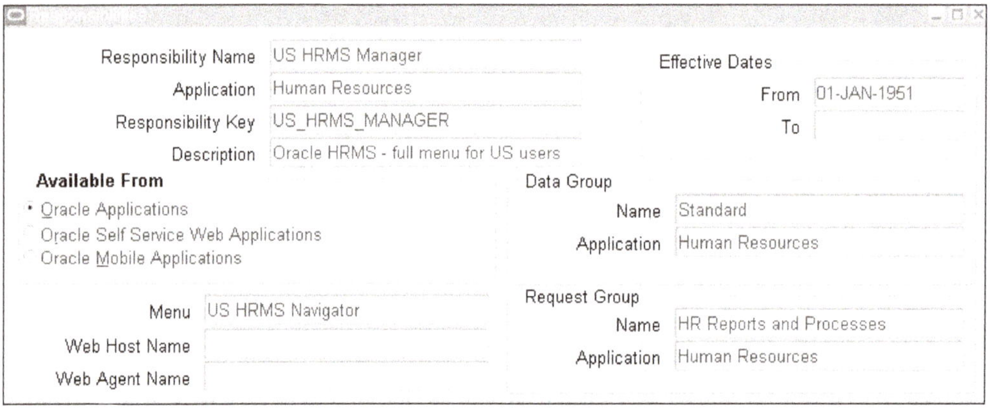

To add the program to a request group, navigate to **System Administrator** | **Security** | **Responsibility** | **Request**:

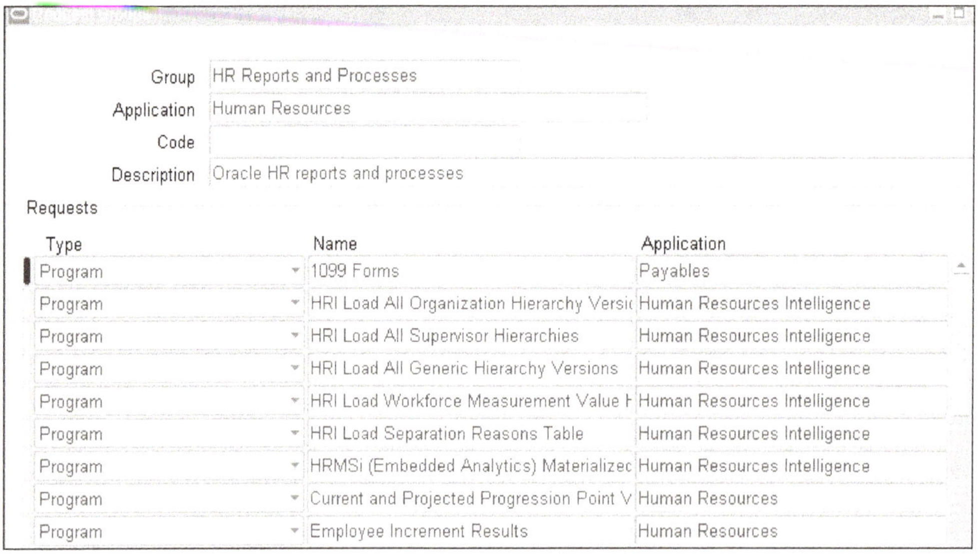

Click on the plus icon on the toolbar to add the program to this group:

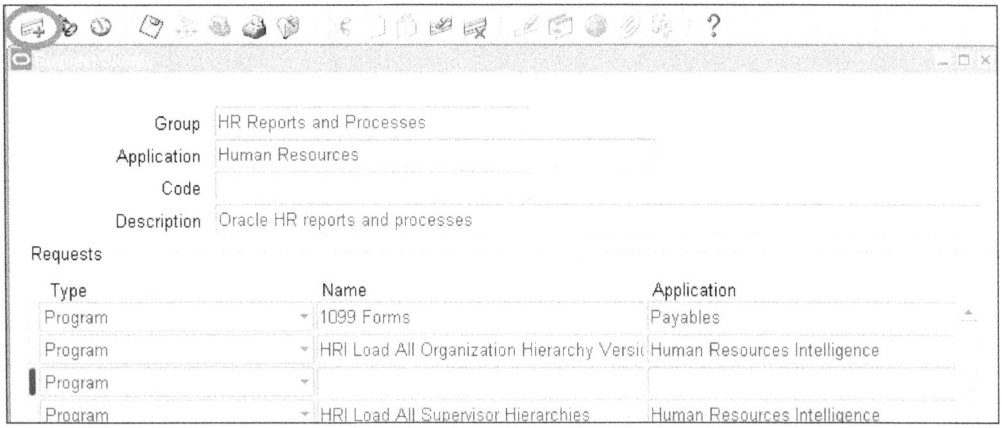

Add the program name `Test Program` in the **Name** field, as marked in the following screenshot:

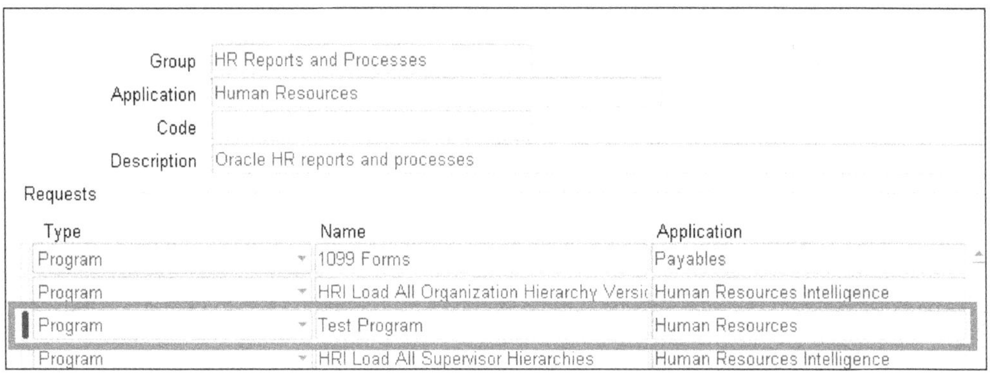

Save the record. You are now ready to run this program using the US HRMS Manager responsibility.

Now, navigate to **US HRMS Manager** | **Processes and Reports** | **Submit Processes and Reports** and click on **OK**. Enter the name of the program created earlier. The **Parameters** window will appear automatically.

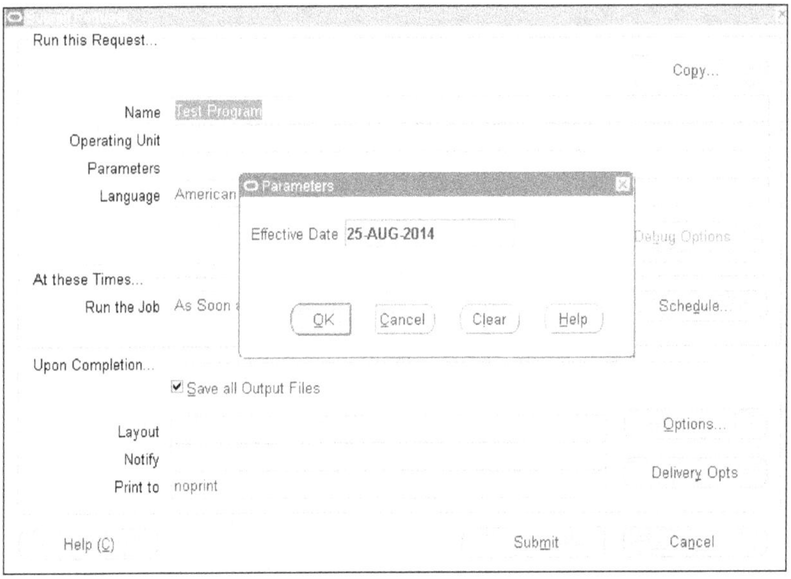

Click on the **Submit** button to run this program. Once you submit the program, it will prompt you to submit a new request. Choose the appropriate action:

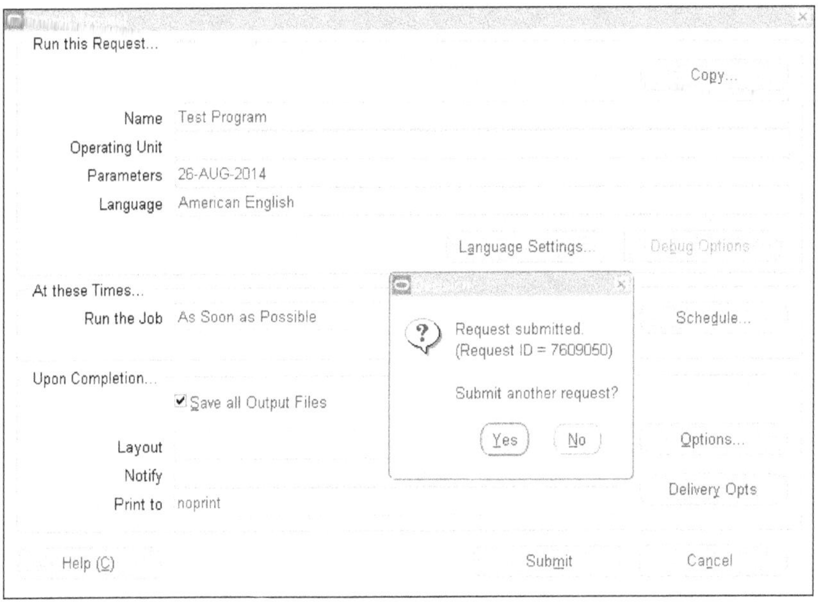

Viewing the output and log

Once the program is submitted, the application creates a unique request ID. Each submitted program will have a unique request ID. To view the submitted program, navigate to **US HRMS Manager** | **Processes and Reports** | **View Requests**.

Click on **Find Requests** to view all the requests submitted by you or to view a specific request, select the **Specific Requests** radio button and enter the request ID.

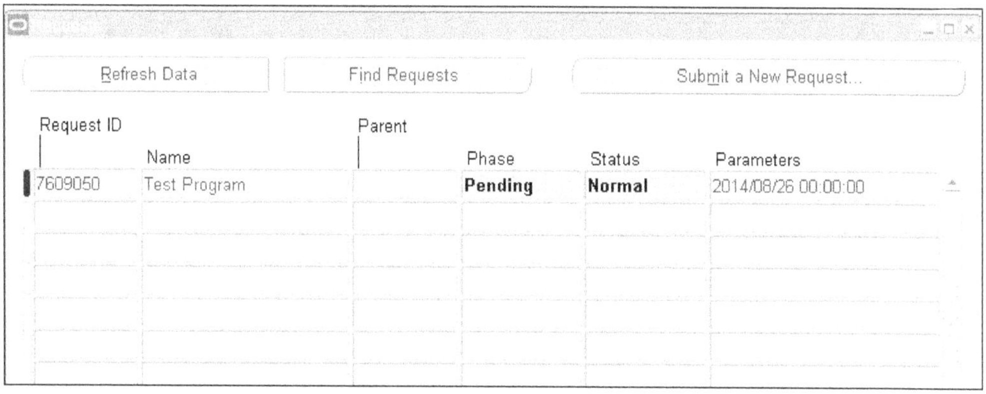

There are four phases when running a report:

- Completed
- Inactive
- Pending
- Running

The value entered in the **Select the Number of Days to View** field will give you the requests submitted by your user for those many days. The default value is set by using the profile option `FND: Default Request Days`.

Scheduling a concurrent program

Scheduling a concurrent program enables a user to run the program as per the schedule defined by the user. Navigate to **US HRMS Manager** | **Processes and Reports** | **Submit Processes and Reports**:

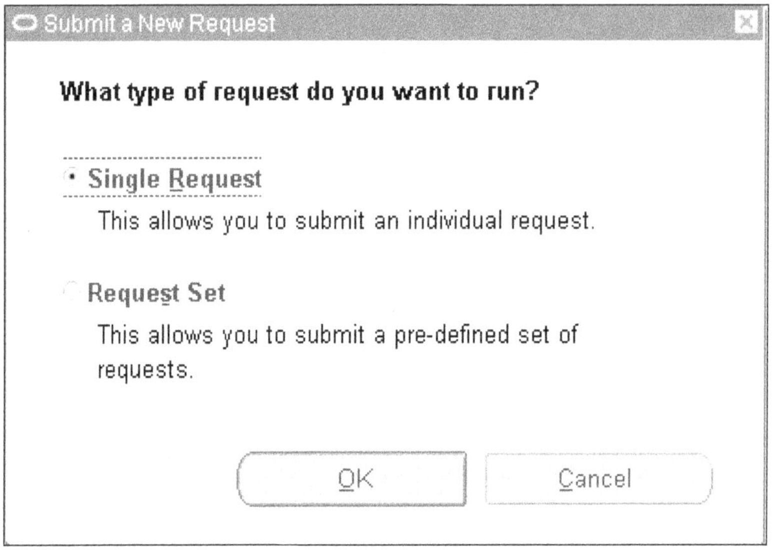

Click on **OK**.

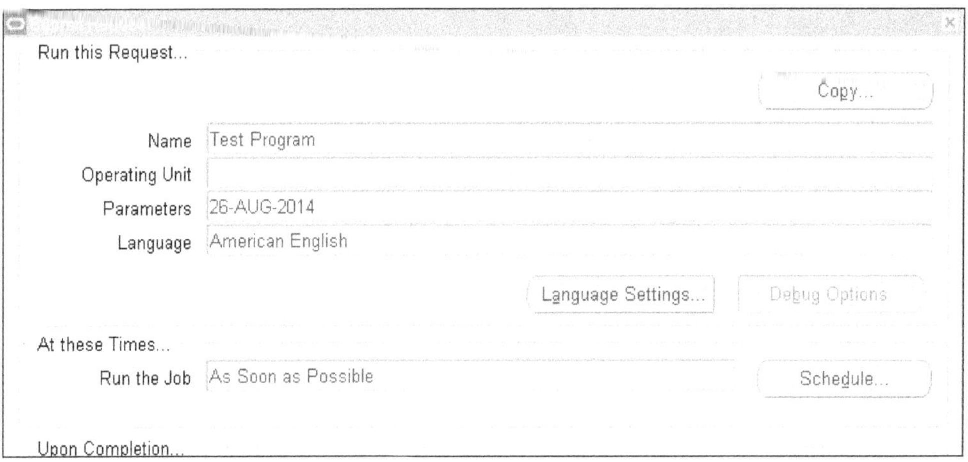

Enter the program name and parameter, and click on **OK**. Then click on the **Schedule...** button.

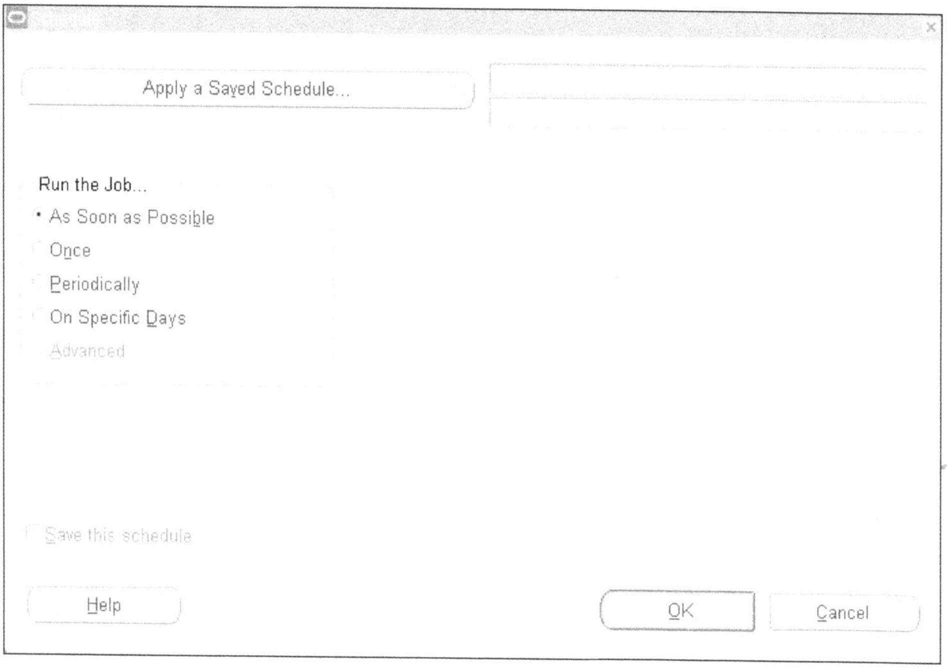

There are a few options regarding the duration you want to run this program for.

Scheduling options

The following are the available scheduling options:

- **As Soon as Possible**: Selecting this option will kick off the concurrent program immediately.

- **Once**: Selecting this option lets you specify at what time and date you want to kick off the concurrent program. The concurrent program will be submitted only once at the specified time and date.

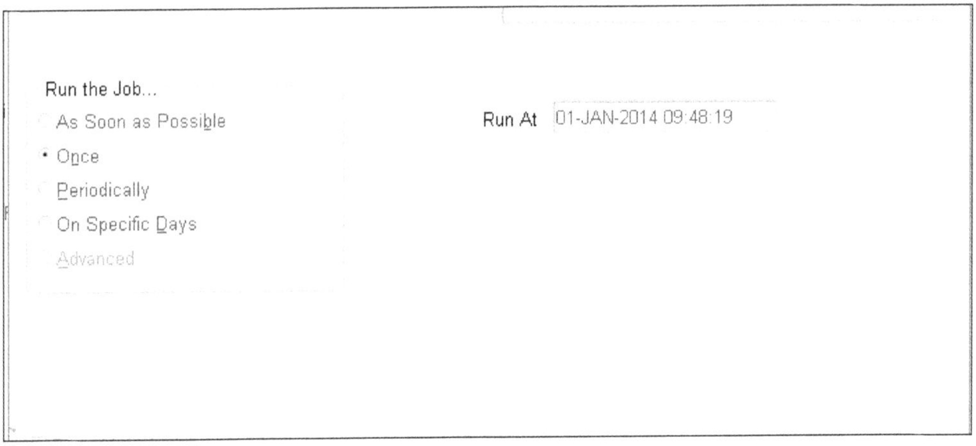

- **Periodically**: This option lets you schedule the program at the specified interval such as once a month/week/day/hour/minute.

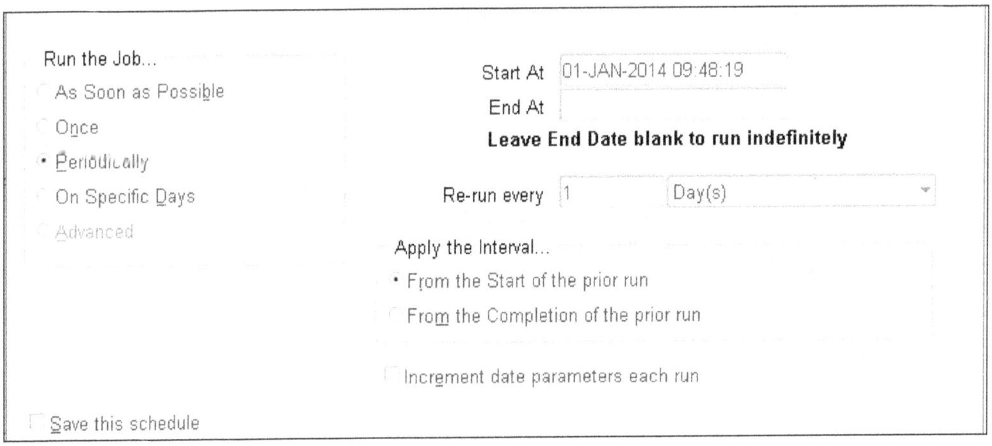

- Start At: This option lets you enter the date and time when you want to start the schedule.
- End At: This option lets you enter the end date for the schedule. Leaving this blank will result in running the schedule indefinitely.
- Re-run every: This option specifies the interval you want to run for, for example—every day or every 2 months.
- Apply the interval: This option specifies how you want to apply the interval, whether from the start of the prior run or from the completion of the prior run; that is, it decides the reference from when then next day the program will be scheduled from. If you select to start the prior run and your program is scheduled to run at 1 P.M. today, then the next schedule will start executing the program from 1 P.M.

If you select the **From the Completion of the prior run** option and your program is scheduled to run from 1 P.M. today and is completed at 5 P.M. then the next schedule will start executing the program from 5 P.M. So the next schedule execution will start at 9 P.M. assuming a program takes 4 hours to complete.

- **Increment date parameters each run**: Use this when one of the parameters for your program is a date. If you check this, the date parameter will be incremented for each run. If not checked, the date given in the parameter will not increment, it will remain the same as entered while scheduling for every run.

- **Apply a Saved Schedule**: If more than one program has to be scheduled in a similar fashion, instead of entering the schedule details for each and every program, you can save the schedule and apply the same schedule for the remaining programs.

- **On Specific Days**: Use this if you want to run the program, for example, on the third day of every month or on every Wednesday. This option lets you choose on what days of every month you want to run a program.

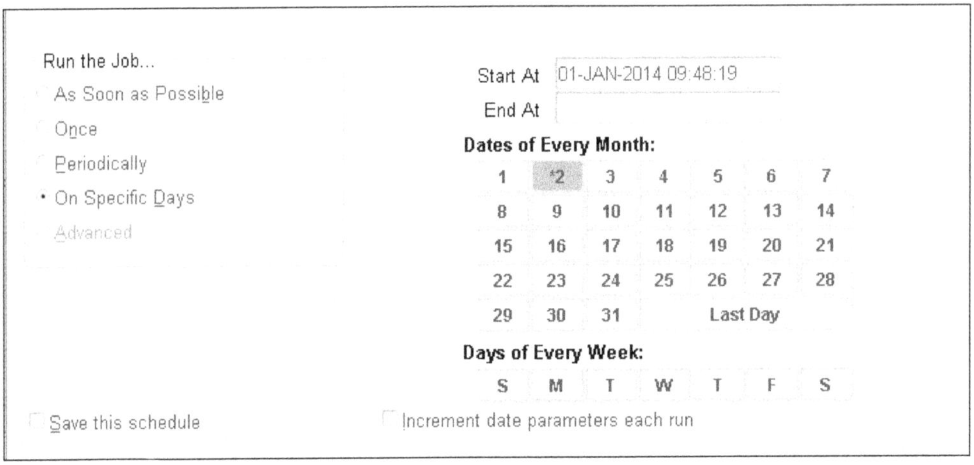

Once you specify the interval you want the program to run for, click on the **OK** button.

We have selected the **Periodically** option to re-run once a day at 1:00 P.M. starting from **01-Jan-2-14** till **15-Mar-2014**, as seen in the following screenshot:

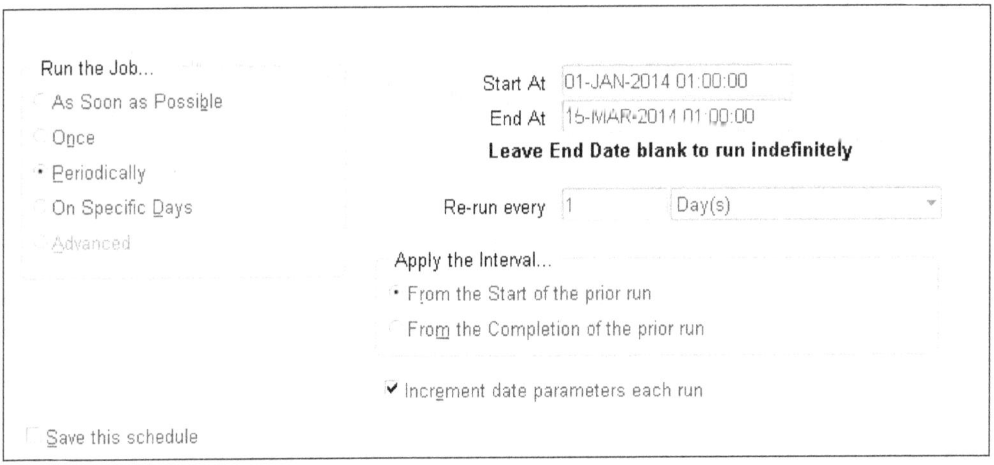

Click on **OK**.

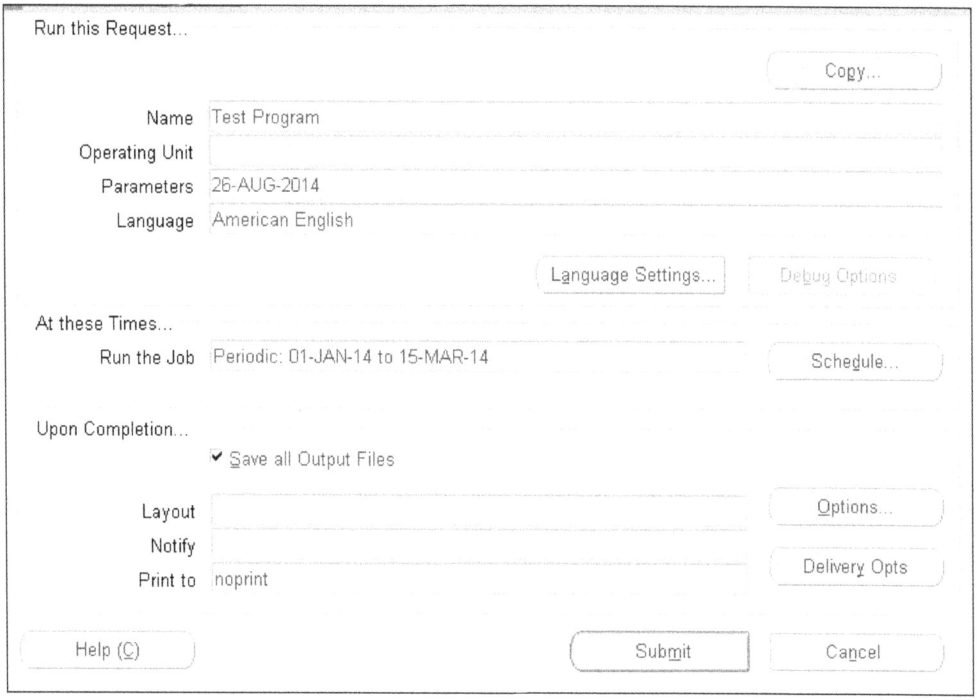

Click on the **Submit** button.

Request set

We need to create a request set if we want to run multiple concurrent programs on a single submit.

This is a way of grouping multiple programs/reports under one set. Navigate to **System Administrator** | **Concurrent** | **Set**, enter the appropriate fields, and save it.

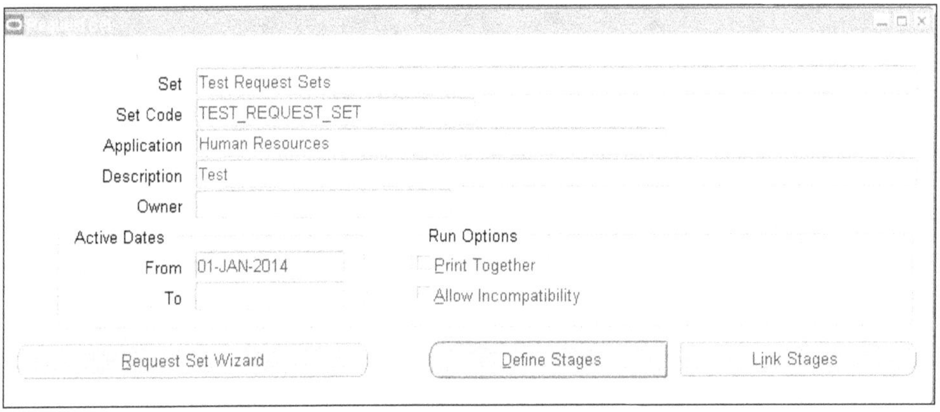

The next step is to define the stages. A request set is composed of one or more stages, and each stage is composed of one or more requests. Stages give the ability to run groups of requests sequentially/parallelly.

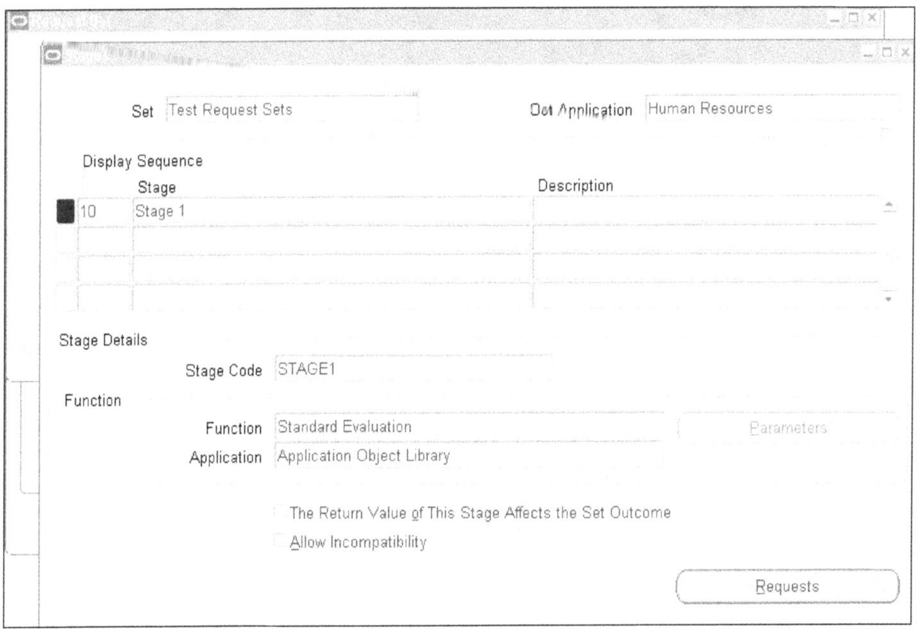

Click on **Requests**.

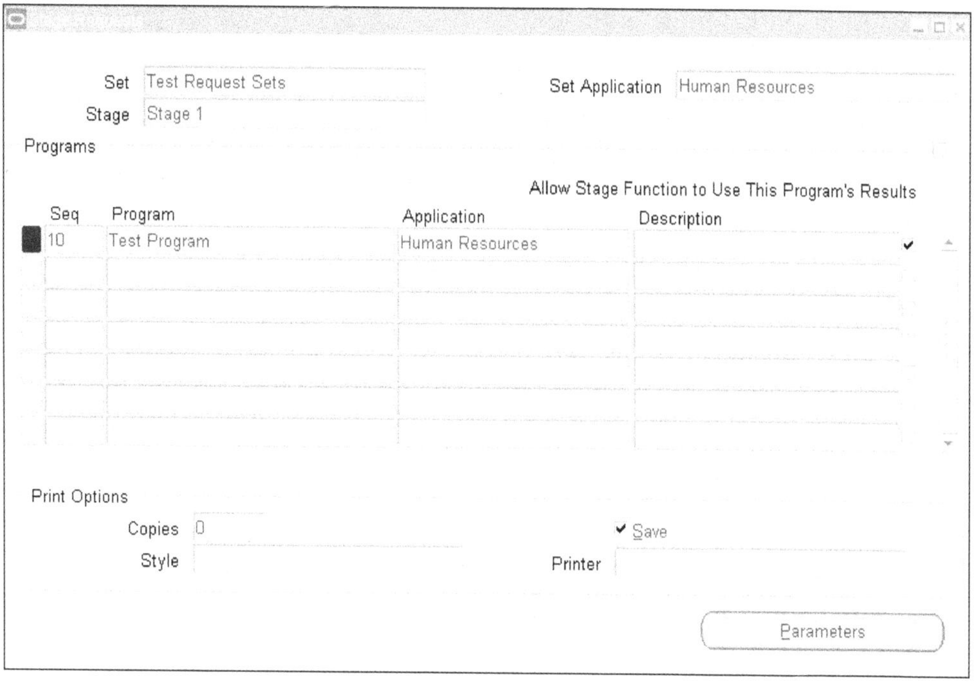

Here, we will specify the program name you want to be a part of the request set. Click on the **Parameters** button. This will open a new form that will allow us to enter the parameters for this program.

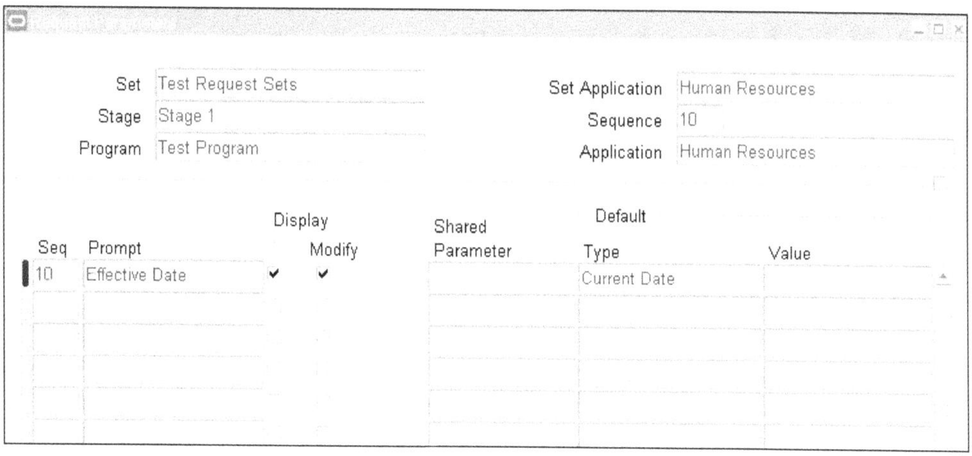

Let's define one more stage, that is, `Stage 2`, which will have some other programs in it.

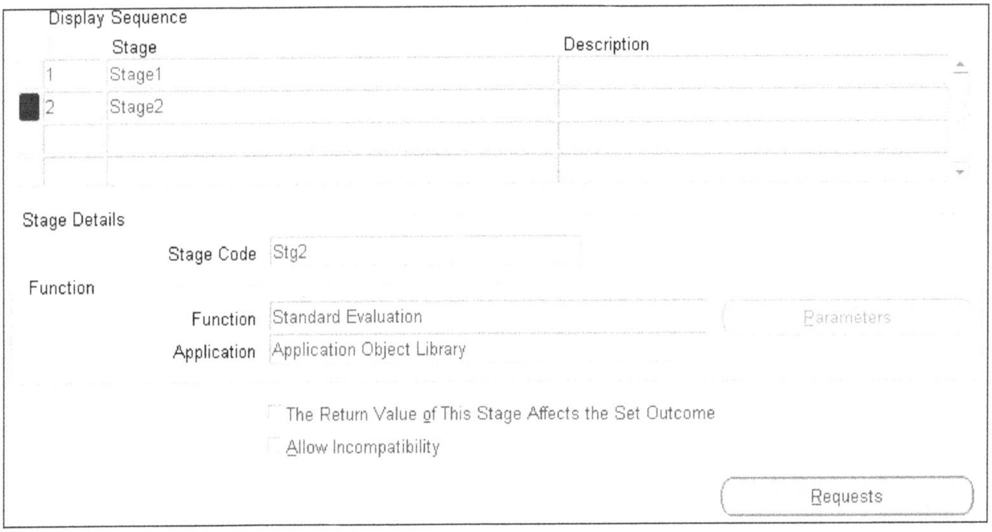

Here, we will add a concurrent program using the **Requests** button, as in the preceding screenshot.

We have added a concurrent program named `TEST` in `Stage 2` of the request set.

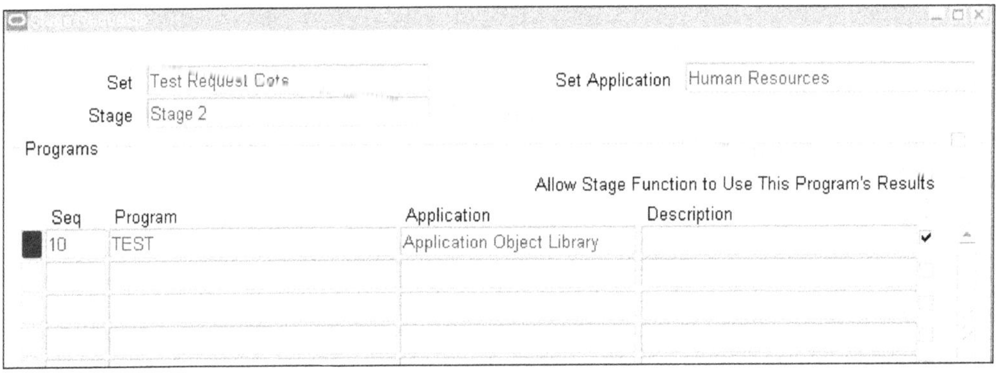

The next step is to link the stages that we have created. As of now, we have two stages and each stage has one concurrent program defined in it. Linking stages will tell the system which sequence to follow once you submit the request set.

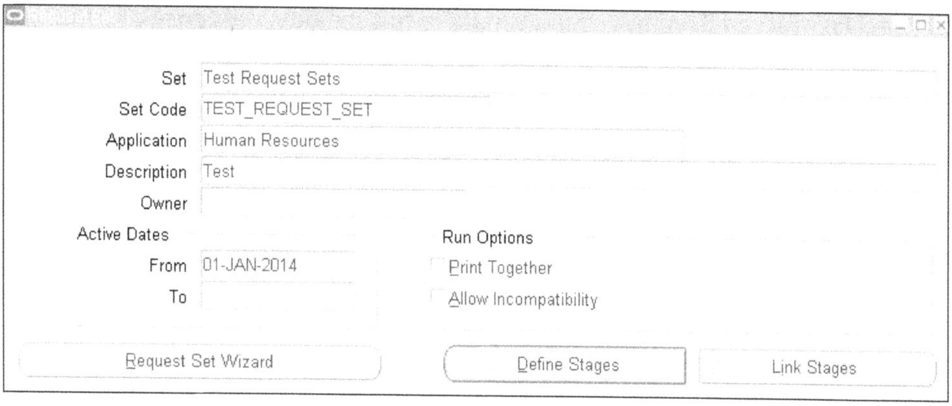

Click on **Link Stages**.

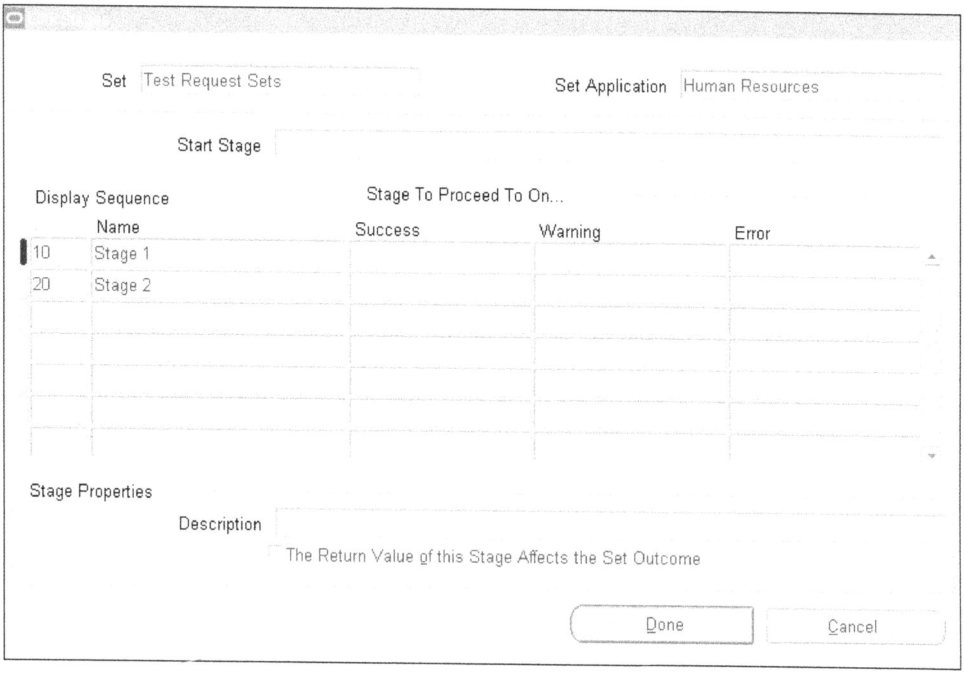

In the preceding form, we need to specify the start stage, that is, which program will be submitted first when you submit the request set.

The **Stage To Proceed To On...** section will specify the next sequence of programs to be executed; that is, if the program's stage is successful/error or in warning state, then what should be the next stage.

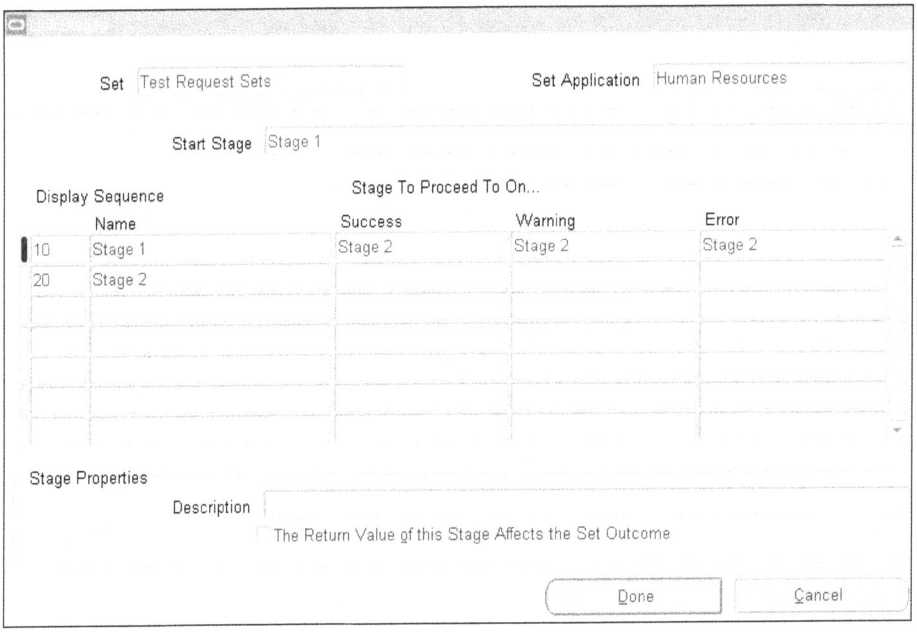

Click on **Done**.

The process to attach a request set to a responsibility is the same as attaching a concurrent program to a responsibility. We just need to add the request set to the request group of the responsibility. Just remember to select the type of request as **Set**.

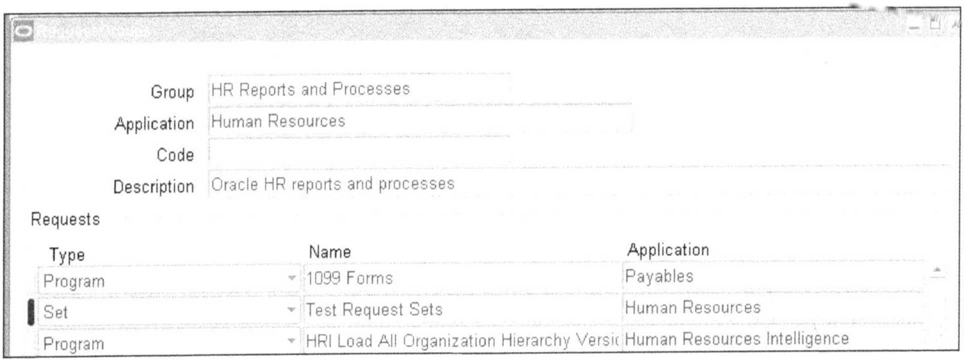

Summary

In this chapter, we covered the role of a system administrator in Oracle applications. We began with covering basic setups performed by the system administrator as part of implementation/rollouts. Furthermore, you understood how to create application users that are used to access the oracle application. We also came across the functionality to create and assign those to the users.

This chapter described menus, the functions which are the basic building blocks of any responsibility. This chapter explained the concept of requests and data groups, which are attached to a responsibility. This chapter also covered in detail the profile option concept in Oracle applications. The profile option is one of the most important functionalities of Oracle apps. This basically controls the behavior of oracle apps.

Then, the chapter explained the concept of SRS, which describes the creation of executables, concurrent programs, parameters, and attaching the concurrent program to a responsibility. It also covered running a concurrent program, scheduling a concurrent program, and the creation of request sets.

In the next chapter, we will see the fundamentals of flexfields and values set along with the configuration of various types of value sets. We will see key flexfields and descriptive flexfields in the Oracle application, which are used extensively in HRMS.

3

Fundamentals of Flexfields / Value Sets

In previous chapters, you learned concepts and functions that are critical to the system administrator role in implementing and managing the Oracle E-Business Suite. In this chapter, we will cover topics that are an integral part of system administration, which includes configuring and the basics of key flexfields and descriptive flexfields, defining value sets, and how we actually use them in our implementation with some examples. Let's begin with value sets.

Value sets

A value set is a set of values or a collection of values. When a user enters a value for a certain field in Oracle, which can be a report parameter or concurrent program parameter, then it validates the entered value.

Navigate to **System Administrator** | **Application** | **Validation** | **Set**.

The **Format Validation** section in the following screenshot will tell us the types of values that are held by the value set. We have selected it as **Char**, which implies that the value in the value set will be of a type character. You have to select the maximum size the value will have. It can be 10, 20, or 100 as per your requirements.

The **Precision** field is used if your value set is of the type number. You can set the precision of the number you want to.

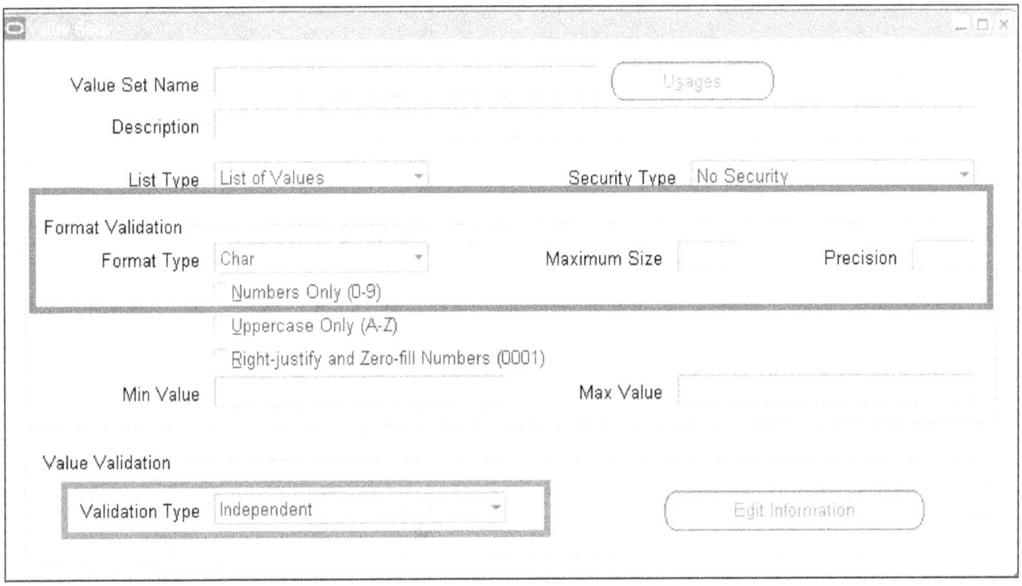

When you create a value set, you need to select the validation type for the value set as indicated in the preceding screenshot.

These are the following types of validation in a value set:

- **None**: This type has no validation
- **Independent**: This type has a defined set of values
- **Dependent**: This type of value set will be dependent on some independent value set
- **Table**: This type of value set will have values for database tables

Independent

After defining the value set in the application, we need to add values in that value set. In order to add values to the value set, we need to navigate to **System Administrator** | **Application** | **Validation** | **Values**.

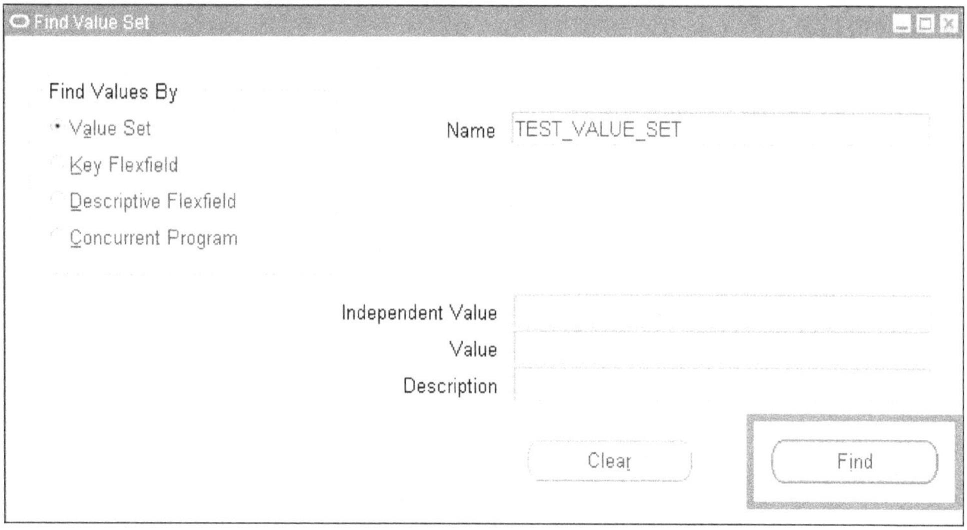

Click on **Find** shown in the preceding screenshot, and then, you should be able to see a screen as indicated here. We will add values 11, 12, 13, 14, and 15 in `TEST_VALUE_SET`. When we say we are adding values in the value set, it implies that this value set will only hold the defined values in it. We can see the details of this usage later in the chapter, where we discuss the use of value sets in various configurations.

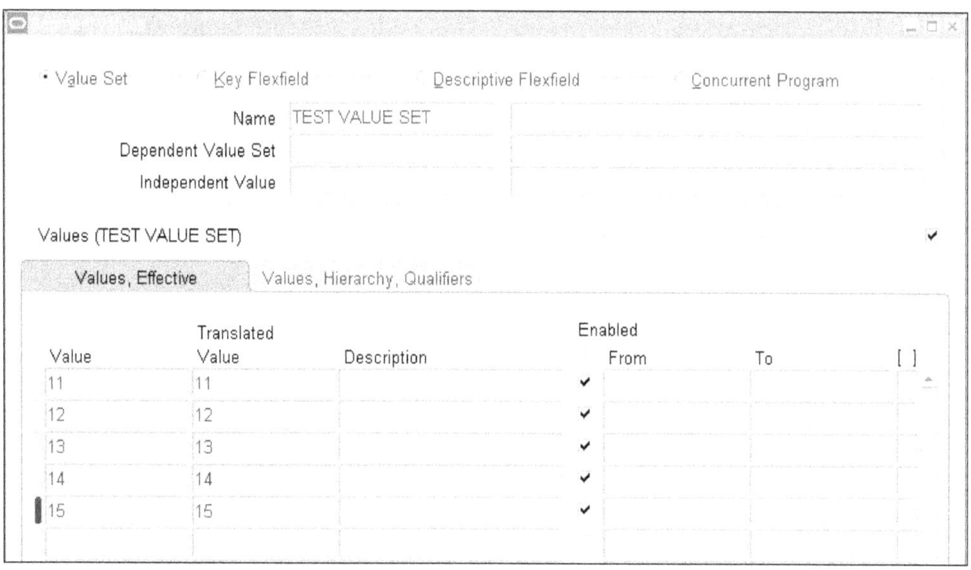

We have added values `11`, `12`, `13`, `14`, and `15` in the preceding value set. After adding the value, we need to save the setup.

Dependent

When I say the value set is of the type dependent, it means that the value set will have a defined set of values in it, and input data is checked against the defined values. Let's look at the following screenshots to get a better understanding:

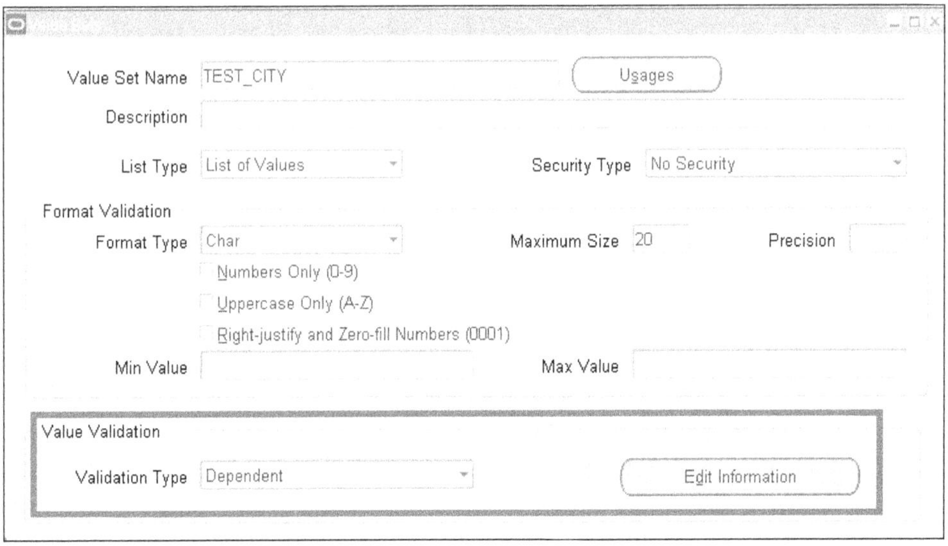

Click on **Edit Information**. It will prompt you to enter the independent value set name. The dependent value set created will be dependent on the values in an independent value set:

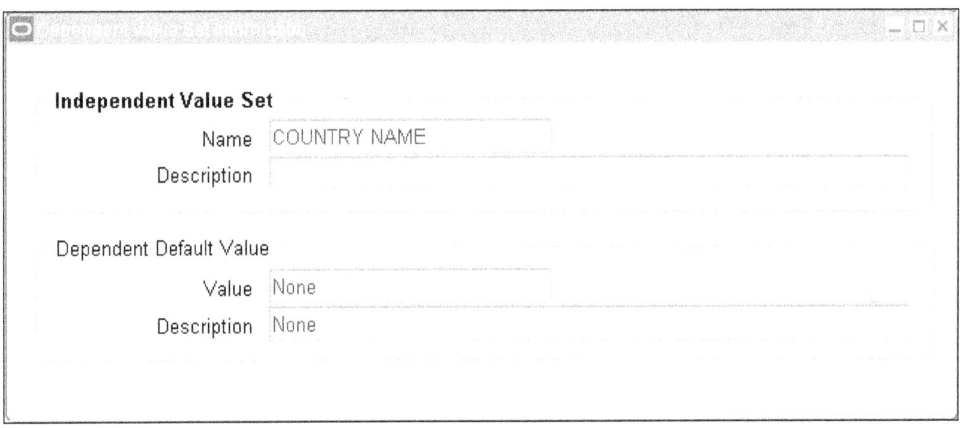

Here, `COUNTRY NAME` is an independent value set with a defined set of values. To view the values in the value set, navigate to **System Administrator** | **Application** | **Validation** | **Values**.

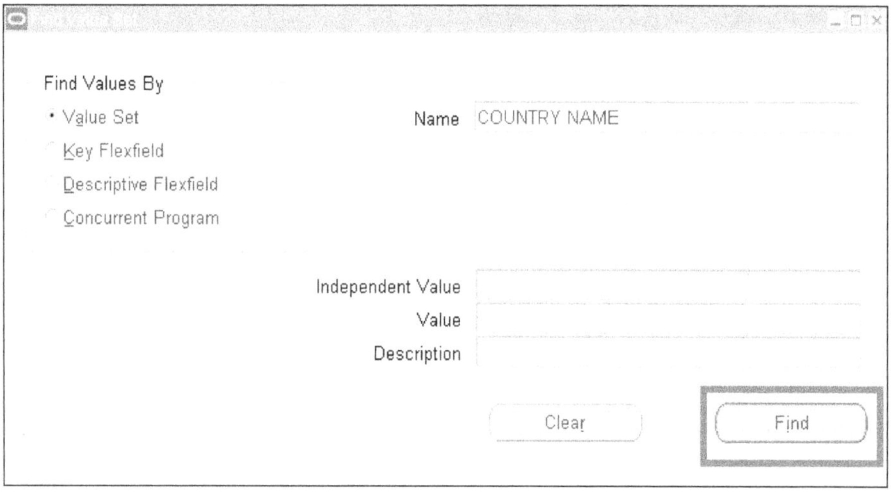

Click on **Find**, and a new form will open to enter the values in this value set.

It has four values defined in it. Now if I want to enter the values for a dependent value set, then I need to find the value set `TEST_CITY` and enter the values.

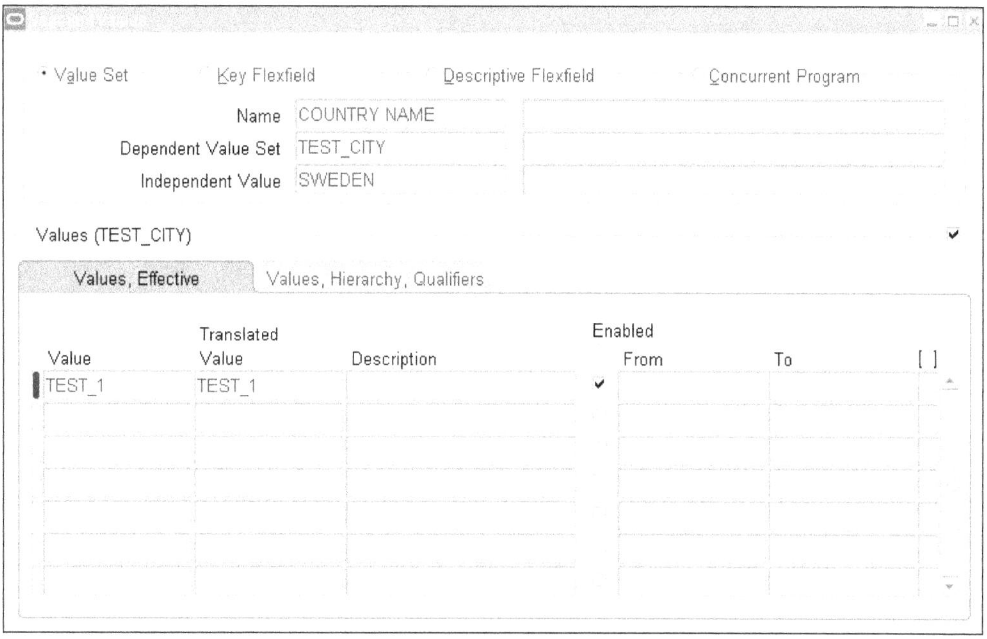

In the preceding screenshot, you can see that I have entered the value `TEST_1` against the independent value `SWEDEN`.

This means that `TEST_CITY` is a dependent value set with the value `TEST_1` that is a subset of the independent value `SWEDEN` of the independent value set `COUNTRY NAME`.

Table

Data input is checked against a table from the database:

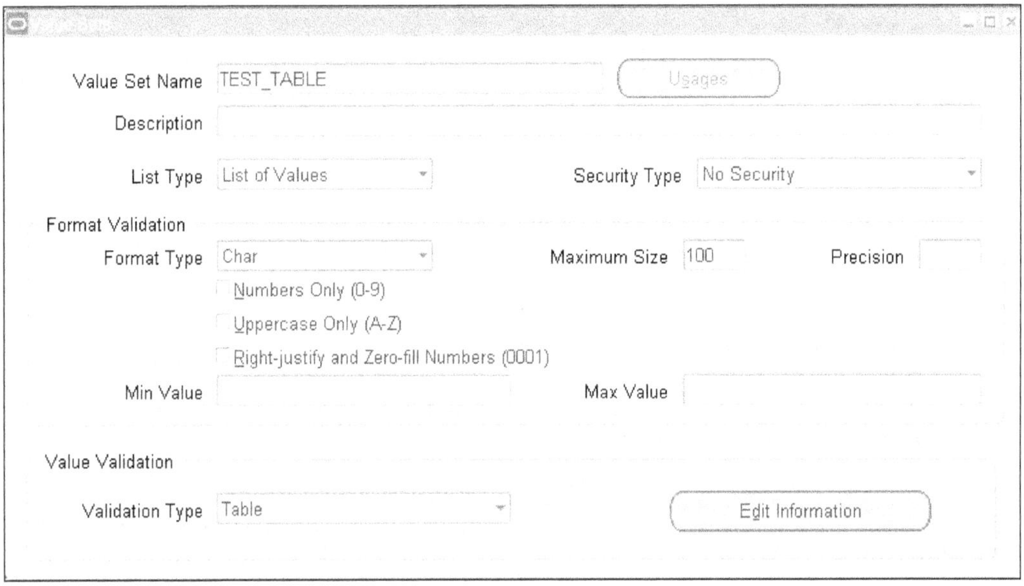

Click on **Edit Information**. The following form will open:

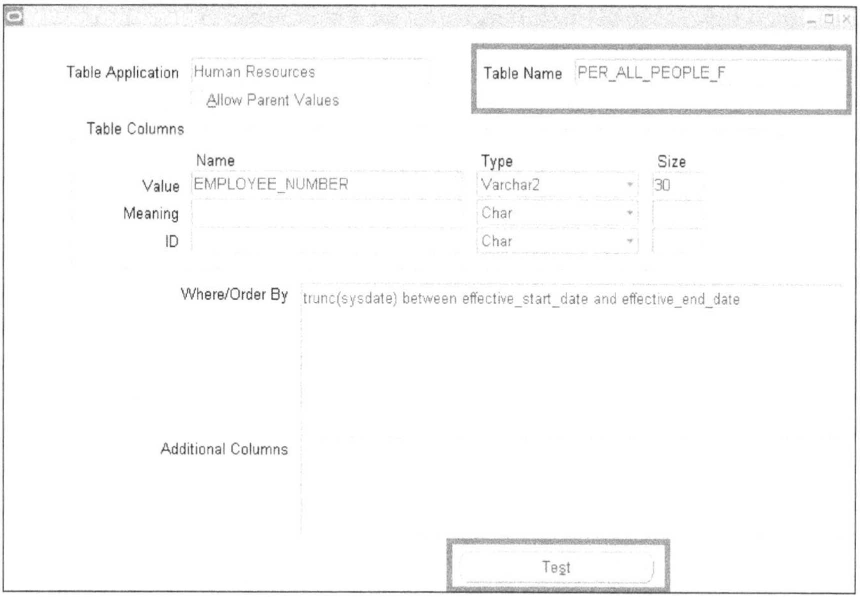

Enter the required field and then click on **Test** to validate the setup. If there is any syntax error in the query written in the **Where/Order By** clause field, then it will give an error; otherwise, it will validate it successfully. The complexity of the query can vary as per the requirement of the value set. In the preceding example, we have written a simple query to fetch a particular column from a single table.

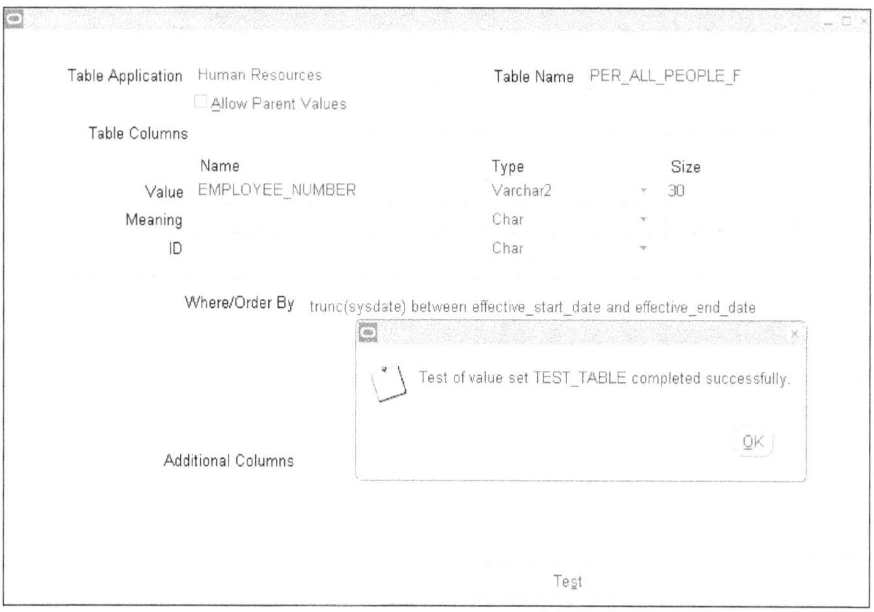

So, if you attach this value set to a parameter of a concurrent program, then the application will fetch employee numbers from the HR table `PER_ALL_PEOPLE_F` and show you a list of all the employee numbers as of the system date.

Significance of $FLEX$

`$FLEX$` enables you to match the prior segment with either a value set name or a segment name. Let `vs2` be the value set definition of the second parameter and `vs1` be the value set definition for the first parameter; then, in the value set, the definition of `vs2` will be `vs2 = value $FLEX$.vs`.

Let's demonstrate the use of these value sets in a concurrent program. This will help you understand the use of value sets in a better way. We will create a concurrent program and attach all the types of value sets created here with each parameter of the concurrent program.

We will use the same concurrent program `Test Program`, which we created in *Chapter 2, Oracle Application System Administration* under the *Create a concurrent program* section.

To view the concurrent program, navigate to **System Administrator** | **Concurrent** | **Program** | **Define**.

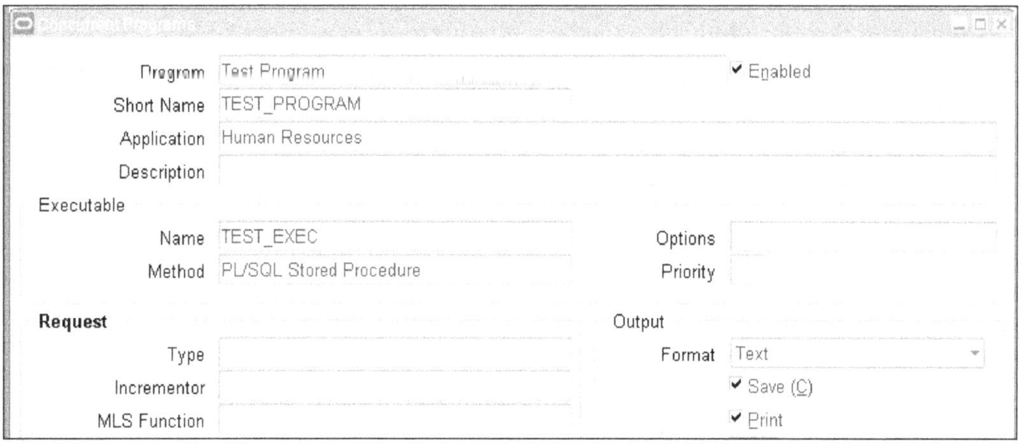

The parameters of the program are as shown in the following screenshot:

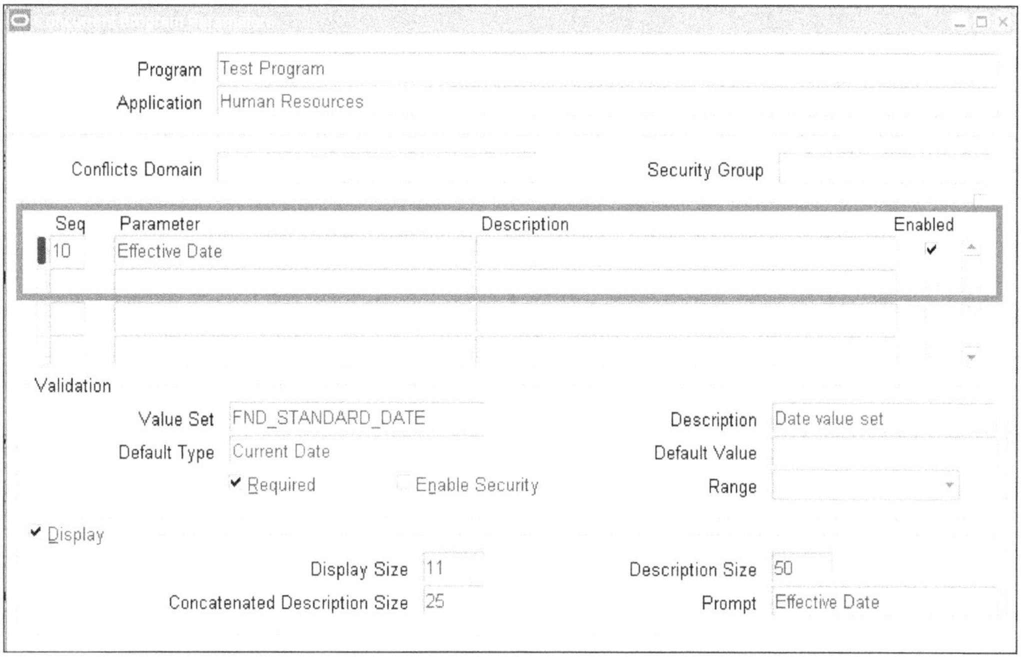

Now, we will add a new parameter in this concurrent program and then attach a value set against that parameter. Parameters can be added with a sequence number and name as marked in following screenshot:

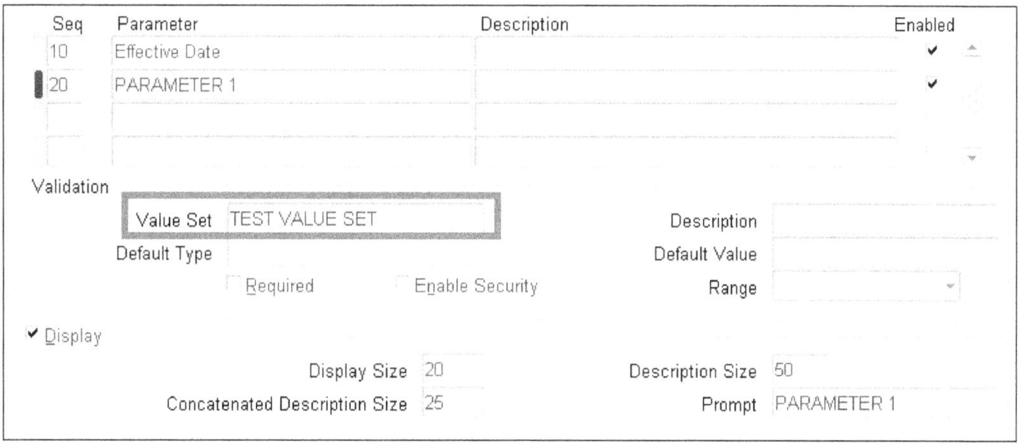

We have attached the independent value set `TEST VALUE SET` to `PARAMETER 1`, as shown in the preceding screenshot.

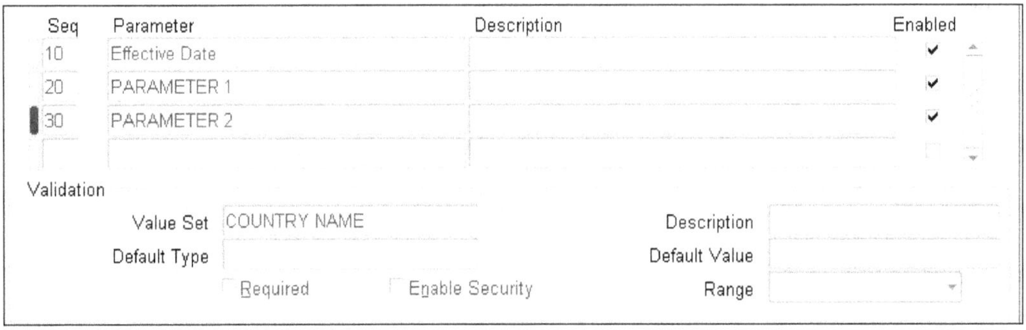

We have attached the independent value set `COUNTRY NAME` to `PARAMETER 2`, as shown in the preceding screenshot.

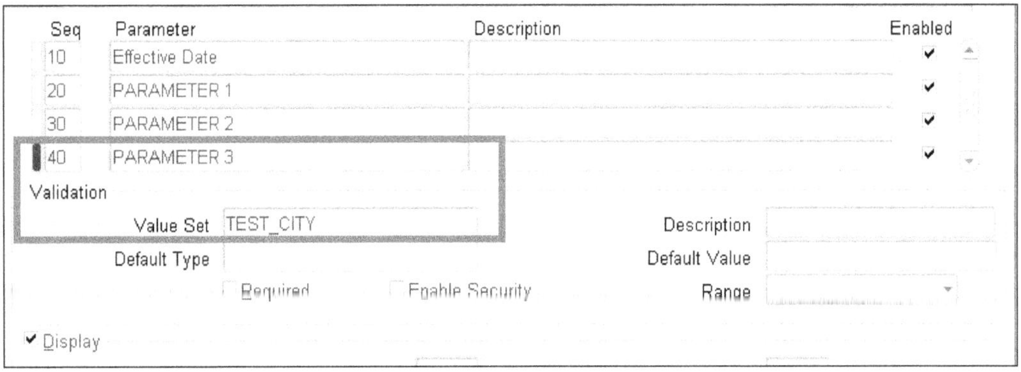

We have attached the dependent value set `TEST_CITY` to `PARAMETER 3`, as shown in the preceding screenshot.

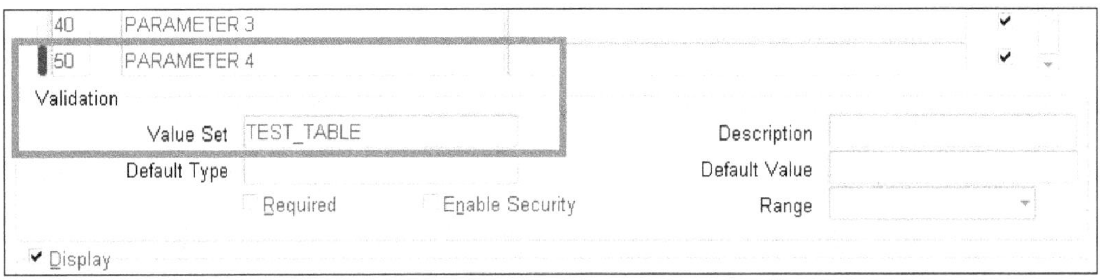

We have now attached the table validated value set `TEST_TABLE` to `PARAMETER 4`. Let's now run the program by navigating to **US HRMS Manager** | **Processes and Reports** | **Submit Processes and Reports**.

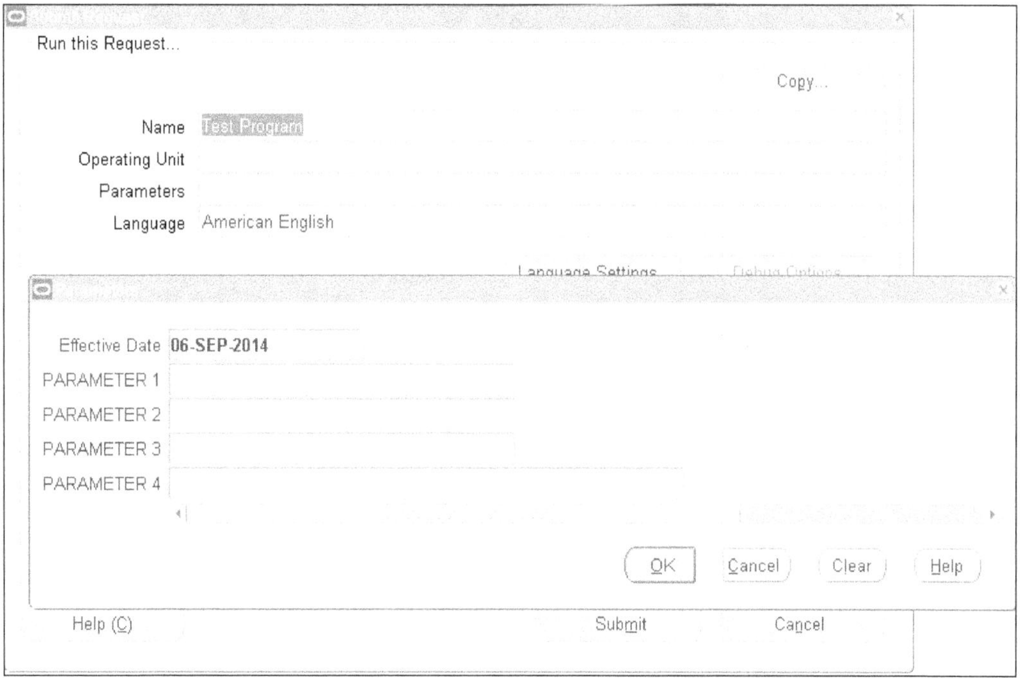

Let's now see the view in each parameter:

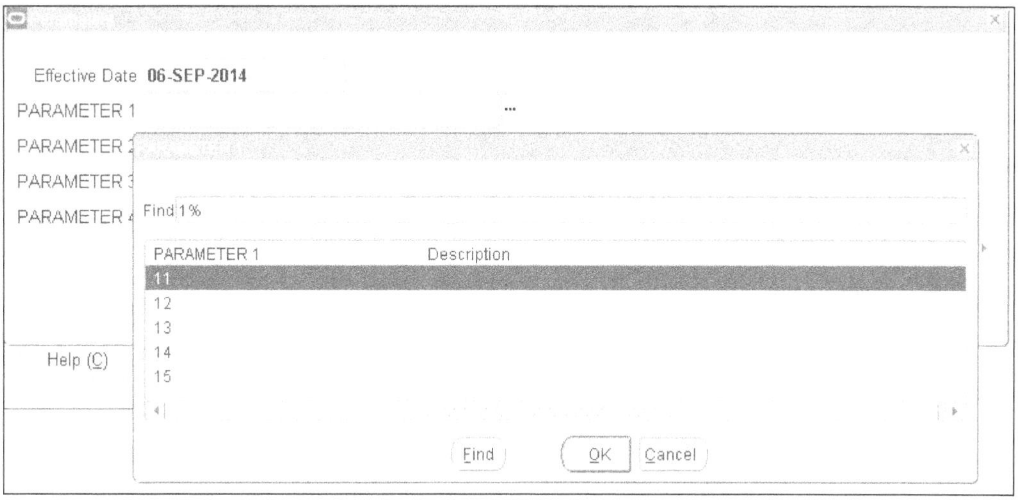

PARAMETER 1 displays all the values we defined, which are 11 to 15.

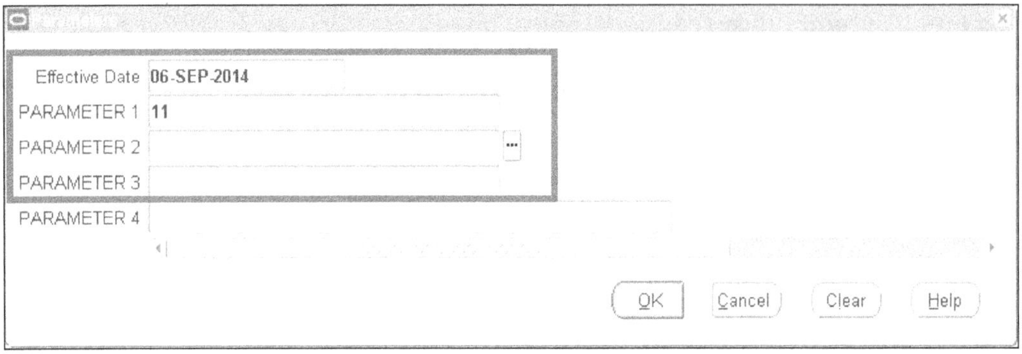

PARAMETER 3 is dependent on PARAMETER 2. Hence, it is grayed out. Once you select PARAMETER 2, it will allow you to enter the values as shown in the following screenshot:

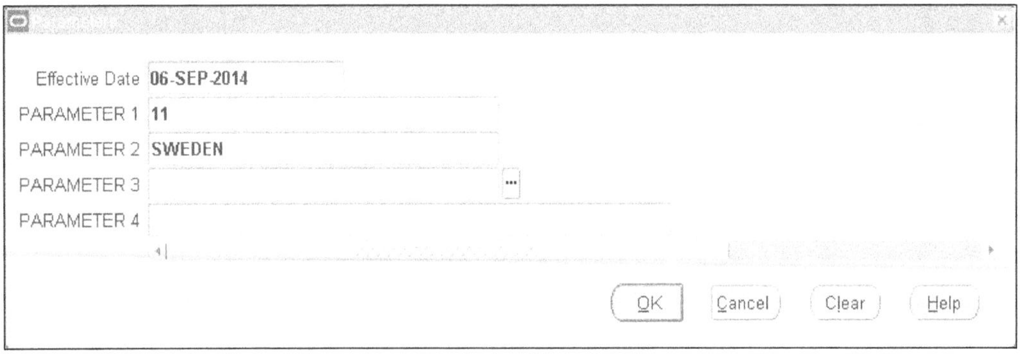

We entered value TEST_1 for the country SWEDEN in the value set. Hence, you have TEST_1 appearing in the selection:

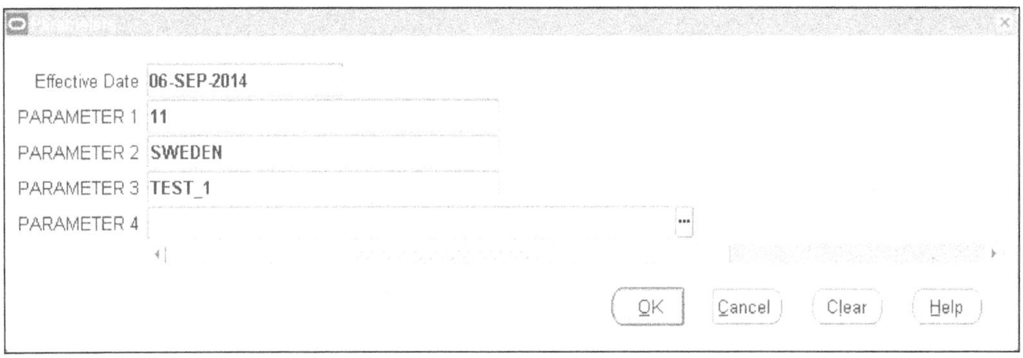

If you select the `PARAMETER 2` value as India (IN), you will not get any random value in `PARAMETER 3`, as we have not defined the `CITY` name in the value set for `IN`.

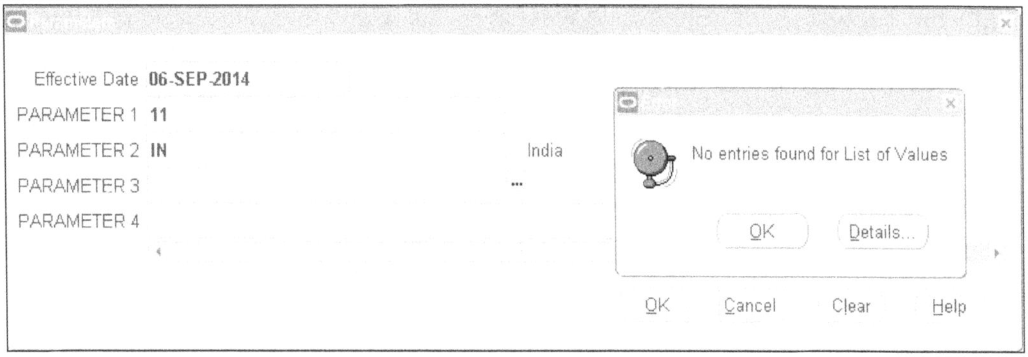

`PARAMETER 4` will show you all employee numbers from the table as it is a table dependent value set and will show values as per the query written in the value set definition:

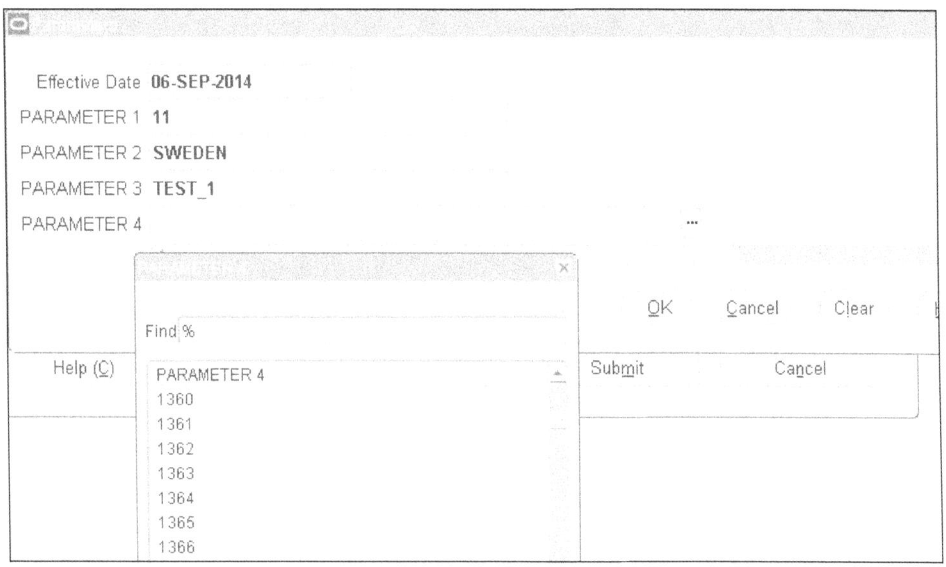

Thus, we have seen an example of using a value set in a concurrent program.

Flexfields in Oracle apps

As the name suggests, a flexfield is a flexible field. It is made up of various subfields or segments. Each segment in a flexfield will have a name and optionally a set of values. A segment is validated using a different value set. You can assign a single value set to more than one segment, and you can even share value sets among different flexfields. This means you can have two segments having the same value but different prompts.

A flexfield structure is a specific configuration of segments. You can add or remove segments, or rearrange the order of segments in a flexfield to get a different structure. There are two types of flexfields—**Key flexfields** and **Descriptive flexfields**.

Key flexfields

In Oracle HRMS, there are a total of eight **Key flexfields** (**KFF**). Out of these eight KFFs, only six are mandatory in HRMS. What I mean by mandatory is, they are required while creating a new business group. You cannot create a business group until you define these KFFs in your application. The mandatory six are as follows:

- Grade
- Job
- Position
- People Group
- Cost Allocation
- Competency

The following are nonmandatory:

- Bank
- Personal Analysis

Let's take Grade KFF and explain it with an example.

Say you are from the IT company. Obviously, your company will have different departments in it. Employees in each department will have a specific grade. The grade signifies your relative level in a company.

Now, you decide to assign grades to your employees. How will you go about it? At this point, you might have various questions. What naming convention shall I follow? Should I use the same names for all departments or different naming conventions for each department so that I can easily distinguish employees based on grades? The answer to all these questions will tell you the grade structure for your company.

So after a lot of thinking, you decide that you will follow a structure for grades that will have both the department and grade name in it.

Suppose you keep grade names starting from one to five and consider you have three departments in your company that are IT department, HR department, and Admin department. So your grade structure will be `Department.GradeName`. Hence, employees will have one of the following grades:

- IT.1, IT.2, IT.3, and so on
- HR.1, HR.2, and so on
- Admin.1, Admin.2, and so on

Now, once you have decided that your grade will be as `Department.GradeName`, the real task of defining grade KFFs starts. In Oracle app terminology, your Grade KFF structure is a two-segment structure; segment 1 is a department name and segment 2 is grade name.

Let's see how to define a KFF. Navigate to **System Administrator** | **Application** | **Flexfield** | **Key** | **Segments**.

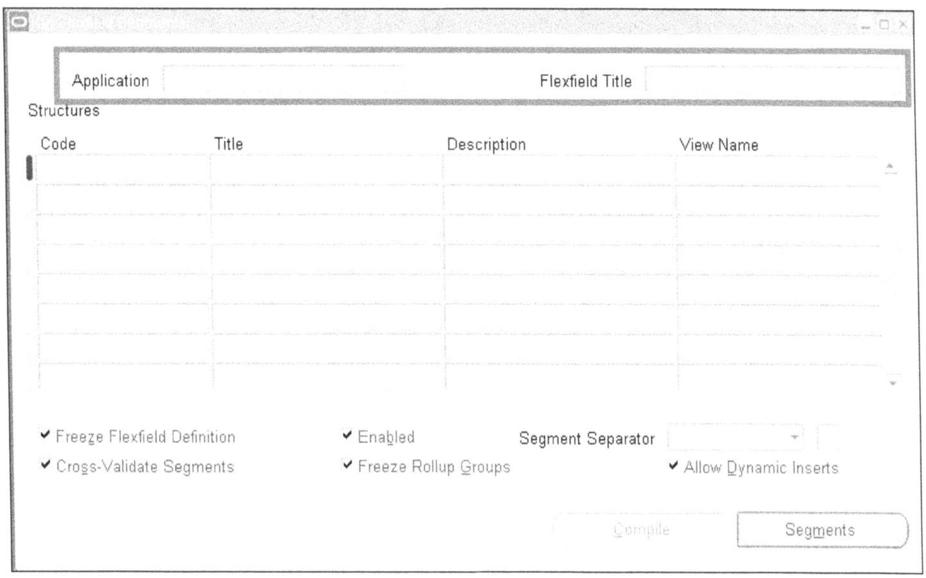

The preceding form is used to define the KFF in an Oracle application. The application field marked will decide the application of the KFF it is related to, for example, Human Resource, Payroll, Receivables, and so on.

The flexfield title, in our case, will be `Grade Flexfield` and the application will be `Human Resources`:

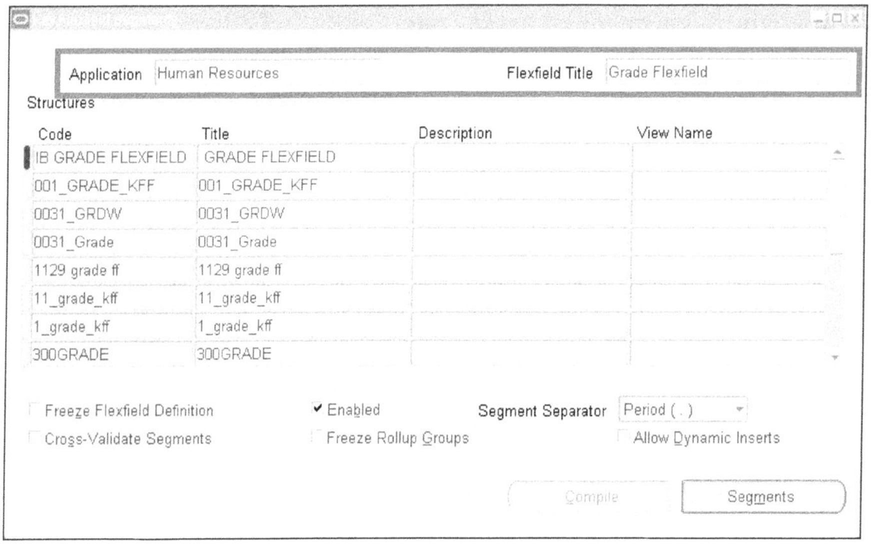

Let's create a new grade structure `TEST_GRADE`. Navigate to **File** | **New**. Enter the **Code** and **Title** fields as `TEST_GRADE` and click on **Save**.

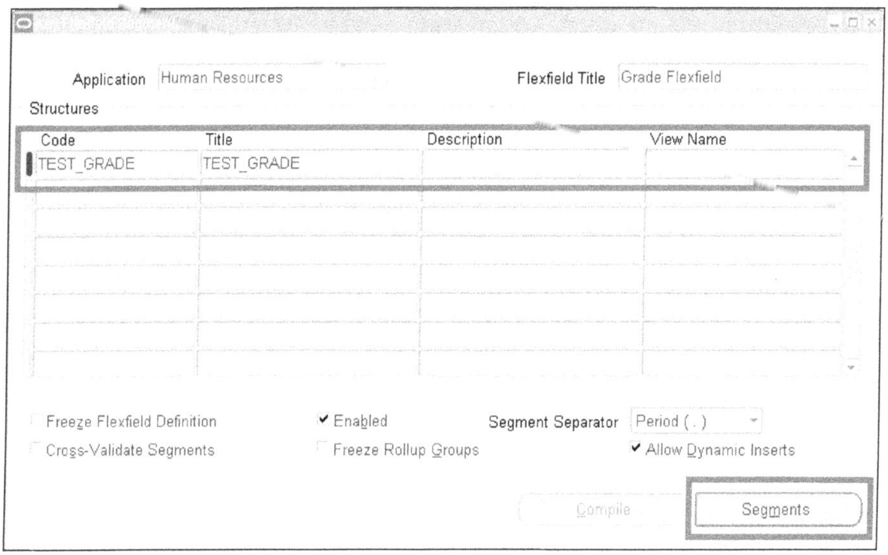

Click on **Segments**.

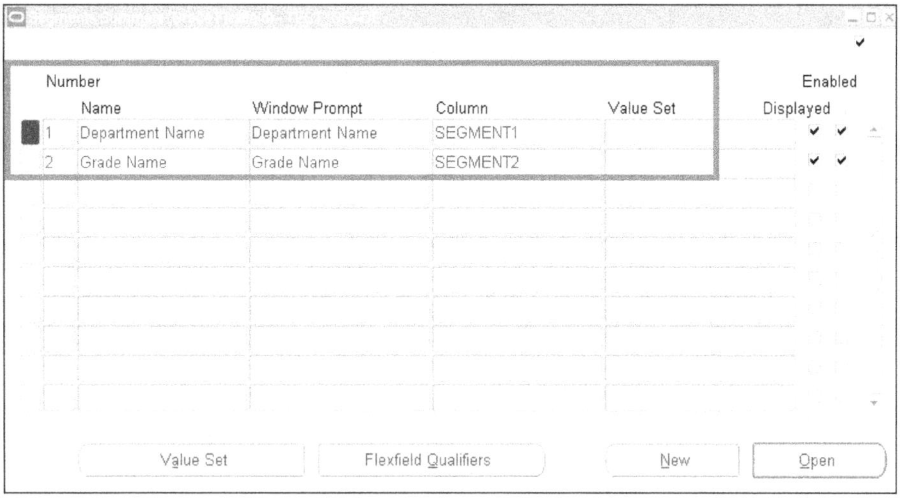

In the preceding screenshot, we have defined two segments `Department Name` and `Grade Name`. Currently, we have not attached any value sets. If you do not attach any values using the value set for the segment, then the field becomes a free text that will enable the user to enter any text of his choice. However, this is not the best practice. So let's define two value sets for each segment.

Let the defined value set for `Department Name` and `Grade Name` be `TEST_DEPT` and `TEST_GRADE` respectively. Both will be independent value sets.

We have seen earlier how to define an independent value set.

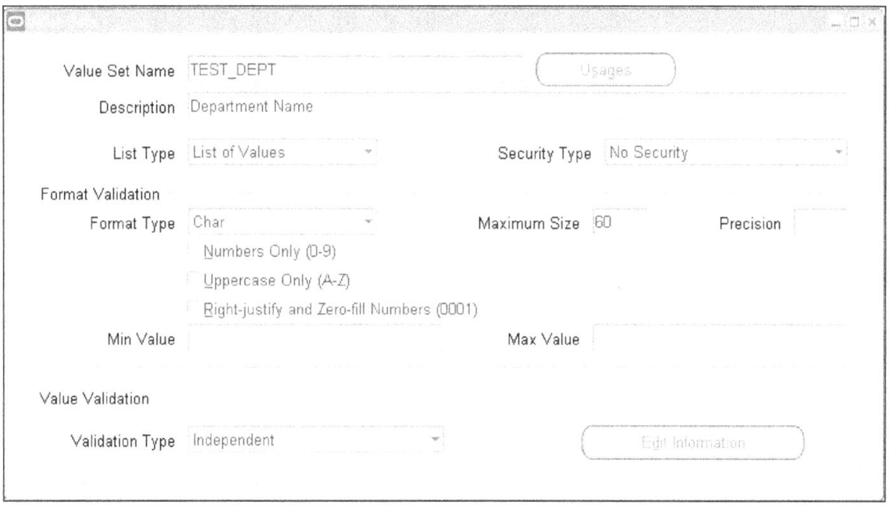

In the preceding screenshot, we have defined an independent value set `TEST_DEPT` that will store the department name. The format type is **Char** and the maximum size defined is `60`.

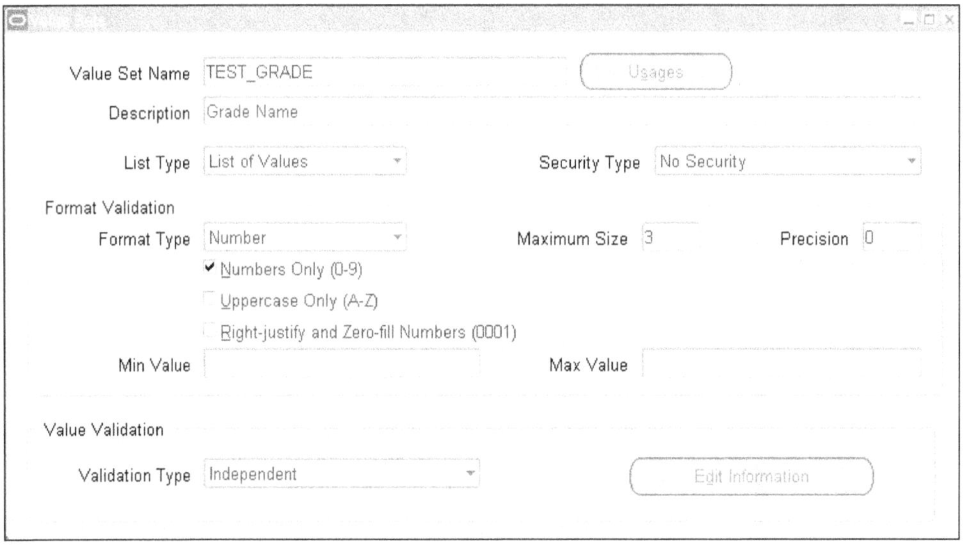

Similarly, we have defined `TEST_GRADE` as another independent value set with the type as **Number** and maximum size as `3`, and we have set a validation that it will have a value in numbers (that is, 0-9).

Let's attach these value sets to the KFF segments.

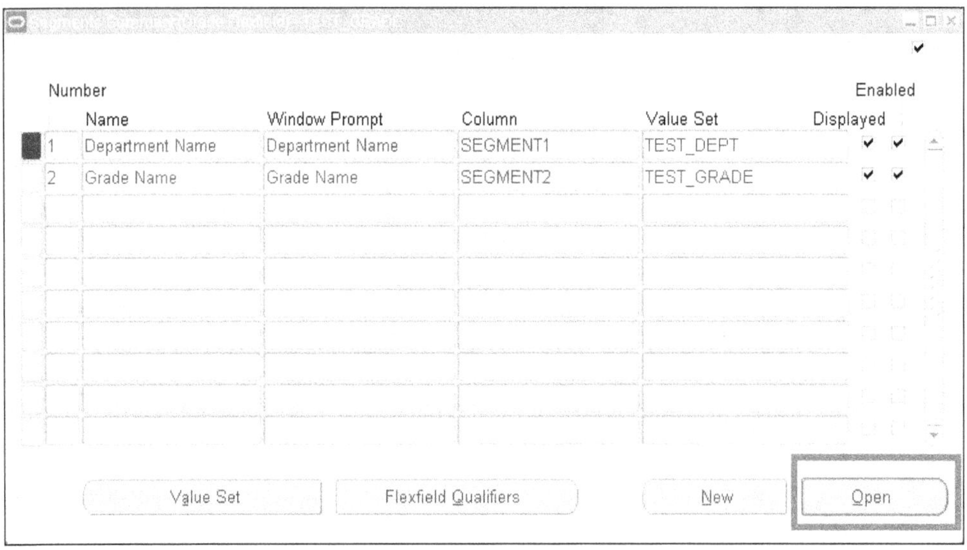

By default, both these fields will be mandatory. Grade is a part of the assignment information for an employee. So, when you enter the assignment information, you have to enter the grade as it is a mandatory field. There might be a requirement in which grade is nonmandatory. For example, an employee in your organization might not have a grade. So, in such cases, you have to make these segments nonmandatory. Whatever property you set, it will be applicable to all assignments in your organization. To make it nonmandatory click on **Open**.

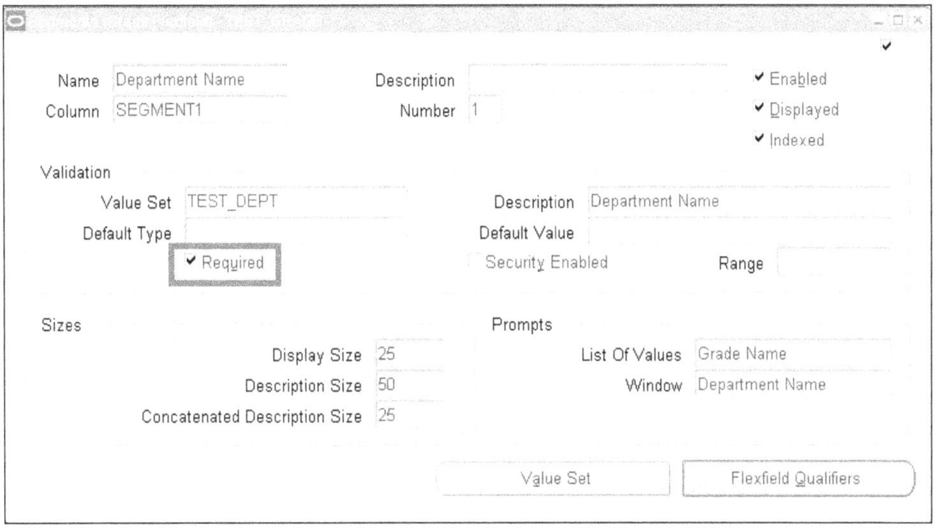

Uncheck the **Required** checkbox in the **Validation** section.

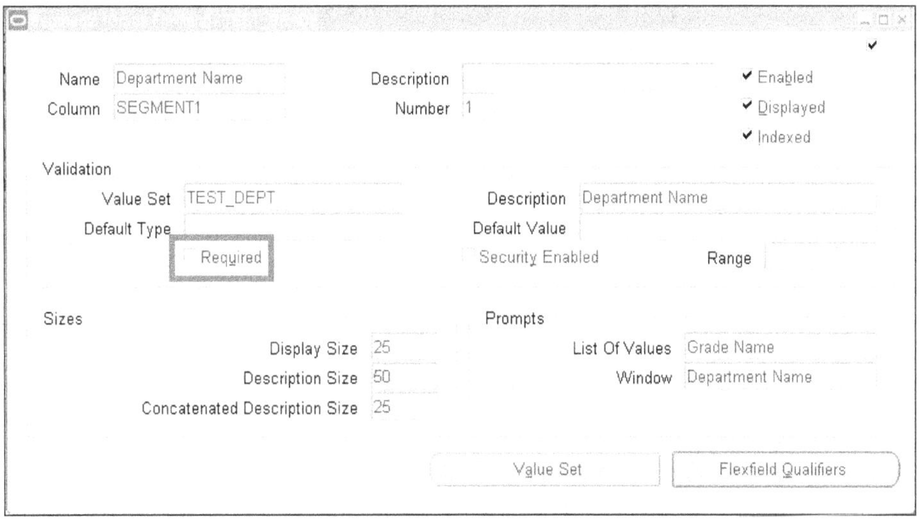

The same goes for `Grade Name`.

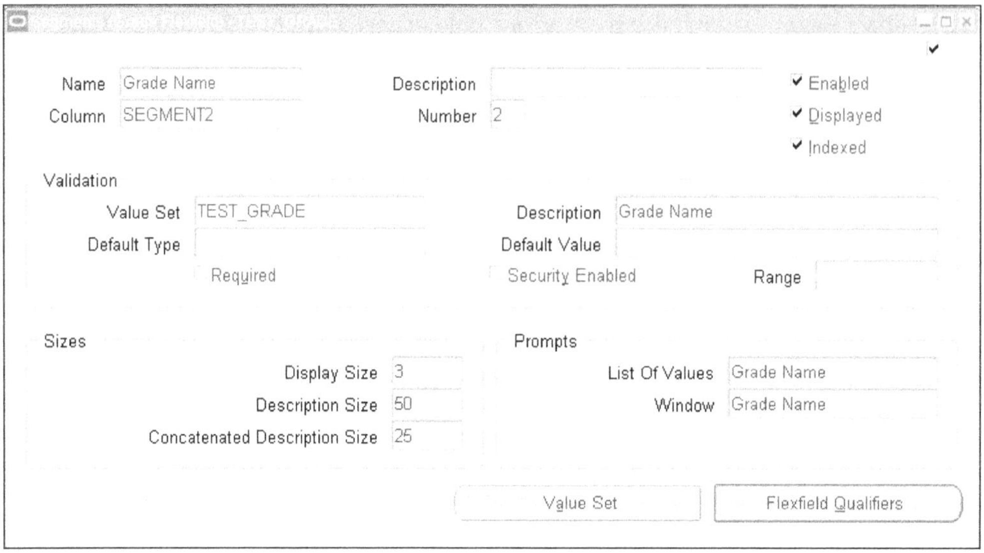

Once you define your required KFFs, you have to attach them to your Business Group. This will be demonstrated in the next chapter.

Let's now learn about **Descriptive flexfields** (**DFF**).

Descriptive flexfields

Descriptive flexfields or DFFs are the extra attributes offered along with the standard table structures to hold the extra data needed by the enterprise. They are generally used for extra reporting functionality.

A seeded table has an extra set of columns/attributes to store the DFFs. If an enterprise has to store any particular data that is not stored in any of the standard columns of the table provided by Oracle EBS, that column can be stored in the database using a DFF. For example, if you want to store whether the employee in your organization is Oracle certified or not, then you can use DFF.

DFFs can be context-specific. We can configure the DFFs in such a way that the data will appear based on the value filled in a specific table. For example, if we want to keep the visa details of the employee. But visa detail fields should only appear if the employee is Expatriate, which is if the employee is not a resident of the country he/she works in. In this case, we can use the work status as a context column. If the value of the field is Expatriate, we will use the DFF to store the visa details; otherwise, the DFF will not appear at all.

So, the DFF can be customized in such a way that data entered in one attribute depends on the data entered in another, whichever is the context.

There can be two types of context as follows:

- Global contexts / Global data elements
- Business contexts

The Global data elements will always appear on the form, whereas the Business context-specific data elements appear only when there is a context specified. The context can be set from any value in the form or might just be another value from the DFF. If the value is seeded from the forms, then it is called a reference field; whereas, if it is just another attribute inside the DFF, it is called a context field. Mostly, context fields are used and are put in the DFF itself. Once the context field is entered, it extends the form to capture the context-specific data elements.

To set up DFF, navigate to **Application** | **Flexfield** | **Descriptive** | **Segments**, as shown in the screenshot:

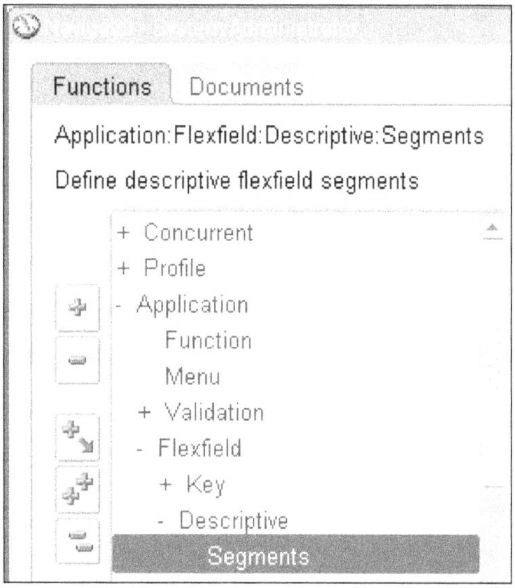

Let's say we want to capture whether an employee is Oracle certified or not. This will be defined in global data elements. Once defined in global data elements, it will be visible across all business groups.

In addition to this, suppose you want to capture data based on the type of employee. If the person is an employee, then you want to capture his old employee number. If the person is an applicant, you might want to capture the current employer.

Both these sets of data will be captured on this person's record.

Let's see how we can achieve this. Navigate to **System Administrator** | **Application** | **Descriptive** | **Segments**.

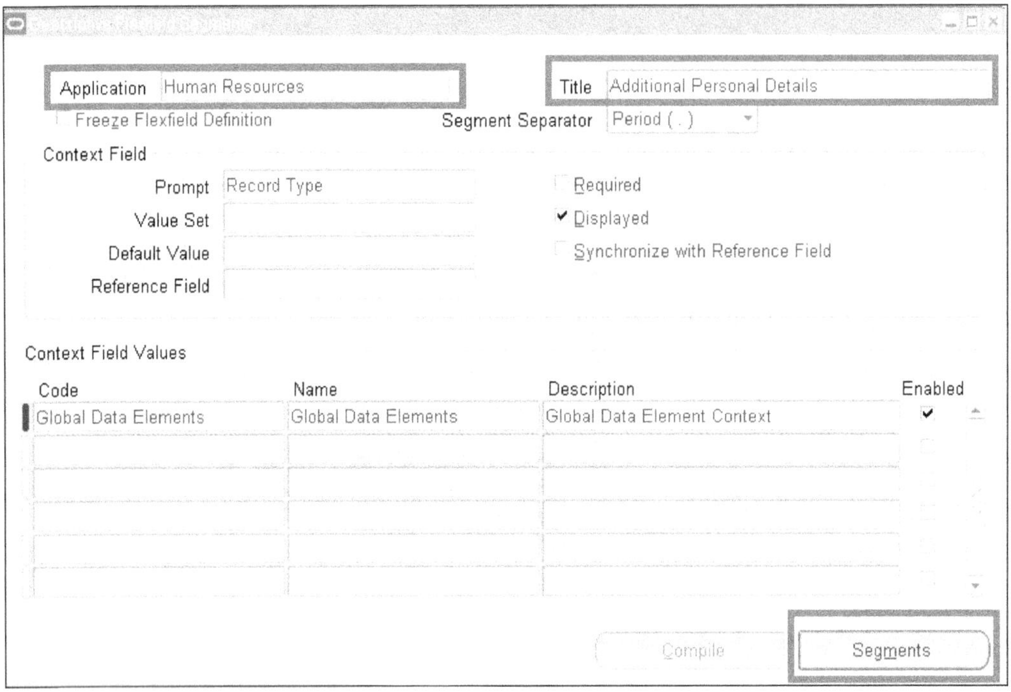

You need to unfreeze the flexfield definition by unchecking the field as marked in the preceding screenshot. **Title** as `Additional Personal Details` and **Prompt** as `Record Type`.

Click on **Segments**.

The segments for Global Data Elements are as shown in the following screenshot:

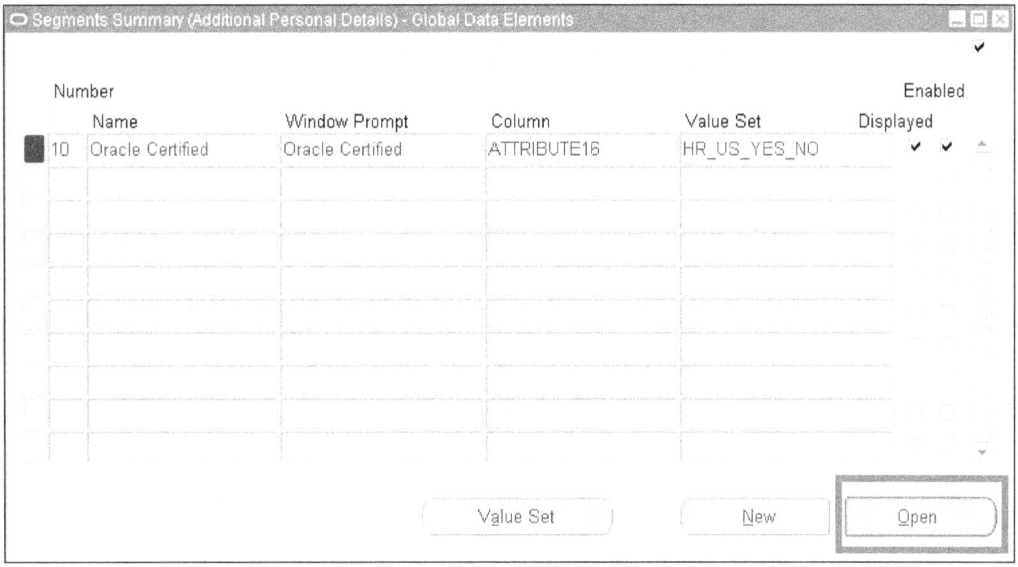

The value set attached is `HR_US_YES_NO`. This will have the value Yes/No. Data will be saved in `ATTRIBUTE16` of the person's table, that is, `PER_ALL_PEOPLE_F`.

Click on **Open**.

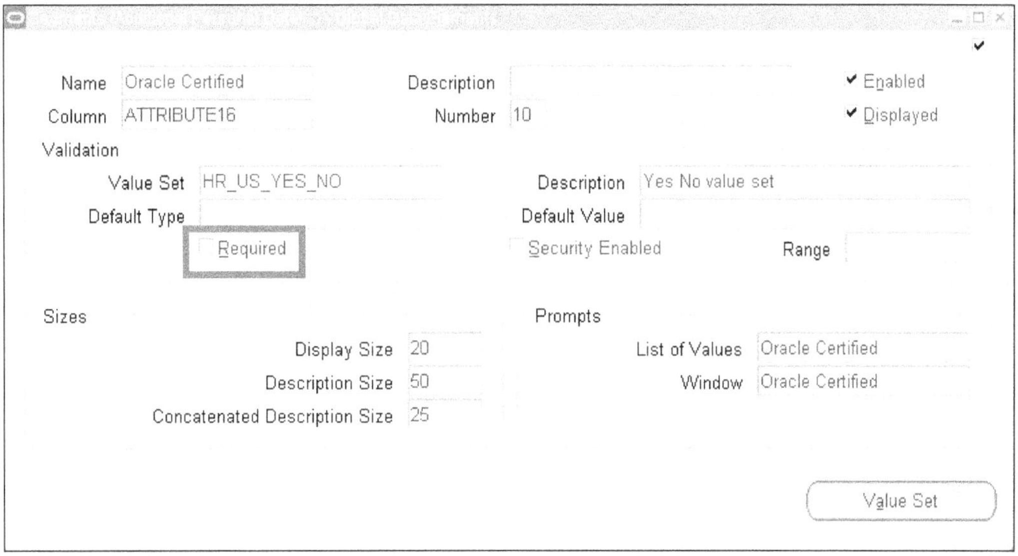

The **Required** field is not set. Hence, it is not mandatory.

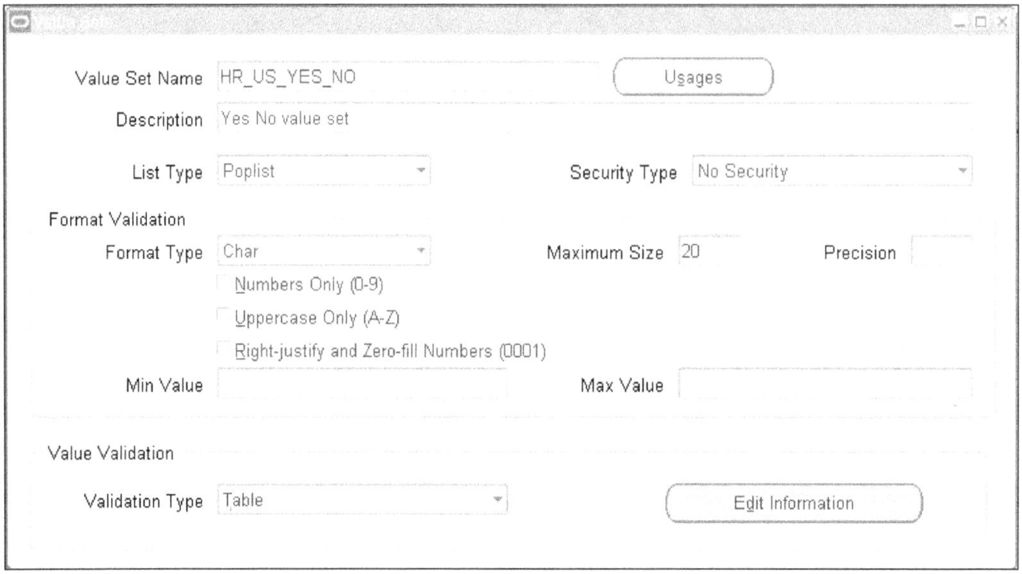

`HR_US_YES_NO` is a dependent value set that fetches values from a lookup.

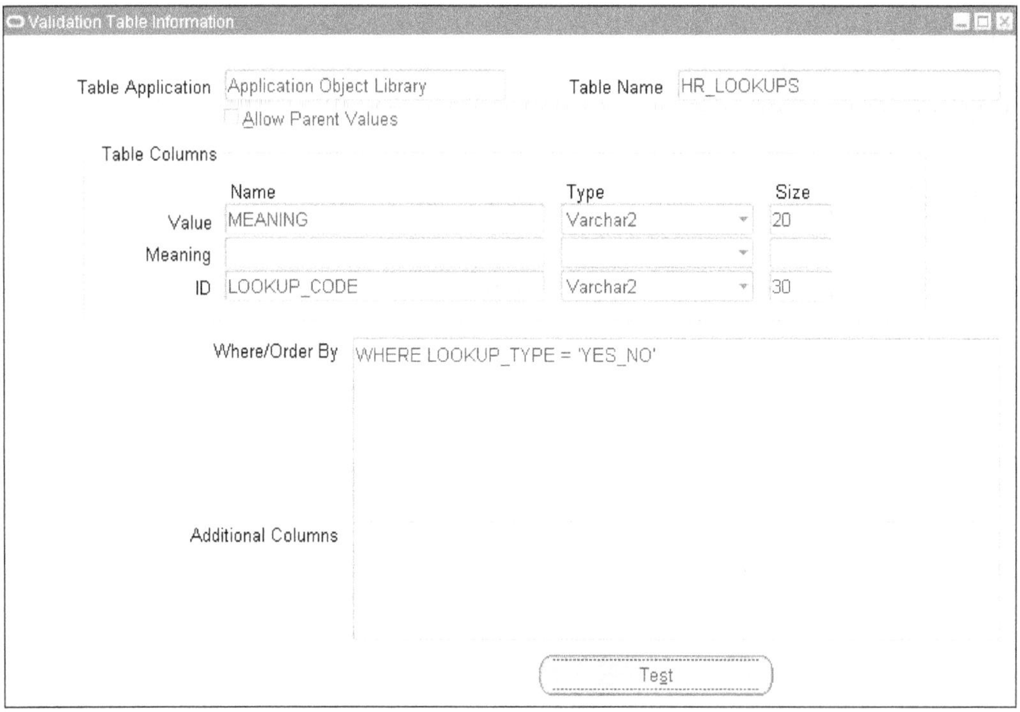

Now let's define one more context for the employee.

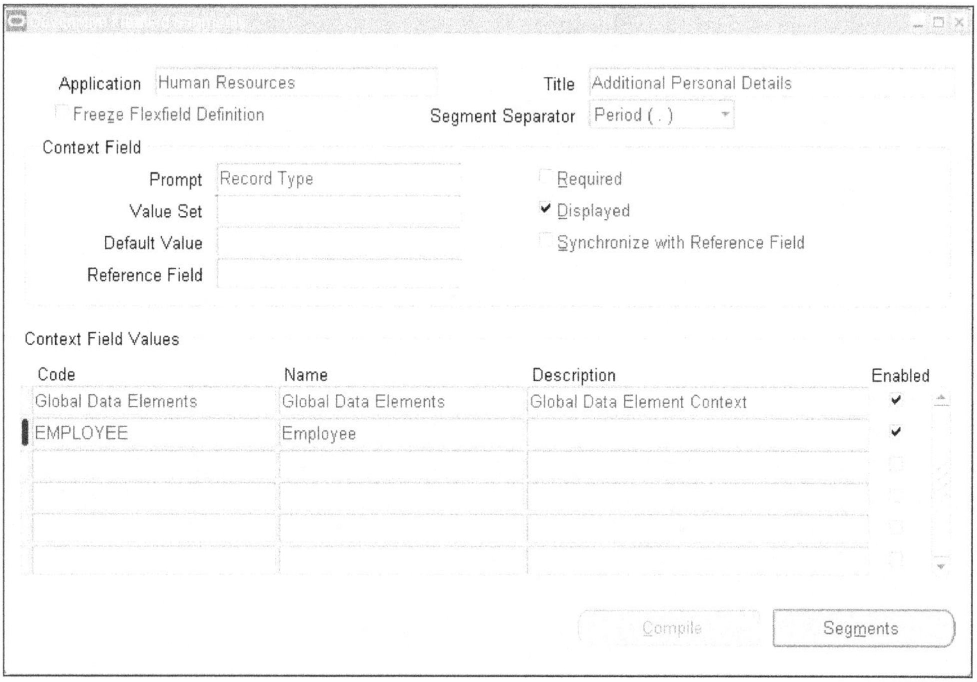

As you can see in the preceding screenshot, we have defined one more context field value. The code is `EMPLOYEE` and the name is `Employee`.

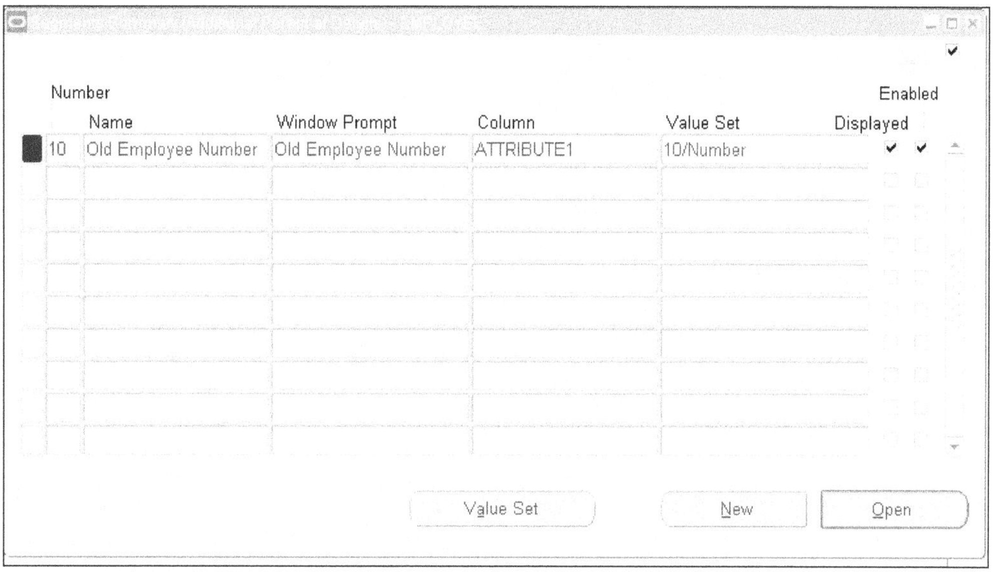

The name of the segment is `Old Employee Number`, which is the same as **Window Prompt**. Window prompts can be changed depending upon the title you want to display on the forms. Data will be stored in `ATTRIBUTE1` of the table and the value set is a 10-digit number.

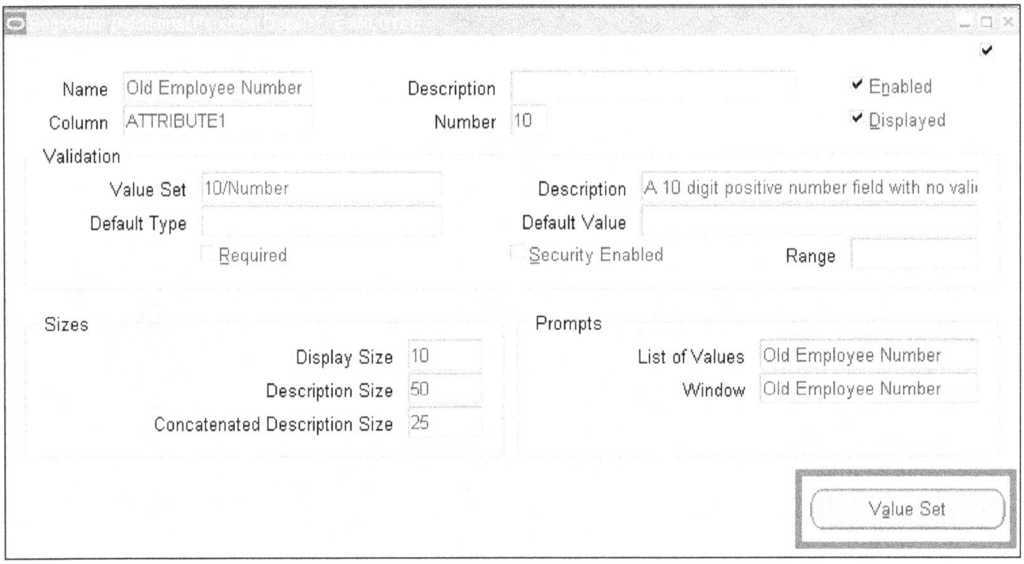

The definition of the value set can be checked by clicking on the **Value Set** button as in the preceding screenshot.

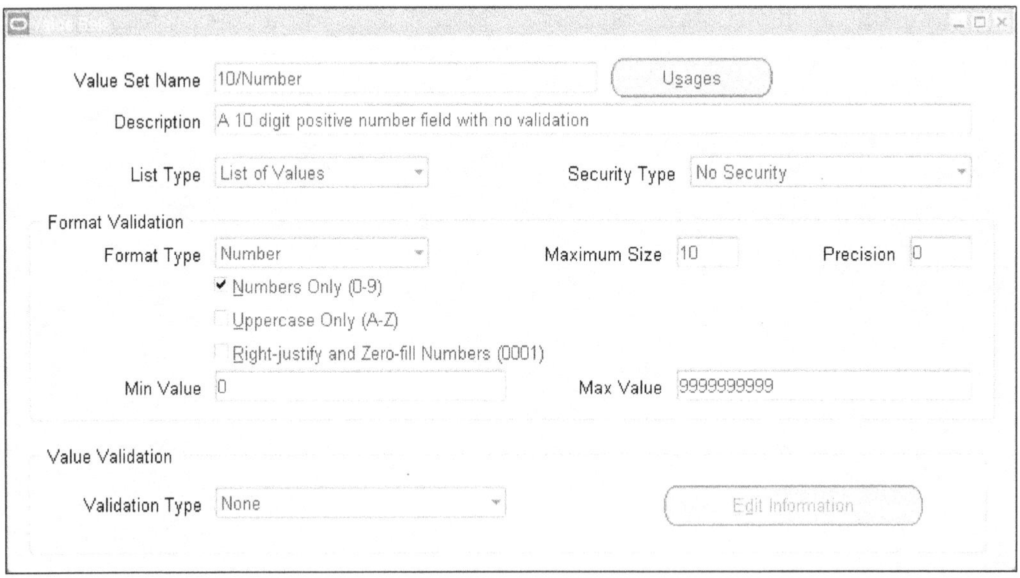

As seen in the preceding screenshot, the value set is a 10-digit positive number. The format type specified is a number with the maximum size as `10`.

The minimum value is `0` and maximum value that can be saved in the field is defined as `9999999999`.

Similarly, we have set one more context for the applicant.

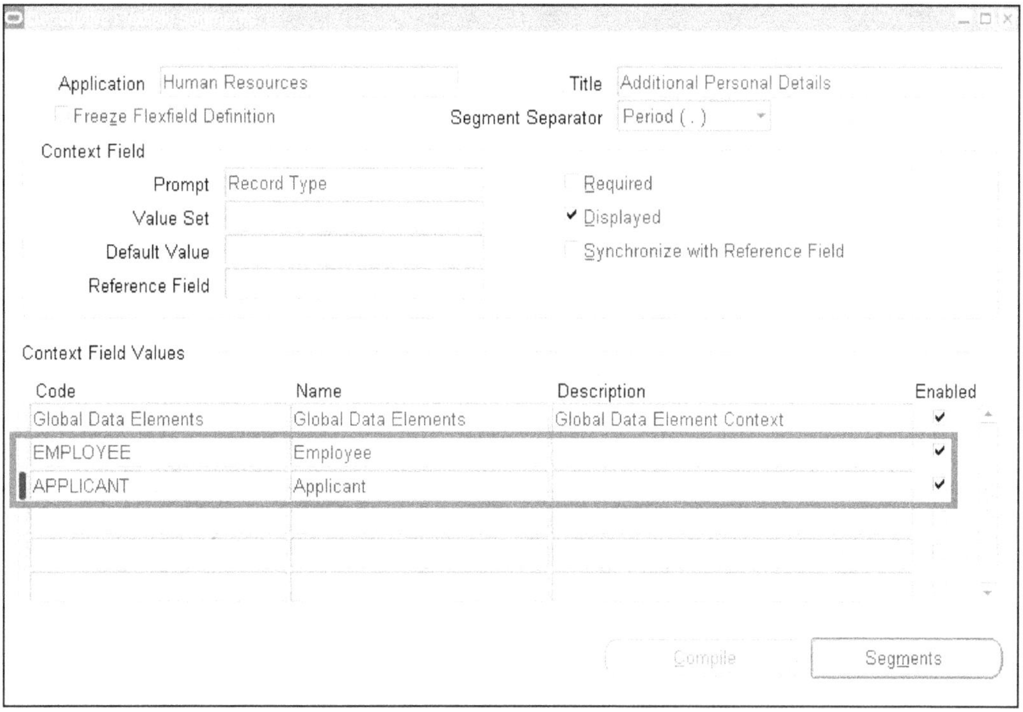

Click on **Segments** to create the segments to be used. We will store the current employer name if the record type of the person is applicant.

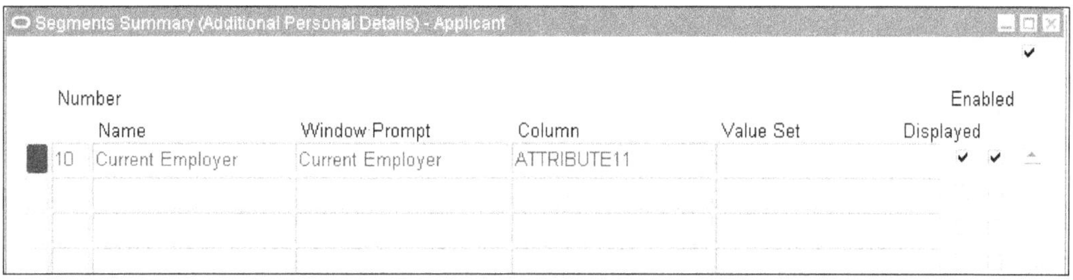

Here, we have not attached any value set. Note this is just an example. It is not a best practice to keep it free text. Now freeze the flexfield definition by enabling the checkbox, as in the following screenshot:

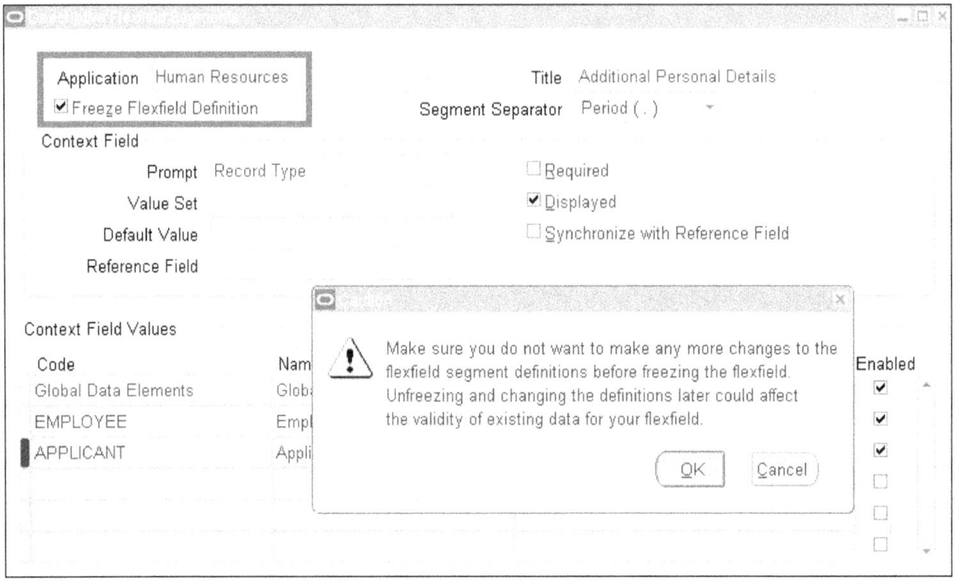

Click on **OK** and then click on **Compile**.

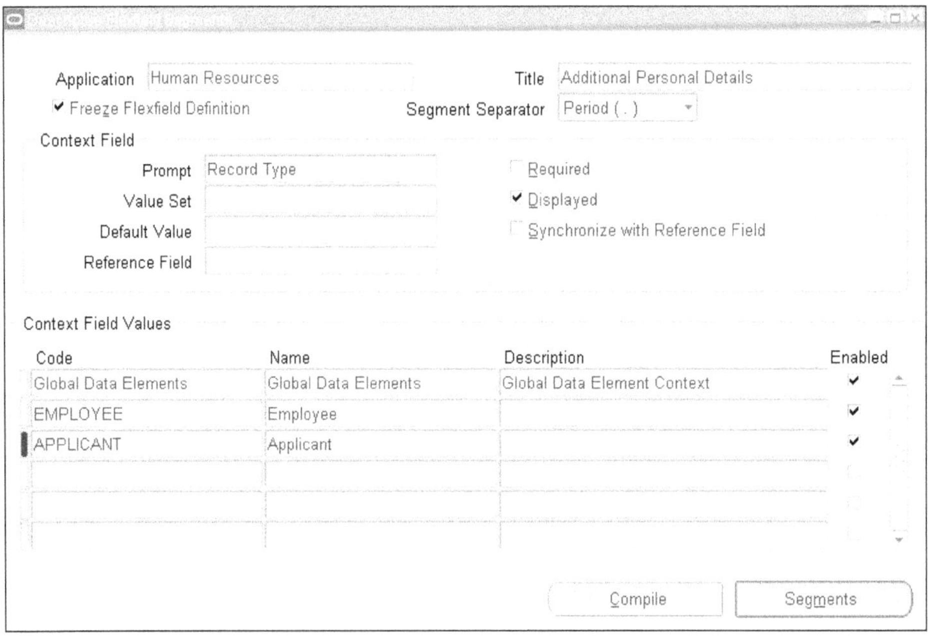

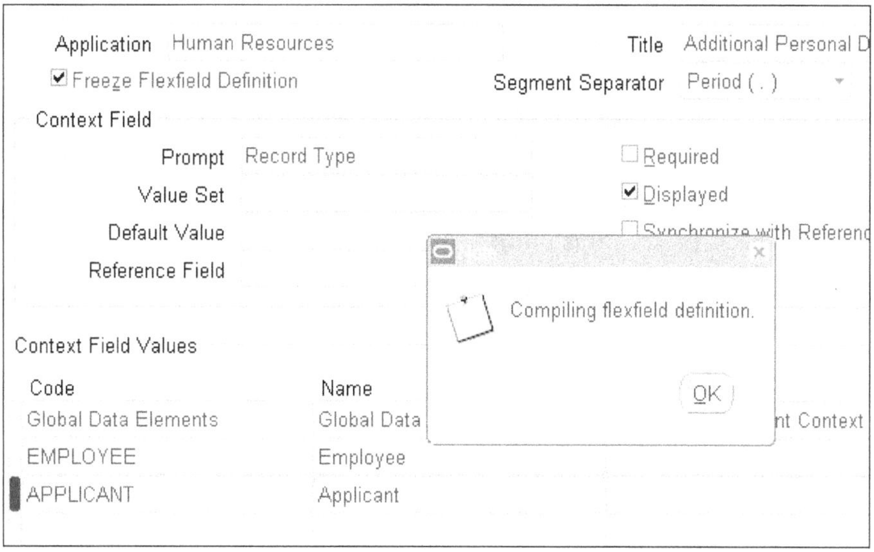

Click on **OK**.

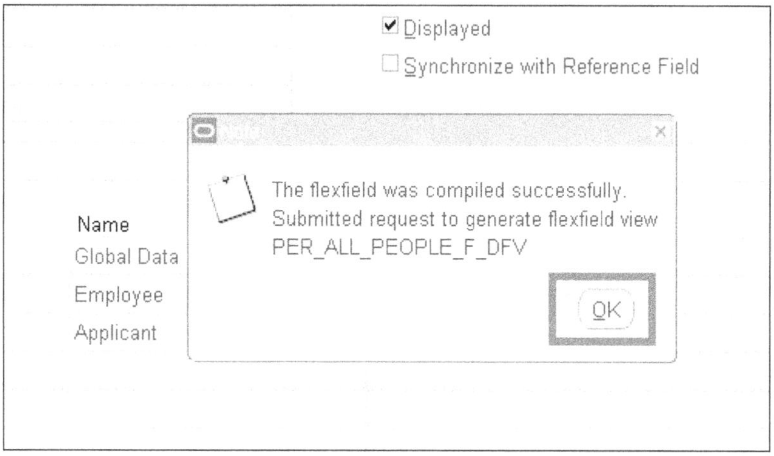

A successful compiled message will be displayed as shown in preceding screenshot, once your DFF set up is proper. In later chapters, you will see how this DFF on the person record is displayed. You can set up DFF on various entities. Examples are Person, Assignment, Address, Locations, and Jobs among others.

Let's now see something we call **Special Information Types (SIT)**.

SITs are basically KFF that are used to capture additional person information. The name of this KFF is **Personal Analysis Flexfield**.

Let's take an example to explain this. Suppose you want to capture information about languages known by your company employees. To capture this data, you can define an SIT. This SIT will store data for languages known by the employees in your company. The next decision will be what exactly you want to store in language data. So let's say we want to capture the languages known by the employee and the fluency of the languages known.

As of now, we need to store this information, so we will need two segments in the SIT, which are:

- Segment 1 is Language Known
- Segment 2 is Fluency

Each segment will have a value set attached to it. Let's say `TEST_LANGUAGE_KNOWN` and `TEST_FLUENCY` are two value sets for each segment respectively.

`TEST_FLUENCY` will have the following values:

- Read
- Write
- Speak

Let's begin with the setup steps. We will first define these value sets and then go on to define the SIT. Navigate to **System Administrator** | **Application** | **Validation** | **Set**.

The following screenshot shows the definition of `TEST_LANGUAGE_KNOWN`.

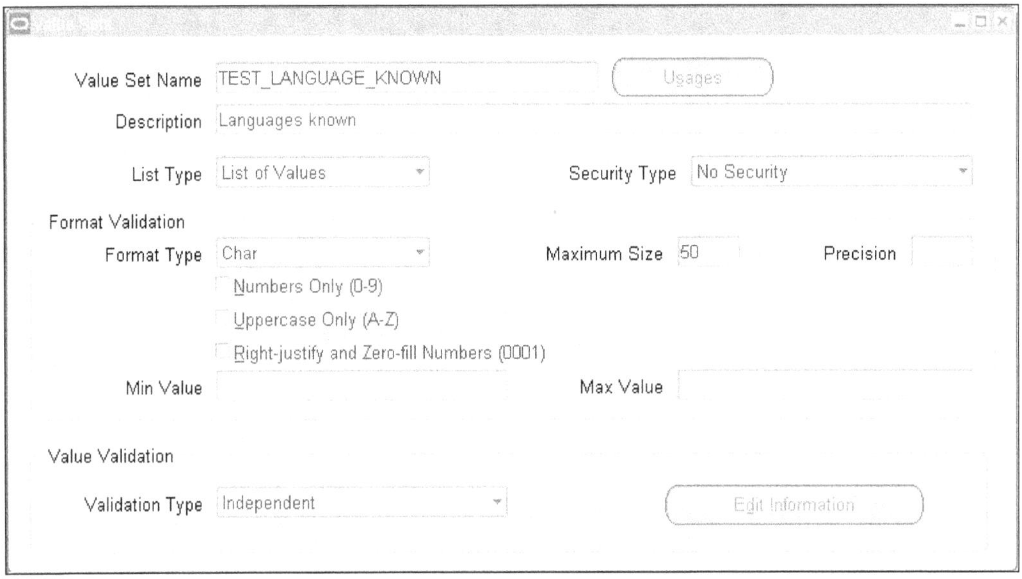

The following screenshot shows the definition of `TEST_FLUENCY`; both are independent value sets of format type **Char**.

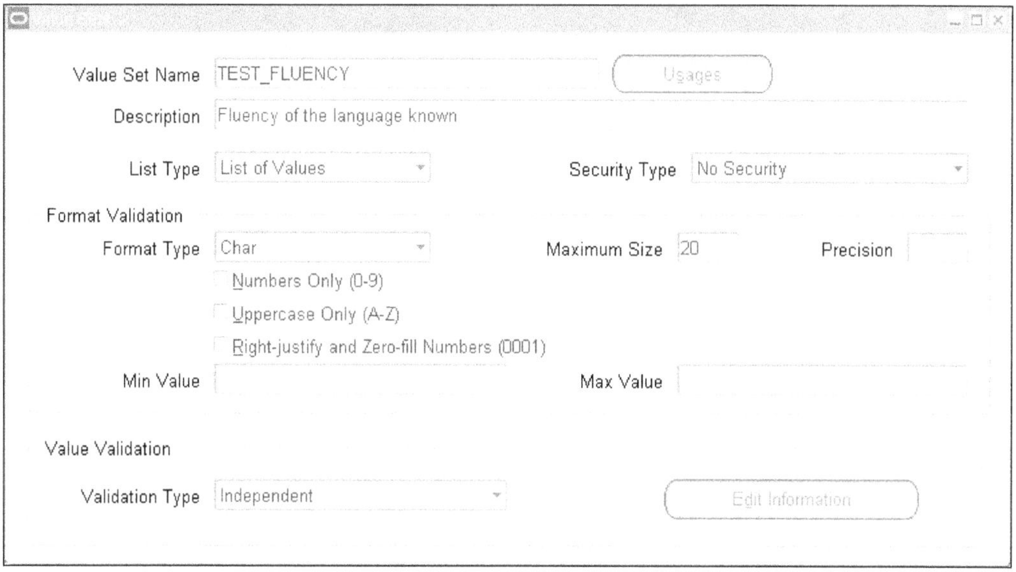

Now we will add values to these value sets by navigating to **System Administrator | Application | Validation | Values**.

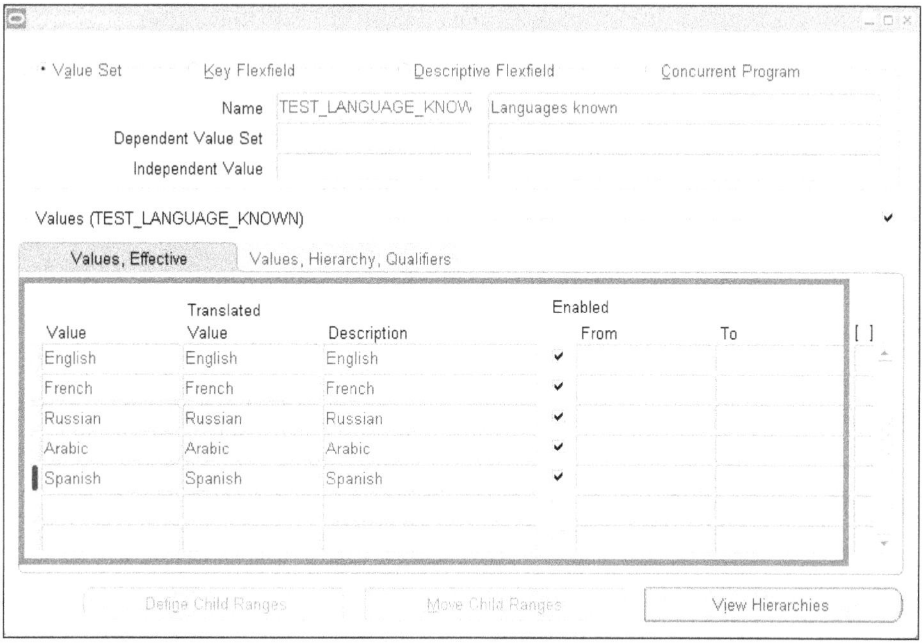

We have added five languages in the `TEST_LANGUAGE_KNOWN` value set. You can enable or disable the values as per your needs by checking/unchecking the **Enabled** field.

Also, there is an option to add **From** and **To** dates for each value. You can add an end date for the value if you do not want to display it from a particular date going forward. Adding an end date will not affect existing records.

Similarly, we will add values for `TEST_FLUENCY`.

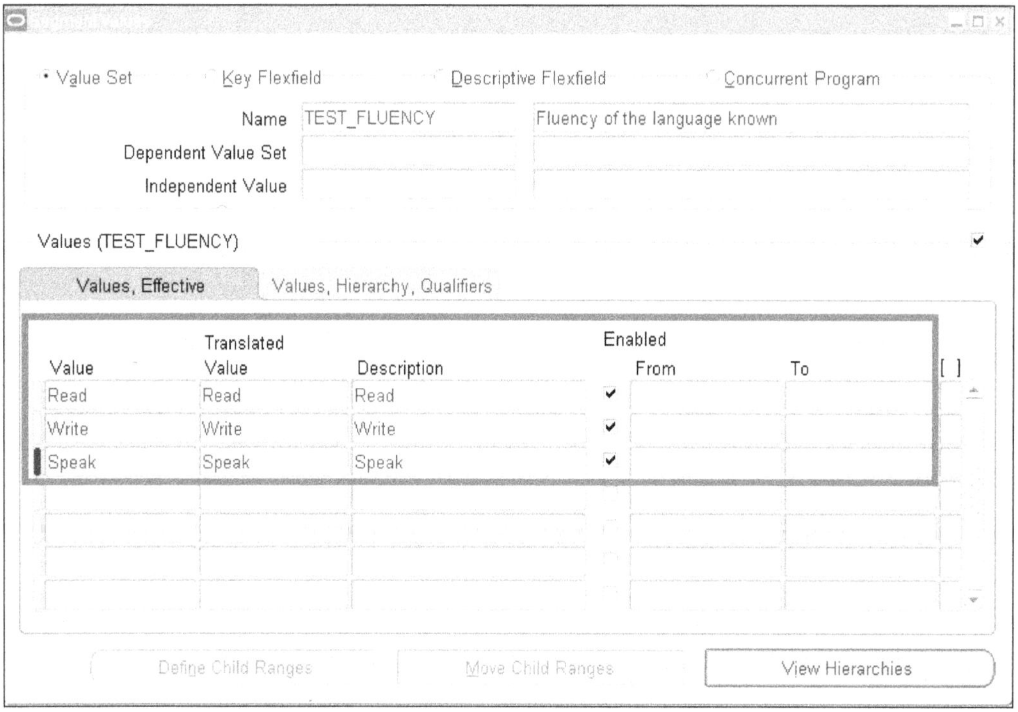

Now we will define the SIT by navigating to **System Administrator** | **Application** | **Flexfield** | **Key** | **Segments**.

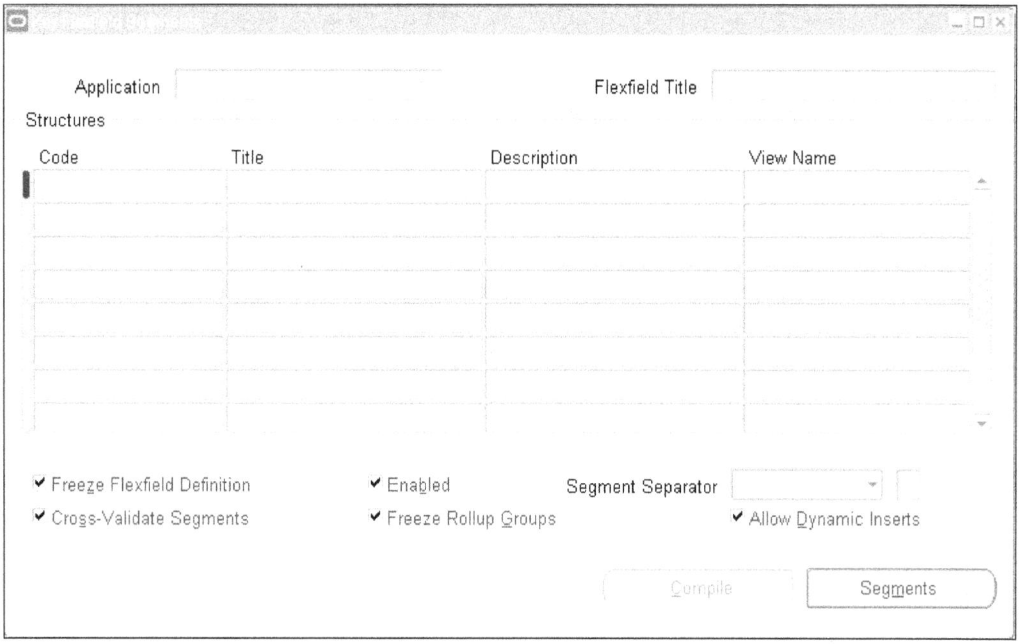

Query for application as `Human Resource` and title as `Personal Analysis Flexfield`.

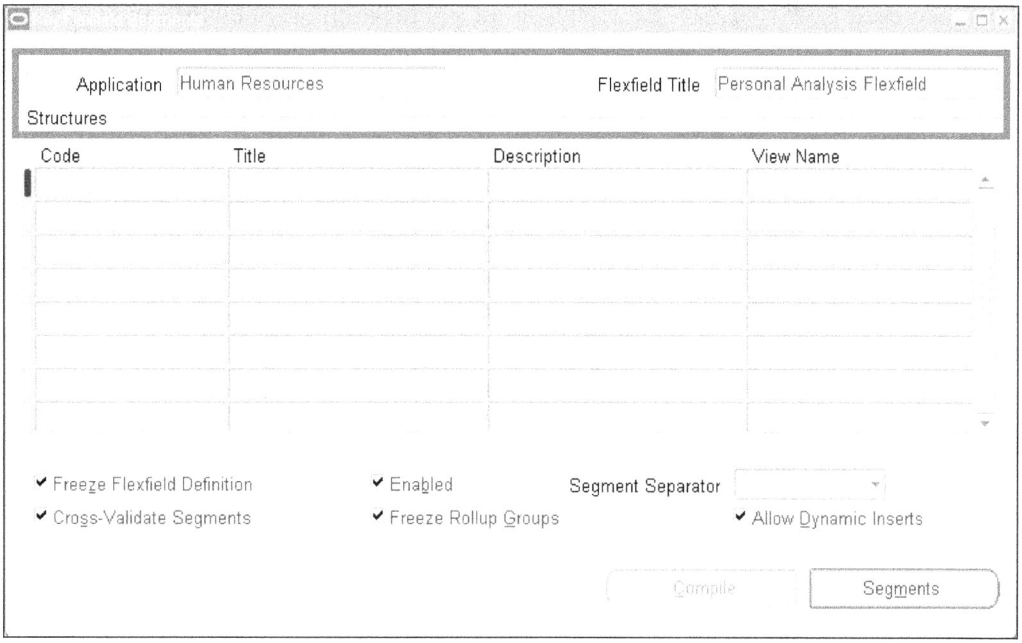

Personal Analysis Flexfield is the title that is used for all SITs. If you want to configure any SIT in HRMS, then we need to configure it here with this title only.

Let's add a new SIT with details as marked in the following screenshot:

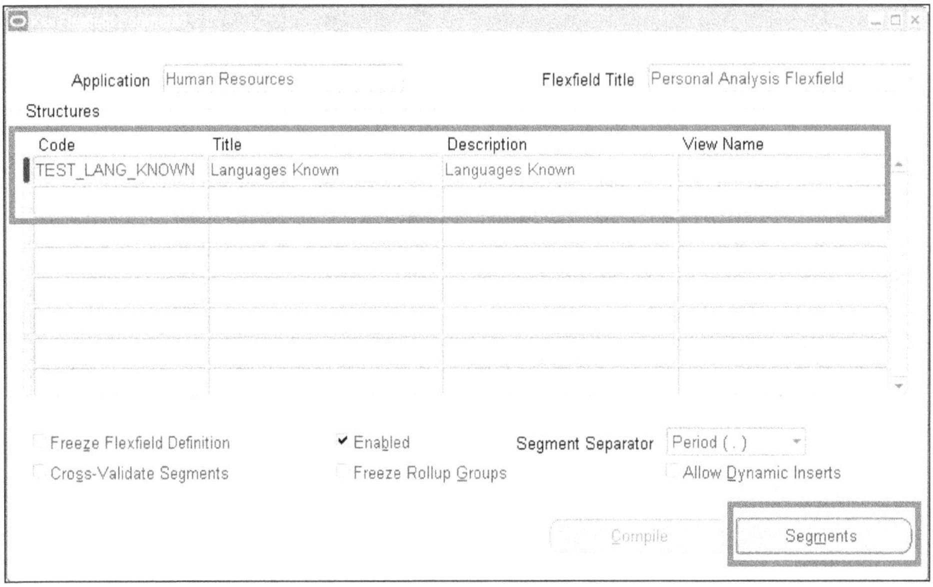

The code used is `TEST_LANG_KNOW`. This is unique for each SIT. The title and description are `Languages Known`. This will be visible to the user. Click on **Segments** to add the segments for this SIT.

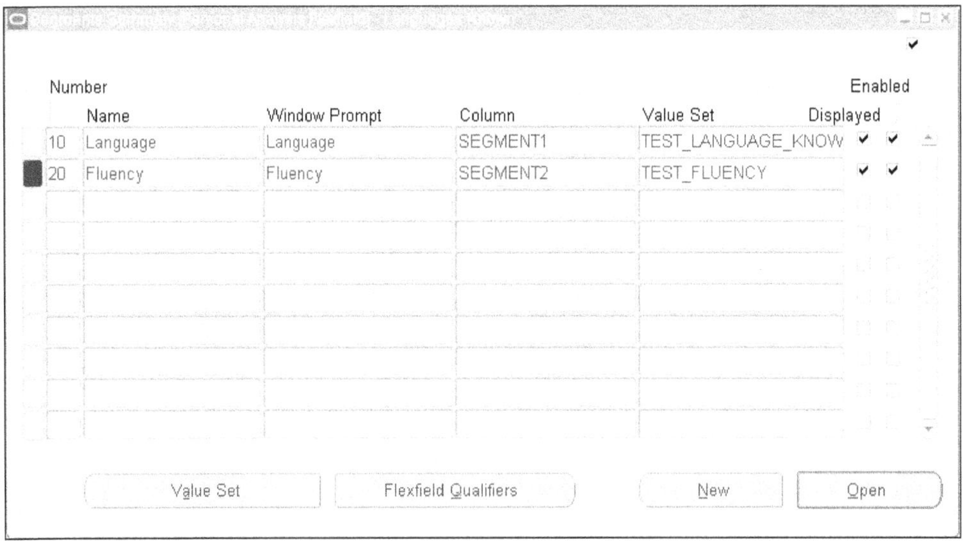

In the preceding screenshot, we can see that there are two segments in the SIT; the first is `Language` and the other is `Fluency`.

Data is stored in a segment rather than an attribute as we saw in DFF.

Click on **Open** to view the value set definition.

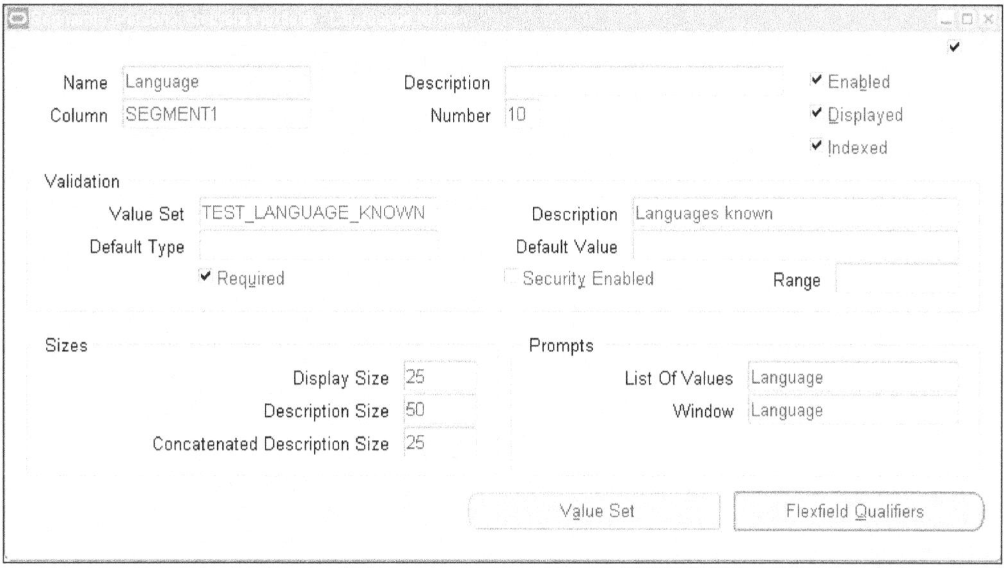

As we can see in the screenshots, both the segments are set as **Required** as marked.

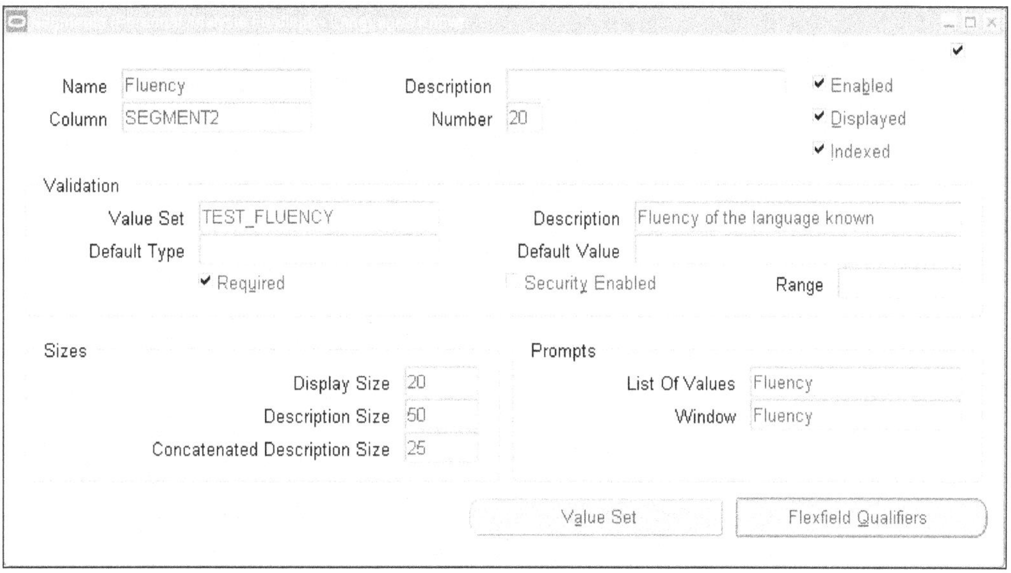

Go back to the main form and enable the checkbox for **Freeze Flexfield Definition**.

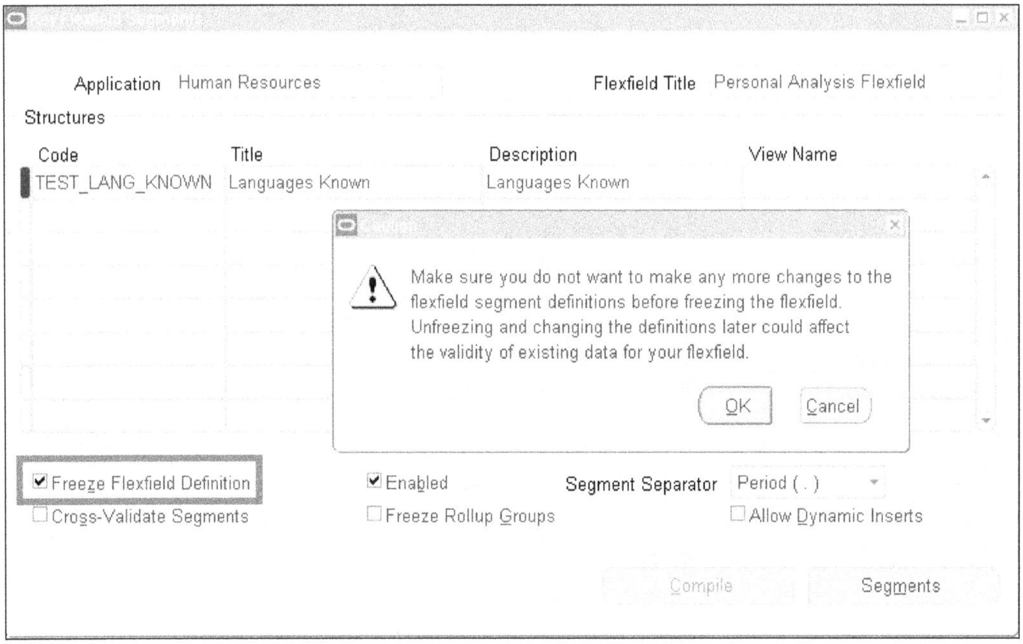

Click on **OK**, and then on **Save**.

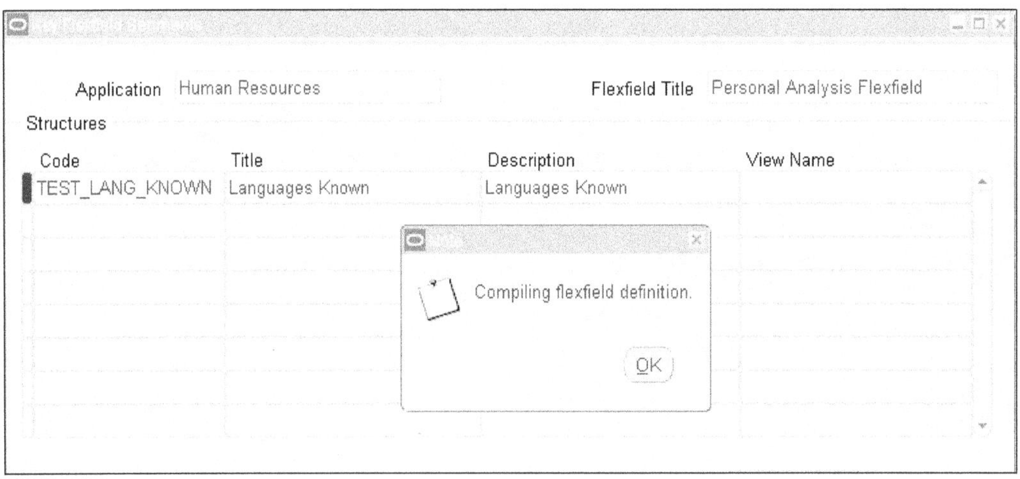

Click on **OK**.

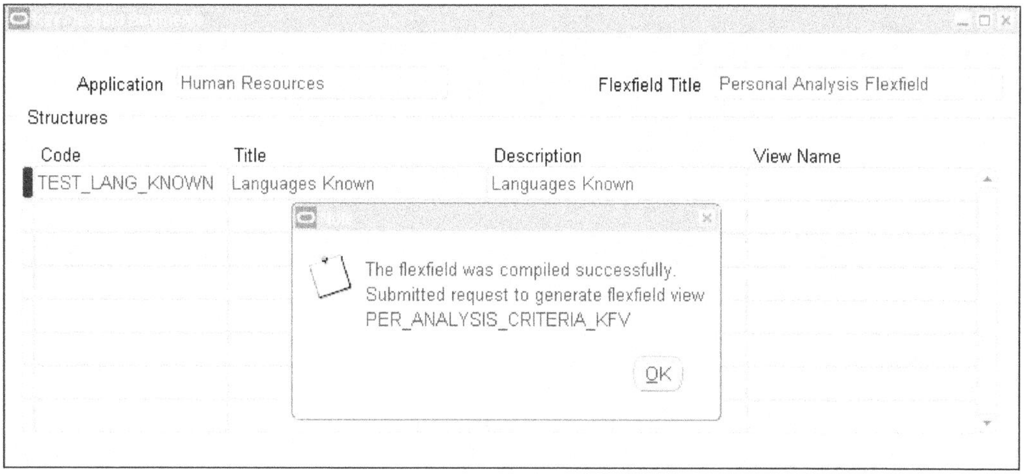

Click on **OK**.

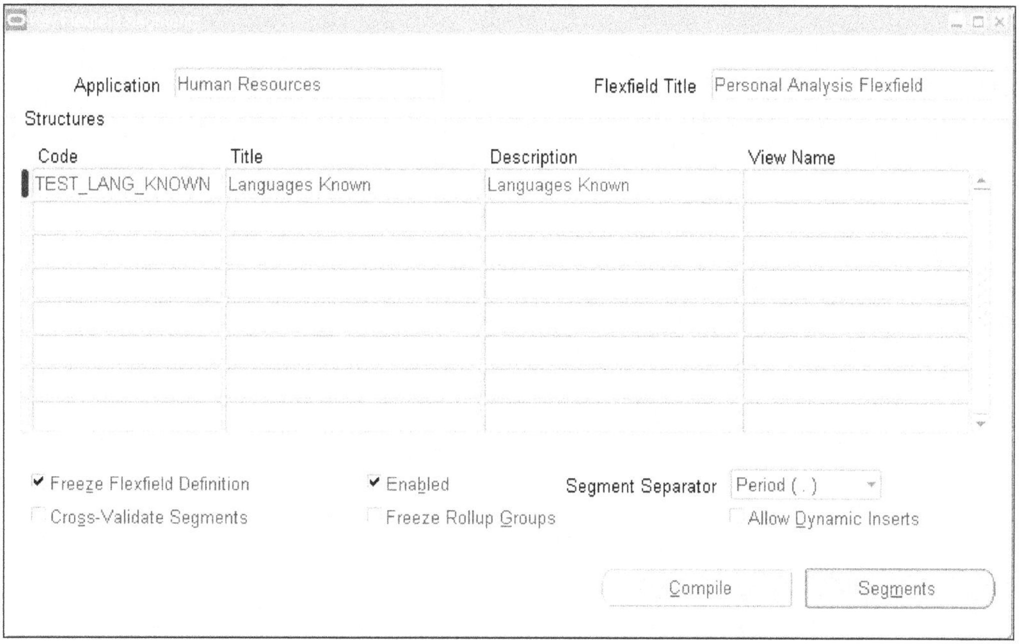

Here, we have completed the setup for the SIT. The next step is to specify the name of the responsibility through which this SIT will be visible. This is referred to as assigning an SIT to a responsibility.

You need to switch to the responsibility to which you need to assign this SIT. In our case, this will be US HRMS Manager.

Once you have switched to US HRMS Manager, navigate to **US HRMS Manager** | **Other Definitions** | **Special Information Types** and search for our SIT `Languages Known`.

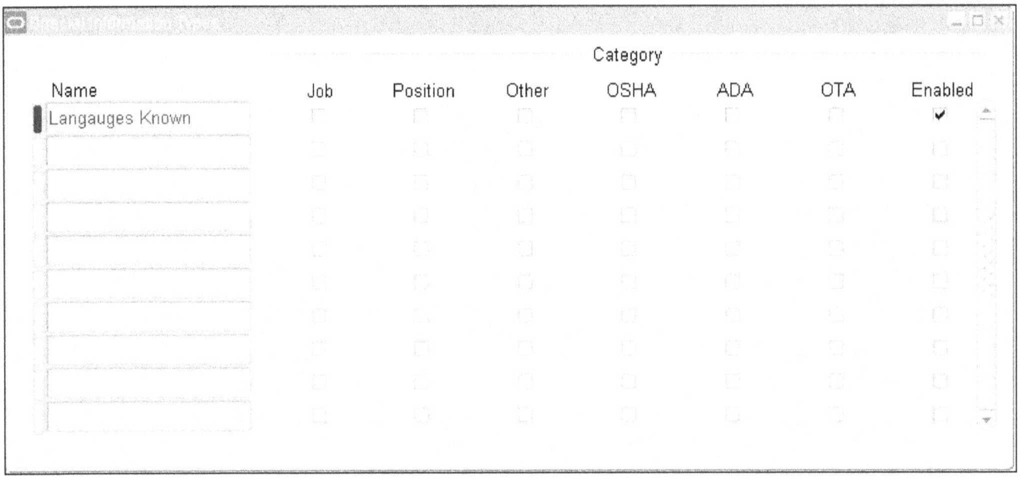

Click on the **Other** checkbox.

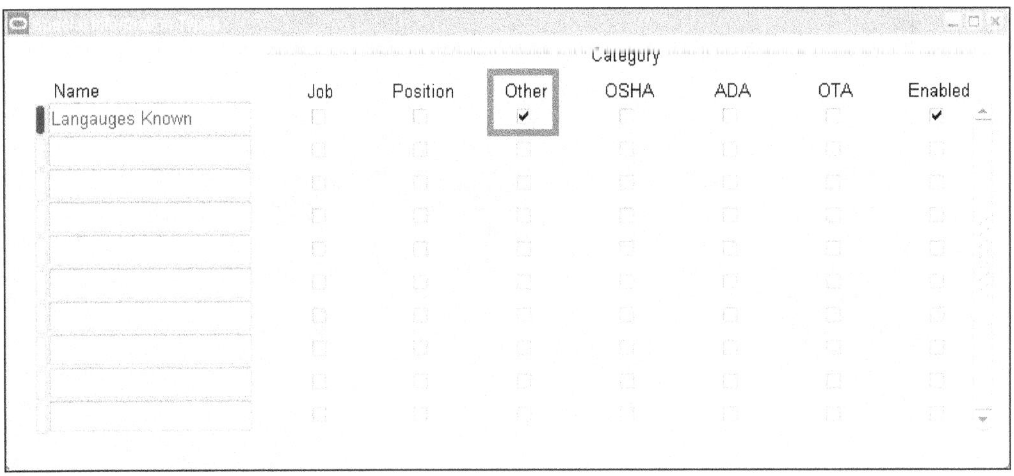

Then, click on **Save**.

This can also be viewed using employee records as follows. The detailed navigation will be shown in the next chapter.

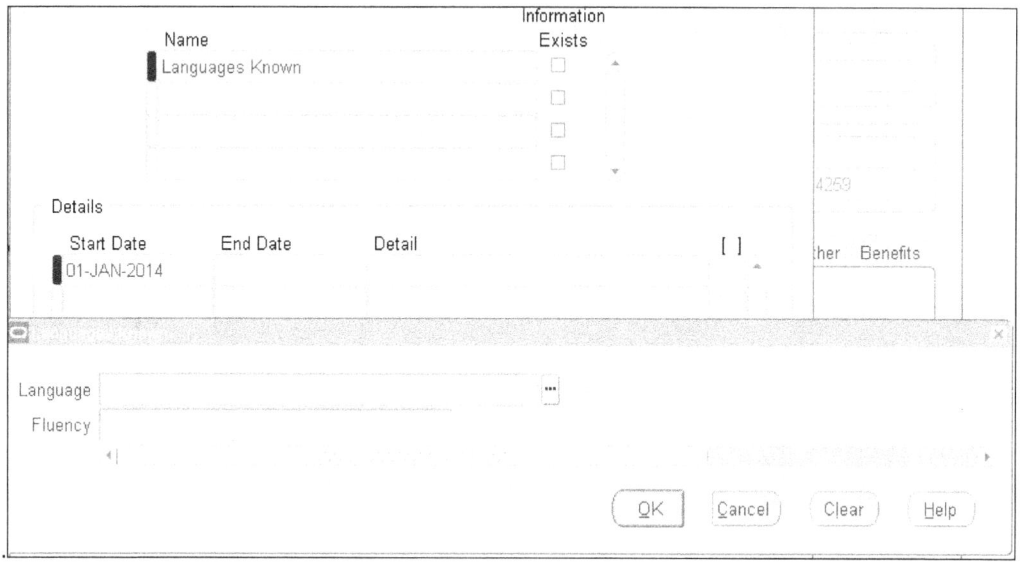

In the preceding screenshot, we can see that we have created the language known SIT with two segments, and both are mandatory.

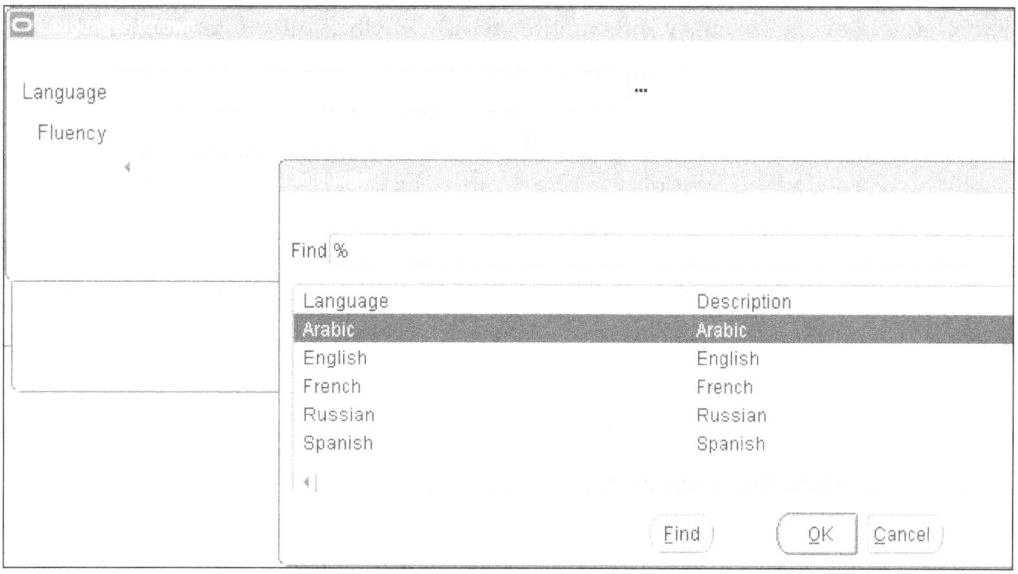

The language segment has the values that are defined in the `TEST_LANGUAGE_KNOWN` value set. In the following screenshot, the **Fluency** segment has the values that we defined in the `TEST_FLUENCY` value set:

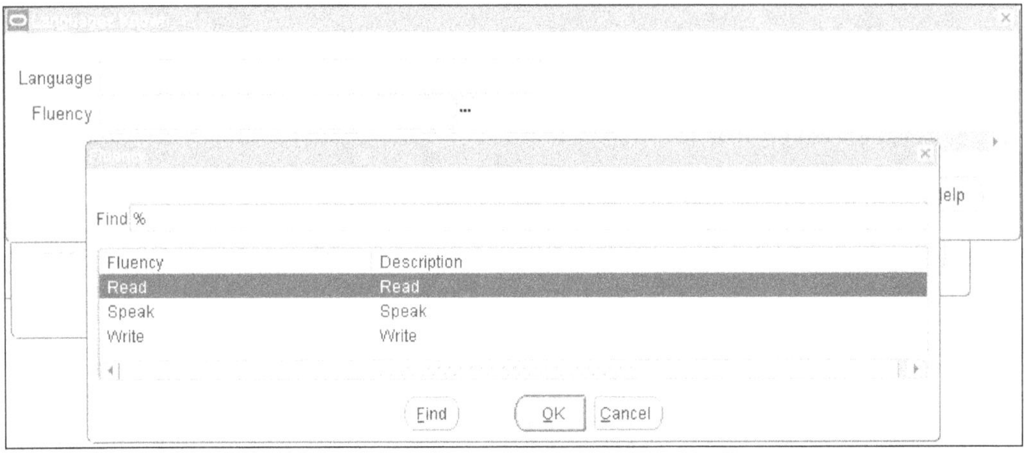

Summary

This chapter covered primary information about Oracle applications flexfields. These are basic setups required to implement core HR. We also discussed, in detail, the concept of value sets. We described various types of value set in detail, the configuration of the value sets, and entering values in these value sets.

Then you learned about flexfields in Oracle apps, basic KFFs in HRMS, along with the configuration of Grade KFFs. The chapter also covered DFFs and their configuration. It also explained configuration of SIT with an example.

In the next chapter, we will cover representing your enterprise, defining business groups, defining various organizations, and defining hierarchy in detail. We will also cover location and basic organization definitions.

4

Business Group, Organization, and Locations

In the previous chapter, we saw architecture, system administration functionality, and also went through the key building blocks of system administration with respect to Oracle Human Resource.

This chapter will cover the concept of work structures in HRMS. We will learn the basics of business group, organization, and locations in HRMS.

Let's start with the business group concept.

Representing your enterprise

The simplest way to represent an enterprise in Oracle HRMS Application is by defining it as a business group.

A business group is the one that holds a complete, self-contained set of information on work structures, remuneration policies, and the employees of the company. It represents the consolidated enterprise, a major division, or an operation company.

The most important decision while creating a business group is whether you need a single business group or multiple business groups. This decision is based on many factors. If your enterprise is operating in a single country then there is no need to create multiple business groups. In this case, a single business group will suffice for your needs.

When your enterprise is operating in multiple countries across the world, then this question arises.

The following generic approach is a business group for each country. The reason for this is that each **business group** (**BG**) is allowed to have just one specific set of segments that is defined for its Job, Position, Grade, Employee Group, and Cost Allocation key flexfields. So if the structures of either the Job, Position, Grade, Employee Group, or Cost Allocation key flexfields are different for the enterprise in each country, then creating a different BG for each country is needed. Another factor that dictates the multiple BG decision is whether you are going to implement Oracle Payroll for your countries. If yes, then we need to create a different BG for each country. The reason is that each country will have its own legislative rules of payroll. Each localization is different and has different payroll rules, which are provided by Oracle.

The decisive factors, other than payroll, for the creation of new business groups, are the legislative requirements of those countries. Also, labor laws and holiday entitlement rules might differ for each country.

Suppose you are operating in multiple countries and not implementing payroll, and out of those countries a few are following the same structure of jobs, grades, and so on, then you can have those countries clubbed in a single business group. This typically happens when your enterprise is spread across different regions; in this case you can also create a BG for each region. An example will be creating a single BG for your enterprises in the Middle East.

Now, once you have decided on the business group count, the next step is to configure it in the system.

The mandatory parameters for defining a BG are the **Key flexfields** (**KFF**), which we have covered on previous chapters.

To define a business group, navigate to **US HRMS Manager** | **Work Structures** | **Organization** | **Description**.

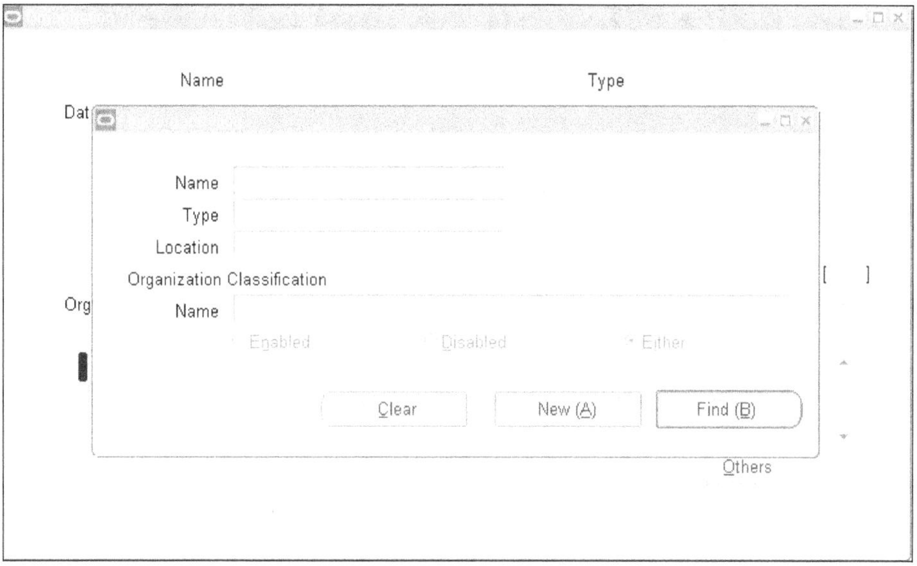

Click on **New (A)**. You can either create or search an organization using this form.

You can use this form to create:

- Business groups
- Internal organizations, including departments, divisions, and sections
- External organizations, including benefit carriers, tax authorities, and recruiting agencies

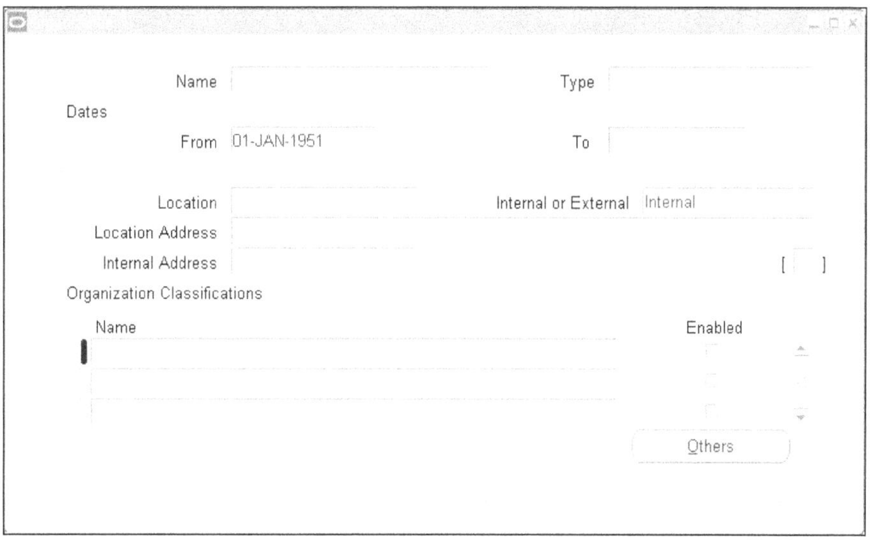

Prerequisites for all organizations

There are prerequisites for setting up an organization in the application. They are as follows:

- Setting up locations (will be covered later in this chapter under the *Defining a location in Oracle Apps* section)
- Entering organization types

A business group is nothing but an organization of type business group. Similarly, you have organizations of different types in your enterprise.

There are various types of organizations that you can define in HRMS. Examples are as follows:

- Corporate headquarters
- Department
- Division
- Operating unit
- Regional office
- Store

Start Date and Name are mandatory for defining an organization. Organization type and location are nonmandatory.

There is no specific use of organization type, but it is mostly used for reporting only. Oracle has provided seeded LOV for organization type, and if required, we can add additional types to that LOV.

As mentioned earlier, organizations can be either internal or external.

Employees can only be assigned to an internal organization (in the **Assignments** screen).

Organizations can be classified under various categories. Once you enter a classification for an organization, then we can enter specific information in accordance with the purpose of the organization.

Examples of classifications are, business group, HR organization, inventory organization, GRE/legal entity, and company cost center.

So in order to define a business group, the classification of the organization must be business group.

You can have more than one classification for an organization, but to assign employees to an organization, you must classify it as HR Organization.

Each classification has a number of organization information types, and each organization information type has a set of fields.

Click on the **Others** button on the **Define organization** screen; the LOV will show various information types for that selected classification.

Some of the information types for the business group classification are as follows:

- Business group info
- Benefits defaults
- Budget value defaults
- Tax details reference
- Work day information

Each of the preceding information types has a specific number of fields associated with it.

We have defined an organization type as `Business Group` and then classified the organization as `Business Group`.

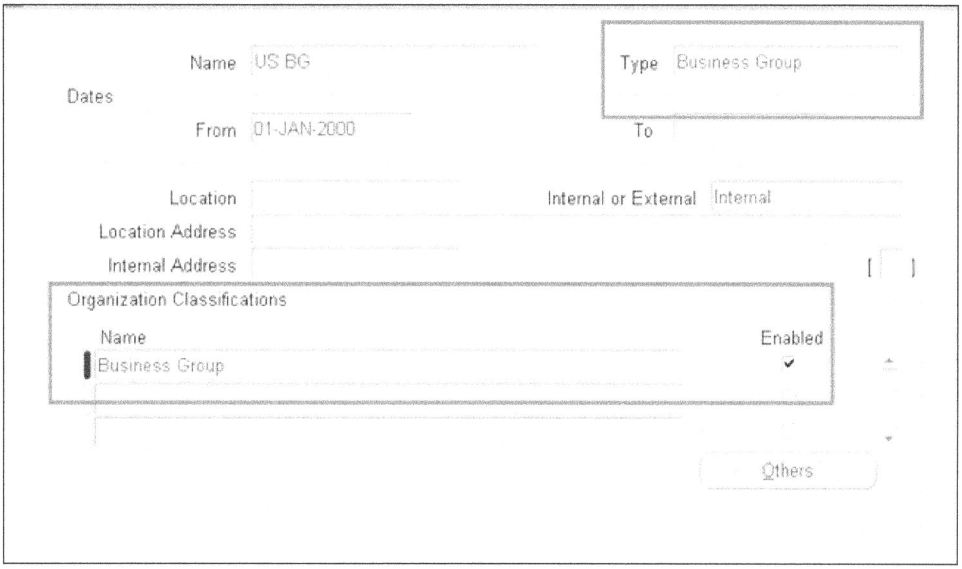

To view the information types, we need to click on **Others** as shown in the preceding screenshot.

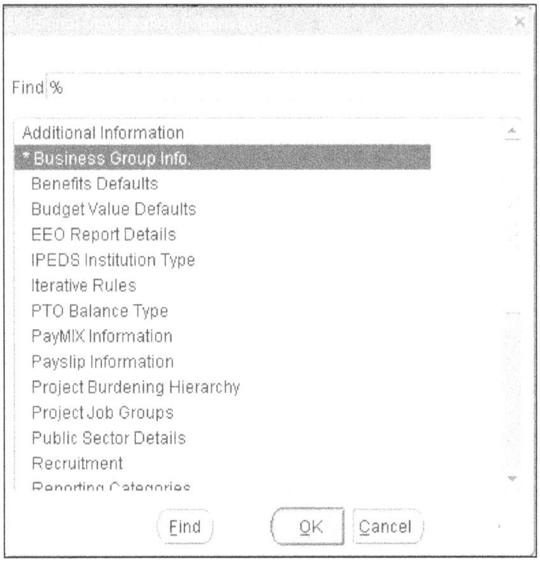

Whenever you define a BG, KFFs have to be mandatorily defined. This can be found in ***Business Group Info**. The following screen appears once you click on the **OK** button.

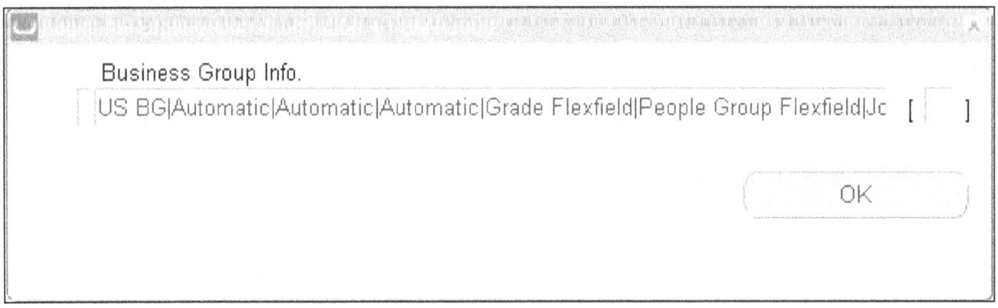

Entering business group information

To enter business group information, perform the following steps:

1. Enter a short name for the Business Group.
2. As employees and applicants in your business group will have employee numbers and applicant numbers, respectively, we need to specify the method to generate the employee and applicant number. The options are:
    - Automatic number generation
    - Manual entry
    - Automatic use of the national identifier (for example, social security number in the U.S., and NI number in the UK). This option is available for employees only.

> We can change from manual entry to automatic but not once we have saved the option, so we must ensure that we chose the correct method of generation.

3. Select the names of the KFF structures you want to use in this Business Group. We have seen this in the previous chapter in the *Flexfields in Oracle Apps* section. These are all mandatory fields.
4. Enter the Legislation Code and default currency for your Business Group. The Legislation Code determines the startup data you can access and the contents of some legislation-specific windows.

> You cannot change the legislation code after entering employees against the Business Group. So, we need to be very precise while selecting the legislation.

5. Enter a Minimum and Maximum Working Age for the Business Group. The application will give you a warning message if we hire an employee, not satisfying the required range.
6. Save your work.

Similarly, you can create many business groups as per your need with different KFF's structures.

Creating an organization

The next step is to create various organizations. There can be multiple organizations under your business groups. These organizations can be classified as HR organizations or any other, as required.

Let's demonstrate this using an example. Suppose you have a company that is in the U.S. and mainly involved in manufacturing. This company is spread across various states in the U.S.. The offices in each state carry out different functions. Some might be regional offices, some will be stores, and some will be product line, and so on. Basically, these are all organization of different types.

One more point to note here is that there will be employees working in these regional offices, stores, and product line. Hence, we need to classify all these organizations as HR organizations. Unless you classify these organizations as HR organizations, you cannot assign employees to them.

Let's define these organizations in the application.

In the following screenshot, we have defined an organization named `West Regional Office` with the type `Regional Office`:

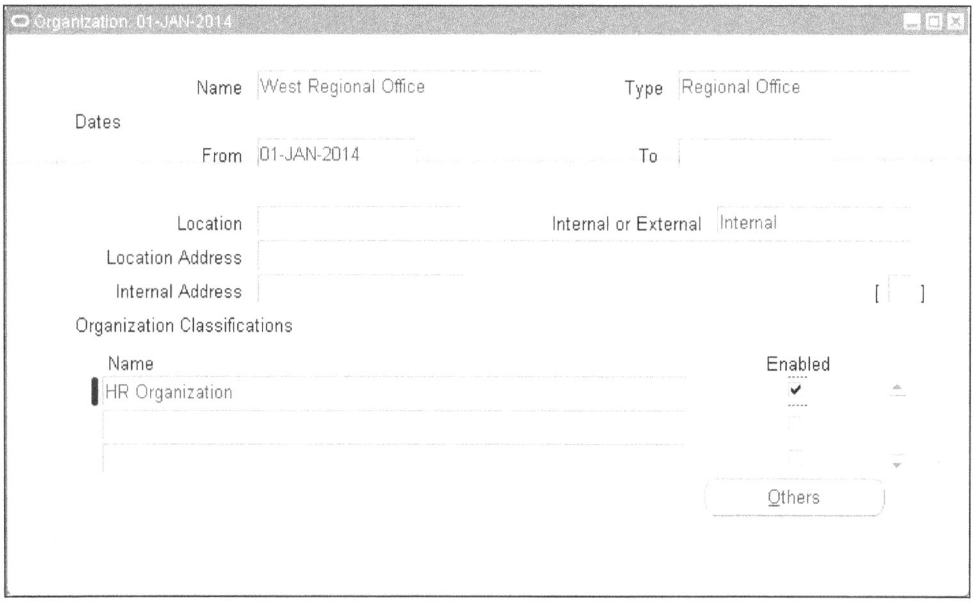

Now, in the following screenshot, we have defined an organization named `Washington Unit` with the type `Product Line`:

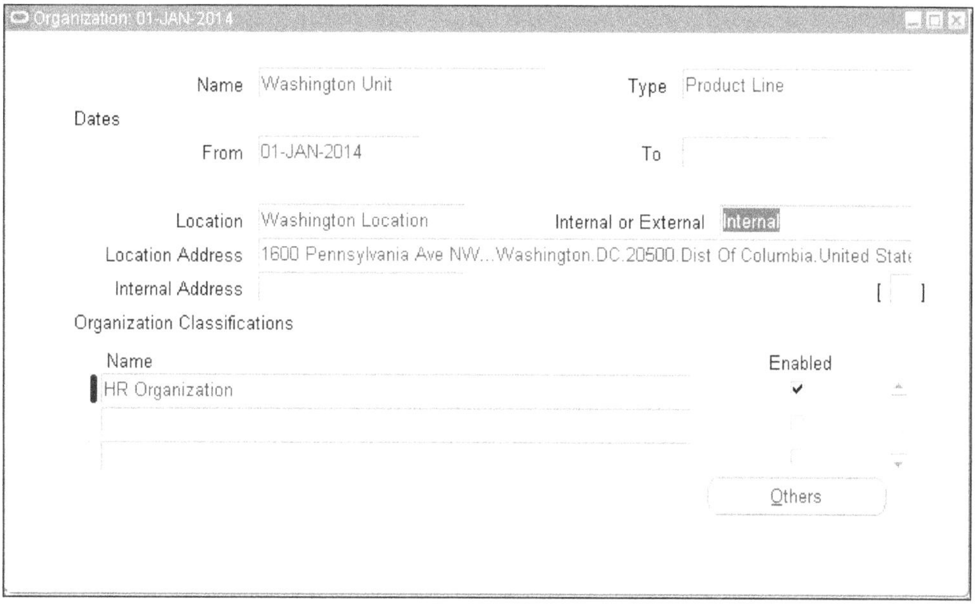

In the following two screenshots, we have defined an organization named `ABC store` and `XYZ Store` with the type `Store`:

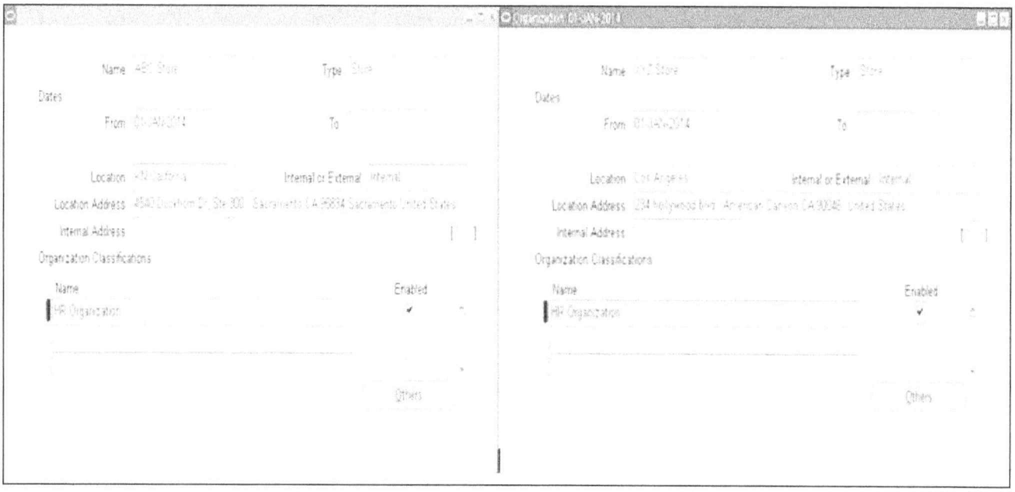

We have now created a total of five organizations including the business group (that we created initially), a regional office in the West, one product line (that is actually a manufacturing unit), and two stores (which will sell the product.)

Just as we entered additional information for each business group, we have an option to enter additional information for each HR organization.

Default working hours can be set up for all employees in the business group or in an HR organization. This information can be captured in an additional information column.

Let's enter work day information for `XYZ Store`. Select the **Work Day Information** option and click on **OK**.

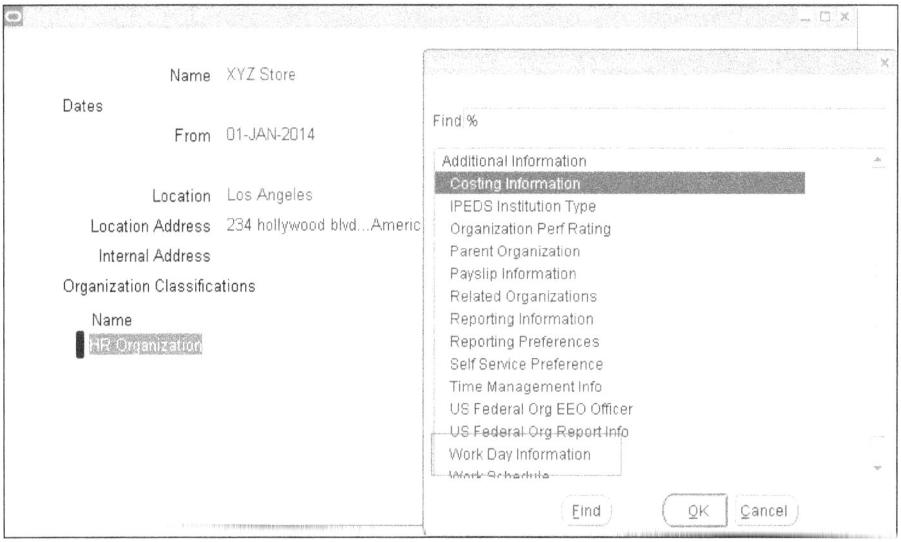

Enter the required values as shown in the following screenshot, such as the normal start and end time of the store and working hours per week.

Employees assigned to this organization (store) will have these default values against them. However, you can also override these values at the employee level.

An introduction to organization hierarchy

We have completed some basic level setup of organizations. As of now, these organizations are independent and are not linked to each other in any way.

We need to set a relationship between these organizations. In other words, we need to set a hierarchy of organizations. Organization hierarchy sets the relationships between the organizations you have defined.

While defining an organization hierarchy, we tell the Oracle application which organizations are reporting to which other organizations. Business group is generally the topmost organization in the hierarchy.

You can create more than one organization hierarchy, and you can create multiple versions of an organization hierarchy

In our case, US BG is the topmost organization. West Regional Office is second in the hierarchy that reports to US BG.

There is a product line, Washington Unit, that reports to the regional office. The other two stores report to the product line. The hierarchy that we will build in the application can be demonstrated as follows:

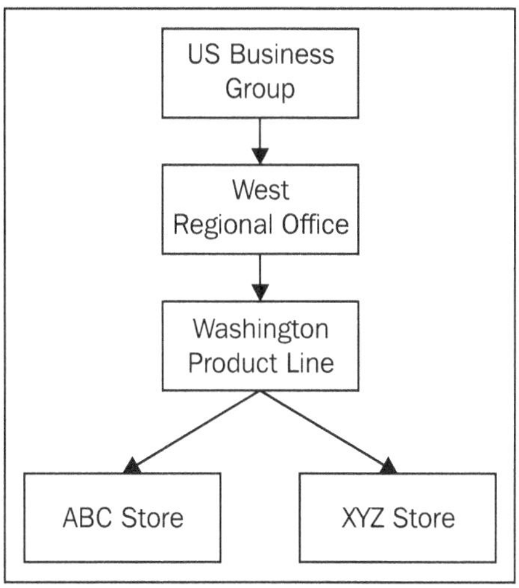

To build this hierarchy, navigate to **US HRMS Manager** | **Work Structures** | **Organization** | **Hierarchy**.

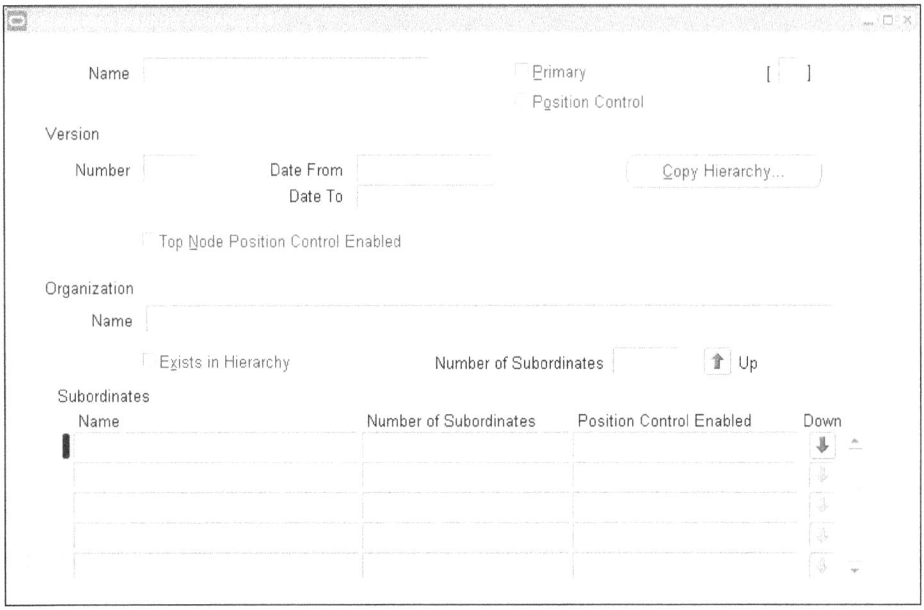

Setting up a new organization hierarchy

To set up a new hierarchy, we need to follow these steps:

1. Enter a unique name for the hierarchy, and select the **Primary** flag if it is the main reporting hierarchy in your enterprise.
2. Enter the start date and version number.
3. Query the top organization name in the **Organization** block.
4. Select the immediate subordinates for the top organization in the **Subordinates** block.
5. Check the **Down** checkbox for the organization in order to add organizations below one of these immediate subordinates. The **Organization** block will show the organization that you have selected. You can add subordinates to this organization. To return to the previous level, check the Up checkbox.

   Go to **Subordinates** and add the organization you want in this hierarchy in the following manner:

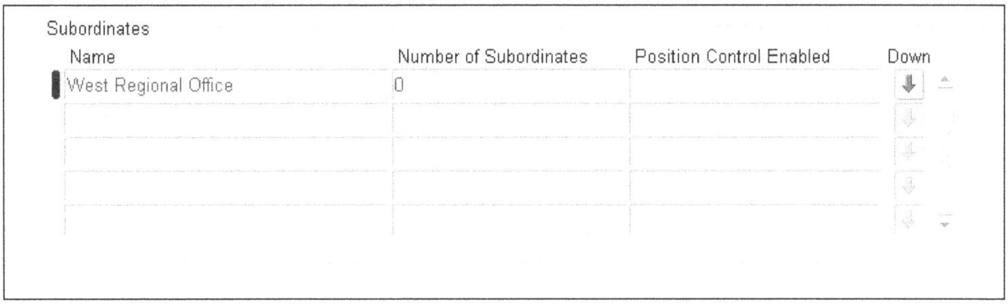

6. Click on the **Down** arrow to add reporting organizations to the West Regional Office.
7. Click on **Down** to add reporting stores.
8. Save the record.

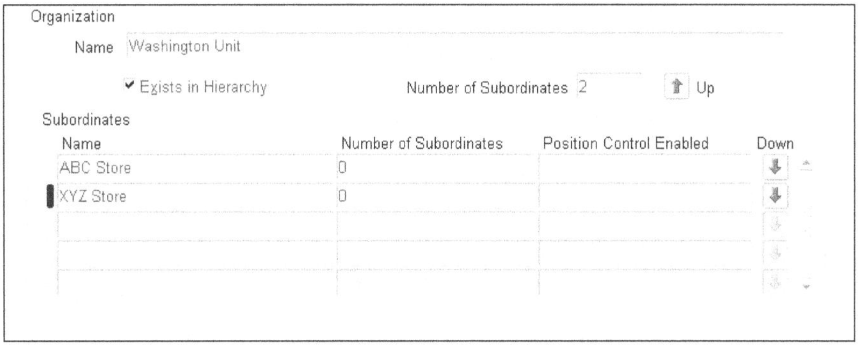

In this way, we have defined the hierarchy of the organization.

The hierarchy can be viewed diagrammatically by navigating to **US HRMS Manager | Work Structures | Organization | Diagrammer**.

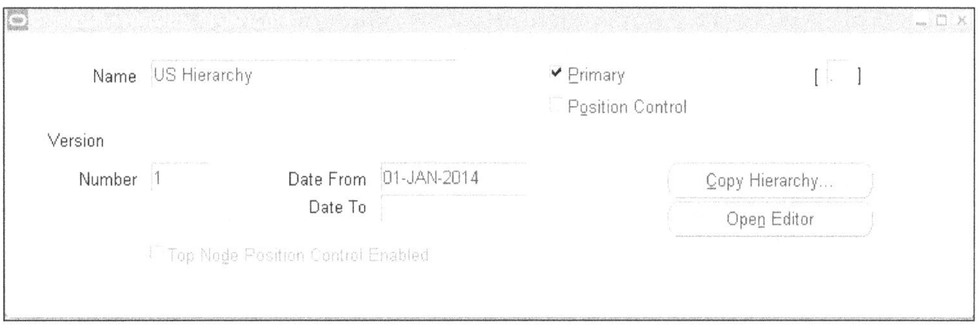

Then, click on **Open Editor**.

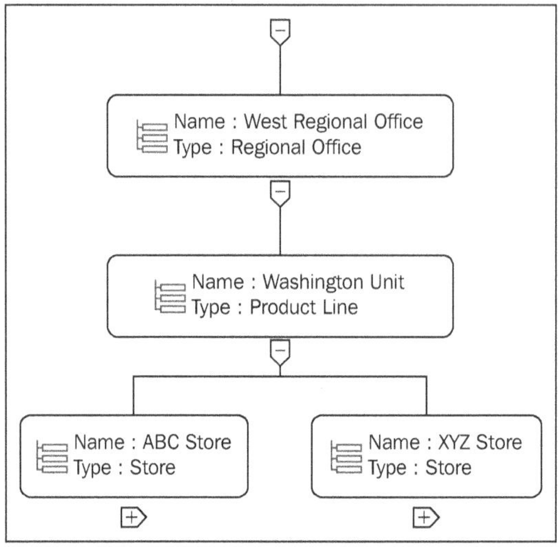

Thus, you learned how to create organization hierarchies in the Oracle application. This organization hierarchy is used for various purposes such as approval mechanisms and reporting.

Changing the organization hierarchy

If you need to update organization hierarchies, then you have three options. They are as follows:

- **Add new organizations in hierarchy**: To add new organizations in the hierarchy, we need to follow these steps:
    1. Query the hierarchy and version you want to update.
    2. Query the parent organization for which you need to add a new organization. Select the new organization in the **Subordinates** block.
    3. Click on **Save**.
- **Changing the top organization of an existing hierarchy**: To change the top organization of an existing hierarchy, we need to follow these steps:
    1. Query the hierarchy and version you want to update.
    2. Query the new top organization.
    3. Select the previous top organization in the **Subordinates** block.
    4. Click on **Save**.

- **Move an organization and all of its subordinates into a hierarchy**: To move an organization and all of its subordinates into a hierarchy, we need to follow these steps:
    1. Query the hierarchy and version you want to change.
    2. Search for the new parent organization. This will be the one for which you wanted to move.
    3. Select the organization to be moved in the **Subordinates** block.
- **To delete an organization hierarchy**: To delete an organization hierarchy, we need to follow this process. Initiate from the lowest level and delete the reporting organizations from the hierarchy.

> The organization hierarchy cannot be deleted if some other version exists or the security profile uses the hierarchy.

The organization hierarchy report

There is a standard organization hierarchy report to show the relationships between organizations in a hierarchy.

You run reports by navigating to **US HRMS Manager** | **Processes and Reports** | **Submit Processes and Reports**.

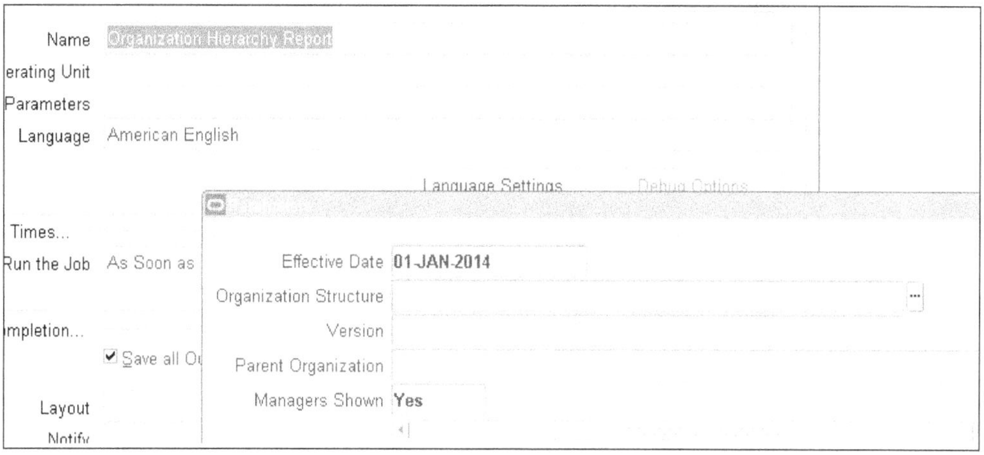

To run the organization hierarchy report, follow these steps:

1. Enter `Organization Hierarchy Report` in the **Name** field.
2. Enter the effective date for which we want to see the report.

3. In the **Organization Structure** field, select the hierarchy. Select the appropriate version if multiple versions exist.
4. In the **Parent Organization** field, select the highest organization in the hierarchy.
5. If you want to see the manager name, then select **Yes** in the **Managers Shown** field.
6. Click on the **Submit** button.

We can also assign a manager for an organization. For this, we need to query the organization and enter the value in **Reporting Information** in **Additional Organization Information** by clicking on the **Others** button.

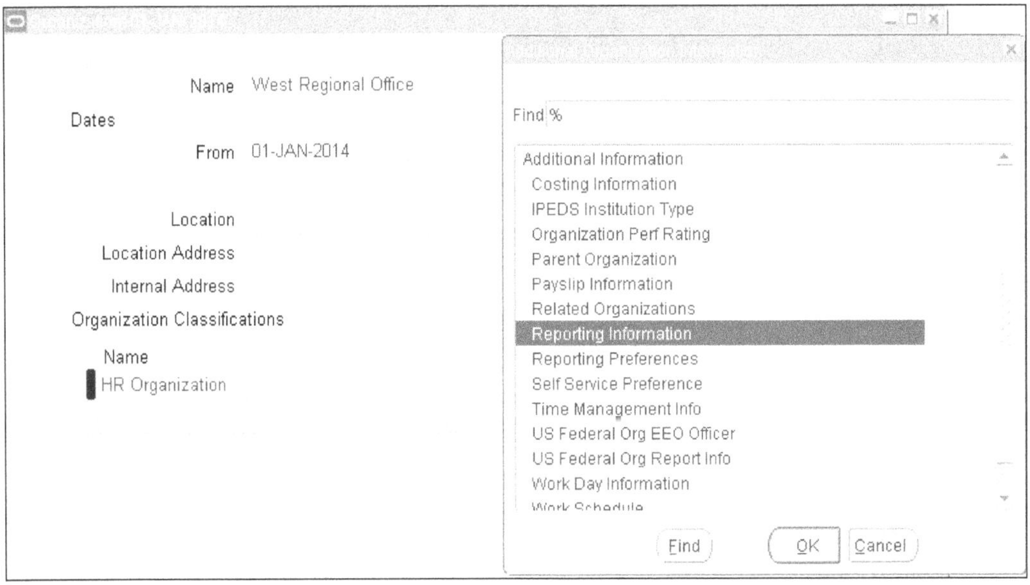

The following is the screenshot that appears after selecting **Reporting Information** and clicking on **OK.**

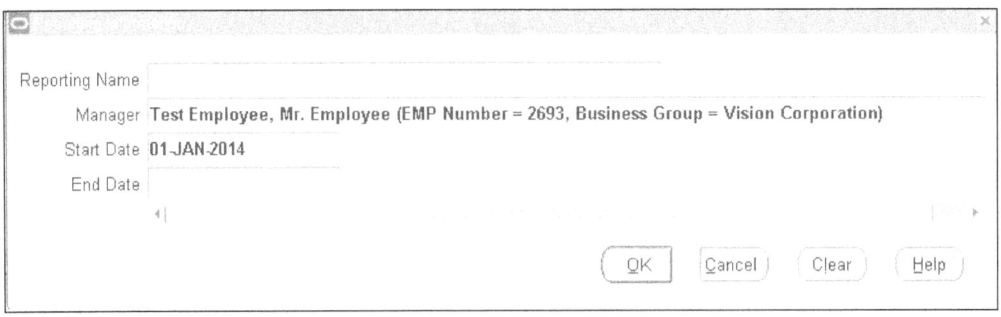

You can add the required reporting information in the fields as in the following screenshot:

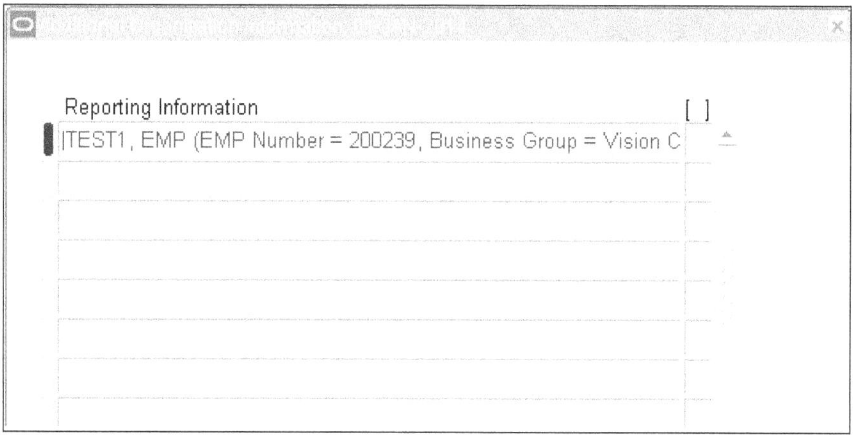

Similarly, other information can also be stored at the organization level. For example, **Time Management Info**.

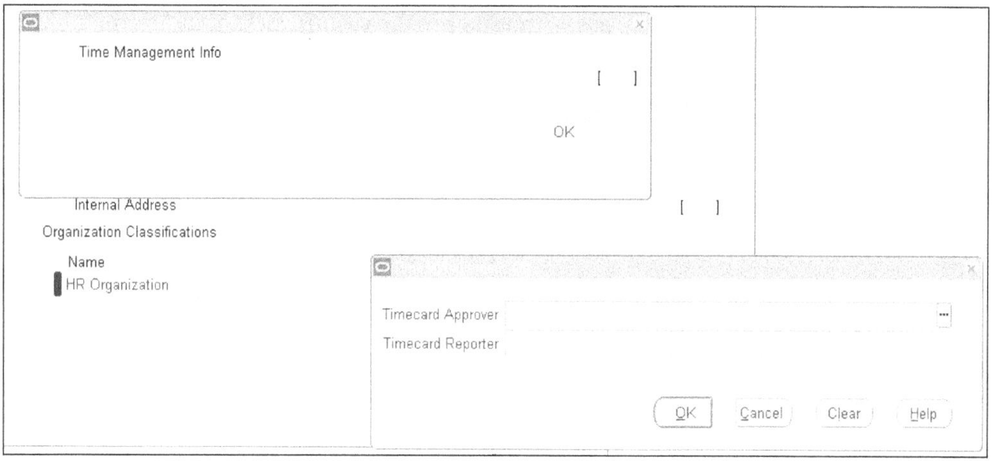

This will store data related to **Oracle Time and Labor** (OTL); that is, **Timecard Approver** and **Timecard Reporter**.

Deleting an organization

If there is a need to delete an organization, there are two approaches that can be used.

In the first approach, you can enter the **To** date in the **Dates** section in the **Organization** form.

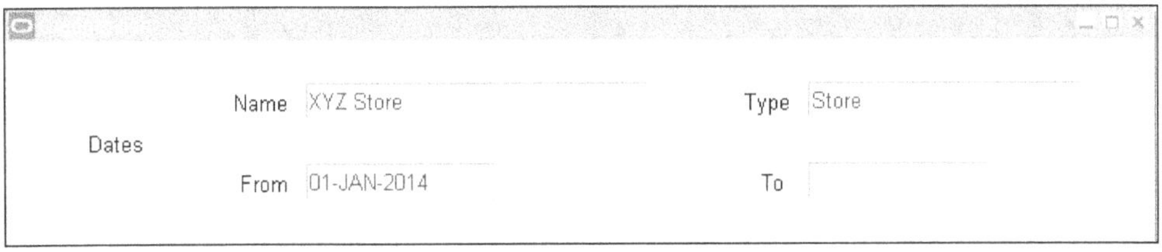

Entering this date will remove an organization from the list of organizations available for employee assignments.

This approach will keep the organization in the system as it is, but you cannot use it further beyond that date.

The second approach is to entirely delete an organization from the application; you must first remove any employee assignments for the organization and then remove the organization from any defined organization hierarchies.

Then, disable its organization classifications in the **Organization** window.

If you follow these steps, only then can you delete an organization entirely from the application.

Defining a location in Oracle apps

We define a location in order to identify the exact address of an organization or employee work location.

If we say that the organization is a location in Washington DC, then we need to specify the exact address of that place. This can be captured in the location definition.

Locations can be local as well as global. Local locations are available only in particular BGs, whereas global locations are visible across all BGs defined in the application.

To define the locations, navigate to **US HRMS Manager** | **Work Structures** | **Location**.

Enter the required field in the form, and enter the name of the location. Here we have used the location name as `Washington DC`.

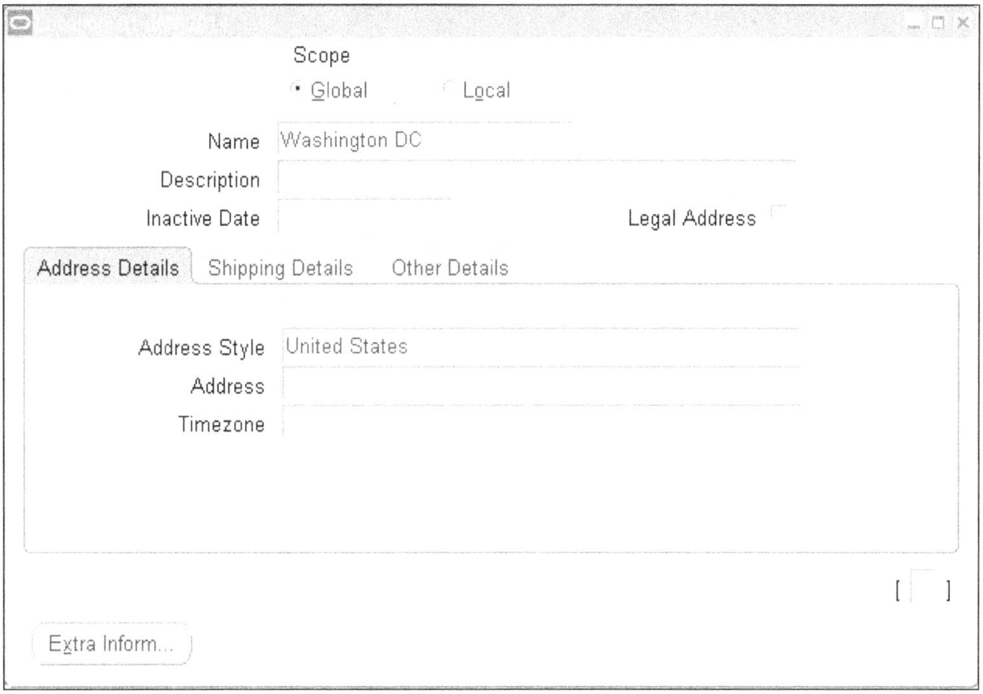

We further need to enter the address. Click on the address field to open the form shown here:

You can also enter the time zone.

Click on the **Shipping Details** tab—shipping details are used for the Oracle Purchasing Module.

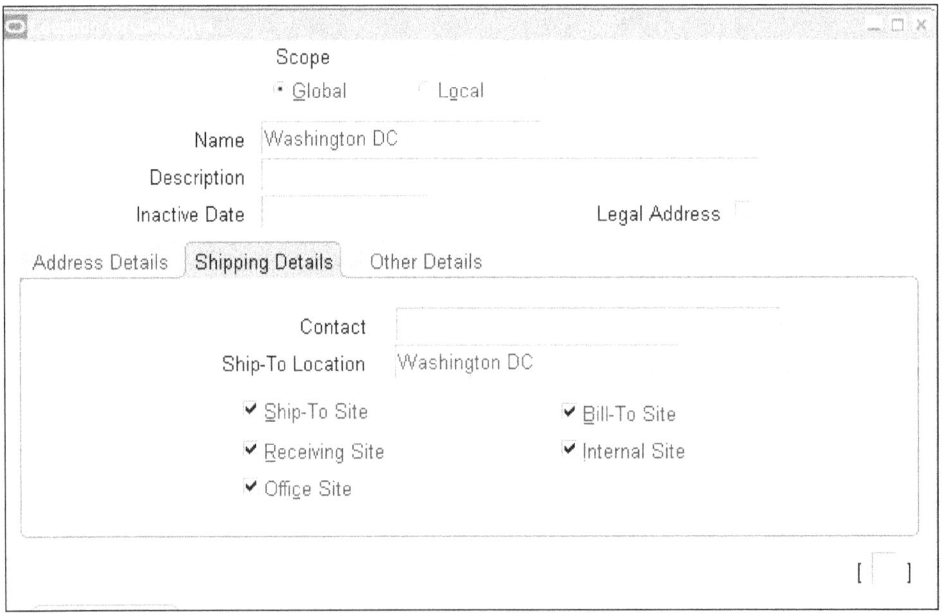

You cannot delete a location from an application, but you can make them inactive by entering a value in **Inactive Date** from when the location is no longer in use in your enterprise.

The location defined can be assigned to an organization you have created. Entering the location of an organization gives us the actual physical location of that organization.

Summary

In this chapter, you learned how to represent your enterprise in Oracle HRMS. We reviewed defining a business group and took the decision to go with single or multiple business groups. We also covered in detail about creating organizations, classifying them, creating an organization hierarchy, entering organization and manager information and how to define a location in Oracle HRMS.

In the next chapter, we will cover in detail about representing Jobs, Positions, and Payrolls in HRMS.

5

Job, Position, Pay Grade, and Payroll

In the previous chapter, you learned the concepts of work structures in Oracle Apps HRMS. You also learned how to define a business group, organization and location, and so on. These learnings were more related to the organizational aspect. We will drill down more in this chapter to see actually what entities are involved in an organization. In this chapter, you will also learn about the concepts of jobs, position, and some fundamental concepts of payroll.

Job and position overview

The work structure provided by Oracle HRMS is quite flexible. It is used to represent the ongoing responsibilities and functions that an enterprise must carry out in order to meet its goals.

Jobs and position are important parts of your enterprise. They facilitate you to differentiate between duty and the person who performs those duties.

Jobs in Oracle HRMS are used to represent the task an employee performs in your enterprise and the necessary skills. An example can be shown as follows:

- Manager
- Developer
- Consultant
- Accountant

Position represents specific details of the job, for example:

- Assistant manager of operations
- Senior SQL developer
- Senior Oracle HRMS consultant
- Payroll accountant

When you actually start implementing Oracle HRMS, you need to decide whether to use jobs, position, or both in your organization. Both these entities are non mandatory for an employee. An employee can have either of these, both of these, or neither of these.

Your organization will generally fall into one of three general categories:

- Rule-based
- Project-based
- Hybrid

For rule-based enterprises such as governments and schools, you control the employment, roles, and payment-related information according to the strict policies and procedures. In these organization types, roles are significant rather than individual. In rule-based organizations, where roles continue to exist after an individual leaves the organization, positions are used.

An IT company is an example of a project-based enterprise. In IT companies, employees are allocated to projects on a regular basis. Here, you have to manage people and their skill sets, instead of fixed roles. Therefore, in project-based organizations, where the role ends when an employee completes a particular project, typically, jobs are used.

A manufacturing company or a corporate is an example of a hybrid enterprise. In this type of company, people are assigned to fixed roles and others to more than one project. Hence, a hybrid enterprise uses both jobs and positions.

Therefore, depending on your requirements, you to have to decide whether to use jobs or positions.

Now, let's see how to define jobs and positions.

Defining a job

Until now, you have learned the concept of using jobs in your organization. In this section, you will learn to define a job in Oracle HRMS.

Navigate to **US HRMS Manager** | **Work Structures** | **Job** | **Description**.

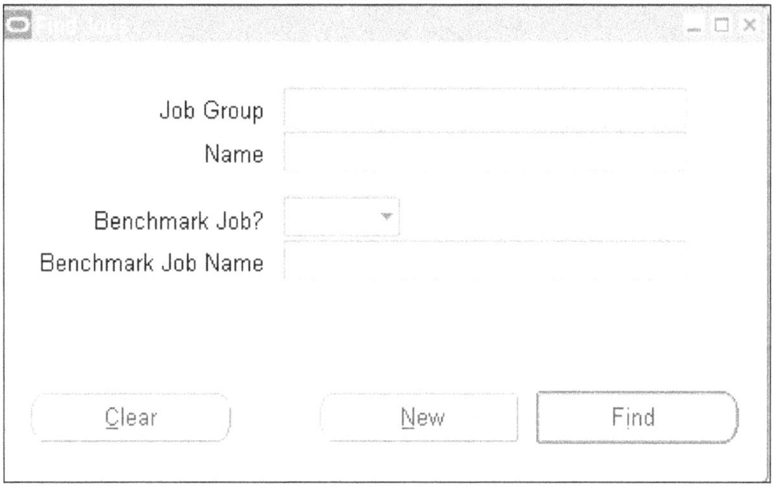

In the screenshot, you can see the form that is used to define a job in your organization or, you can say, in your business group. You can use this window to search for a particular job or to create a new job. Click on the **New** button to create a new job.

Before creating a job you can create a job group. Oracle HRMS organizes jobs in job groups. For each business group, there is a default job group; however, you can define additional groups if you want to. Some statutory reports do require job group as their parameter. Otherwise, there is no such significance of using a job group.

Creating a job group

To define a job group, navigate to **US HRMS Manager** | **Work Structures** | **Job** | **Job Group**.

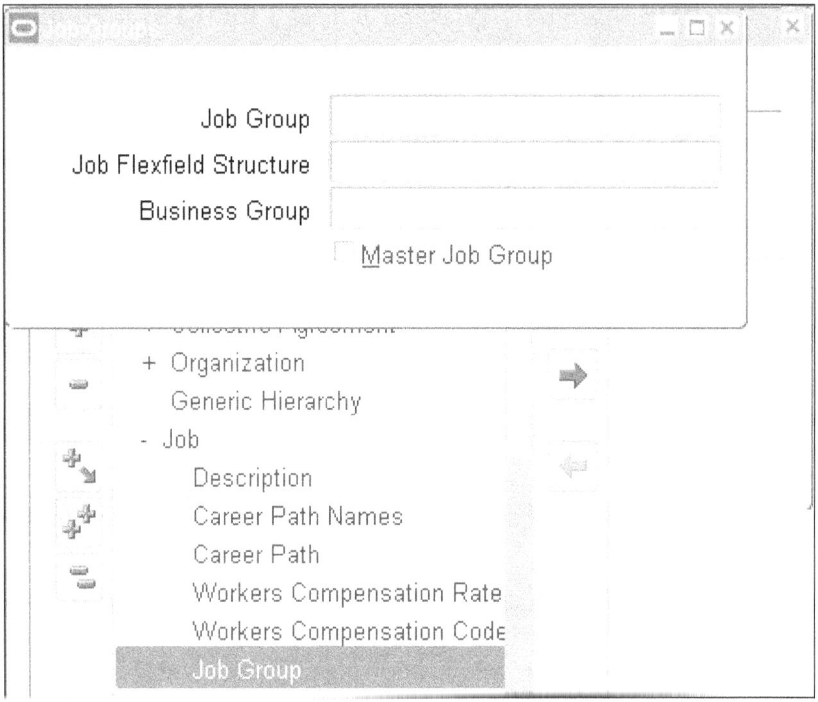

To create a job group, here are the steps:

1. Enter a name for the job group.
2. Select the flexfield structure. This will decide the fields that are displayed in the **Job Groups** window when this job group is chosen. We have seen how to define the Key flexfield in *Chapter 3, Fundamental of Flexfields / Value Sets*, under the *Key flexfields* section.
3. Select a business group if required.
4. Check the **Master Job Group** checkbox if this is to be the master job group. This is used in Oracle Projects. The jobs within the master job group can have jobs from other job groups mapped onto them using Oracle projects.
5. Save your changes.

As we have now created a Job Group, we will use the job group to create a job.

Creating a job

To define a job, navigate to **US HRMS Manager** | **Work Structures** | **Job** | **Description**.

Now, follow these steps to define a job:

1. Enter a date of your choice.
2. Select the required job group.
3. Enter a name for the job. This name should be unique. The name will have segments depending upon your definition of Job key flex.
4. To match employees to roles, which included qualification or valid experience, use the **Requirement** button to enter a job requirement.
5. The **Valid Grades** button is used to enter the grades to which job holders can be assigned.

In our case, we have created a job name `Manager.Job 002` from 01-Jan-2014.

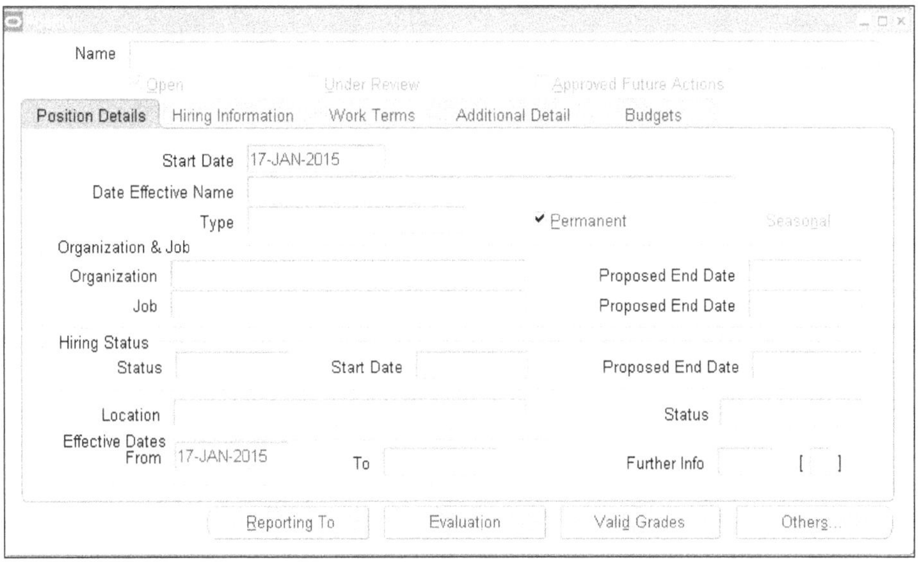

Thus, we have seen how to define a job. This job can be assigned to an employee in assignment information.

Defining position

As seen earlier, the concept of position in an organization. In this section, we will see how to define a position in an organization. Navigate to **US HRMS Manager** | **Work Structures** | **Position** | **Description**.

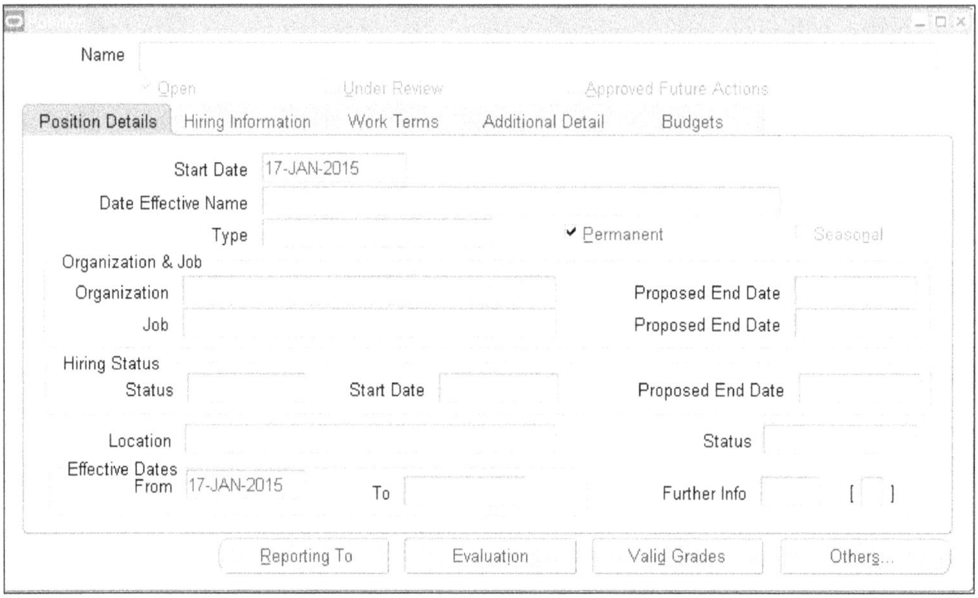

Follow these steps to define a position:

1. First, we need to set the effective date from when we want to create a position.
2. Then, enter the name of the position in the **Date Effective Name** field in the **Position Details** tab. This name must be unique or it will give you an appropriate error.
3. The next step is to enter the position type; there are four options for this field. These are None, Pooled, Shared, and Single incumbent.

Single incumbent means at a given point of time only one employee is allowed to hold that position in the organization.

In case of Shared, there can be more than one incumbent. This value will be as entered in the FTE field.

Pooled (public sector only) means the position is loosely defined, so rules about FTE and hours are not enforced by the system.

1. Select the None option in case you do not need to record position types.
2. In case the position is permanent in your organization. The example for such a case can be CEO.
3. Seasonal, as the name suggests, is used for one season each year (such as a summer teacher), so select the **Seasonal** checkbox for such cases.
4. As position can be for an organization or a job, enter the appropriate organization and job in the respective fields.
5. Enter the proposed end dates in case you know that the position will be transferred to another organization or job in the future.
6. Enter a hiring status.
7. A position can have a location. If not entered, it will be defaulted to the location of the organization.
8. Select a status for the position. This is an optional field.

The **Hiring Information** tab is used to enter further information regarding the position created. Enter the **Head Count** and the **FTE** information. Furthermore, enter the probation period, payroll name, grade, and salary basis (this information will be automatically populated on the person's assignment form when the position is assigned to a person).

In the **Work Terms** tab, enter the working hours and frequency used by this position. Also, enter the normal start and end time. In addition, you can also enter the supervisor, relief, and successor for the position.

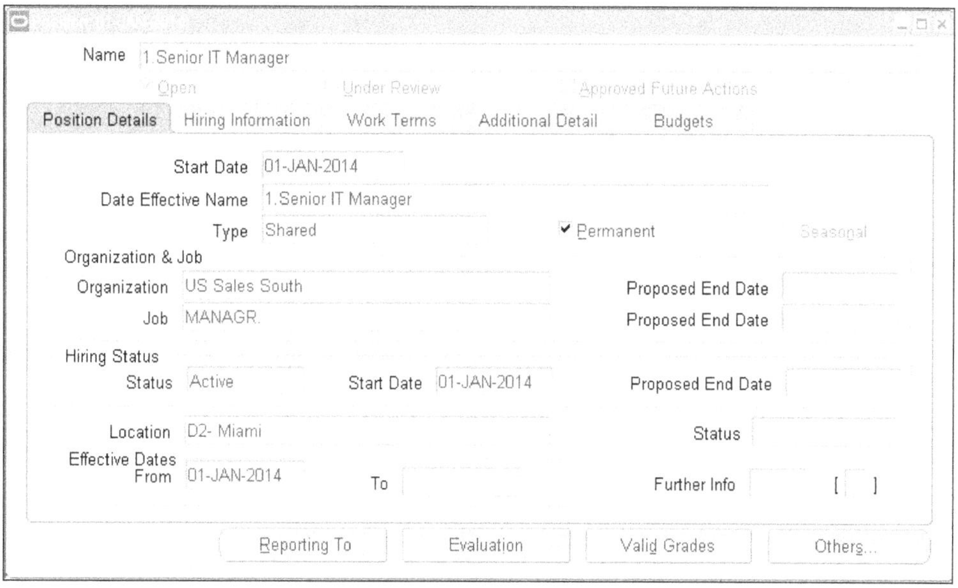

Hence, we have seen how to define a position. There are still many fields used in defining a position, but they are not as significant as the remaining fields that we have seen before.

Now that you learned how to define jobs and position in Oracle apps HRMS, let's see the concept of position hierarchy.

Your organization may route transactions for data entry and approval using different chains of authority. One such chain of authority you can use is position hierarchy.

To define position hierarchy, navigate to **US HRMS Manager** | **Work Structures** | **Position** | **Hierarchy**:

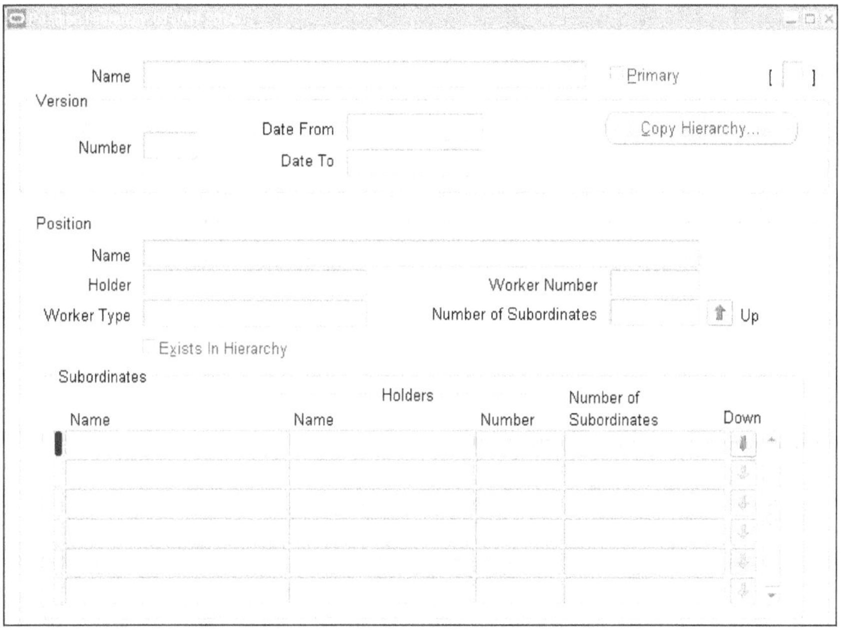

Enter the primary name of the position hierarchy and enter the version number and start date of the hierarchy.

Query the top position name into the position block. The holder field will display the employee name holding this position along with worker type and employee number.

Now in the subordinate block, enter the immediate subordinate for the top position. To add a position below this added subordinate position, please check the checkbox.

To create a new version of an existing hierarchy, follow the same steps as creating a position hierarchy. Use the down arrow in the version field to move through existing versions of the hierarchy until you reach a version number where there is no data.

To copy an existing hierarchy, you have to query the name and number of the new hierarchy and click on the **Copy Hierarchy** button. This is then followed by selecting the name and the version number of the hierarchy you want to copy.

To change the position of the hierarchy, there are three options. They are as follows:

- By adding a new position to the existing one, you have to query the hierarchy and the version you want to change. Then you need to query the parent position for the one you want to add, which is followed by selecting the new position in the **Subordinates** block.
- Change the top position in an existing hierarchy. Again, you have to query the hierarchy and version you want to change, then you need to query the new top position, and this is followed by selecting the previous top position in the subordinates block.
- You can also move a position and all of its subordinates within a hierarchy. To move a position, you need to query the hierarchy and the version you want to change, and then query the new parent position for the one you want to move. This is followed by selecting the position to move in the subordinates block.

In order to delete a positional hierarchy, one must begin by deleting the lowest level and working their way towards the top level.

> You cannot delete a hierarchy if the other version exists or if any security profile uses it.

Thus, we have seen details about the position hierarchy.

In the next section, we will slowly move towards fundamental concepts involved in the Oracle payroll. Before that, let's see the most used entity in Oracle HRMS, that is, People Group.

People Group in Oracle HRMS

People Group is a **Key Flexfield** (**KFF**) in HRMS such as job, grade, and position. Oracle provides People Group KFF for several purposes. If an organization wants to group certain sets of people based on certain parameters such as benefit-eligible types, then you can use the People Group KFF.

People Group is mostly used to store benefit eligibility; however, it can serve many purposes in your implementation. It is one of the fields in the assignment form.

In *Chapter 3, Fundamental of Flexfields / Value Sets*, we have seen how to define KFF. People Group KFF segments can also be defined using the same detail mentioned in that chapter. All KFFs hold information in segments. You can configure a maximum of 30 segments.

The most important use of People Group is to link benefits to group flexfield segments. This will ensure that only employees within groups are eligible for that benefit.

Let me explain this with an example. Let's say your organization wants to pay a car allowance to a few eligible employees. You open a segment in People Group KFF to store this eligibility. This segment will have the value Yes or No. This value can further be used in payroll to pay car allowance for an employee.

Thus we can configure People Group in our business group to a maximum of 30 segments to store data for employees.

Now in the next section, we will see how to define a payroll for our business group.

Defining payroll

A payroll is a set of employees whose pay you process with a single frequency, for example, weekly, monthly, or semimonthly. You can define as many payrolls as you want to meet the requirements of your company. For example, your company has two different types of employee, one of which is paid monthly, and others are paid weekly; then you can define two payrolls for your organization. You can then place those employees on a payroll by assigning him or her to the payroll.

As per the HRMS design, every employee assignment must have a payroll attached to it though this field is nonmandatory.

The entity payroll tells the system about the payroll frequency/cycles, the valid payment methods, and the check dates to which the employee is entitled. Employees which fall into the same payroll share the same payroll frequency and pay dates.

Payroll has only one pay frequency, hence you must define at least one payroll for each pay frequency you use. The following table shows the valid period types for pay frequency:

Payroll Period Types	Periods per Year
Year	1
Semi-Year	2
Quarter	4
Bi-Month	6
Calendar Month	12
Lunar Month	13
Semi-Month	24
Bi-Week	26
Week	52

Before defining a payroll, you need to have an additional setup. This additional setup is the setting up of a payment method for your organization.

Every organization has rules for its payment. Some organizations pay by check, some by deposits directly to your banks, and some even pay by cash. The method of payment that an organization follows in order to pay its employees is known as the **Organizational Payment method**.

The employee in your organization can select the method by which they would like to be paid every pay period. Some employees may opt to get their salaries in their defined bank account, some might want to have a check, or some may like to have half by check and half cash.

Each payroll binds together a set of valid payment methods. Therefore, the available options can be specific to each payroll.

The payment methods differ with the types of banks as well. For example, if your Company deals with three different banks, then it will require three different payment methods defined for each of the banks it deals with, even though all of the payment methods will be of the same type.

To define the payment method, navigate to **US HRMS Manager | Payroll | Payment Methods**:

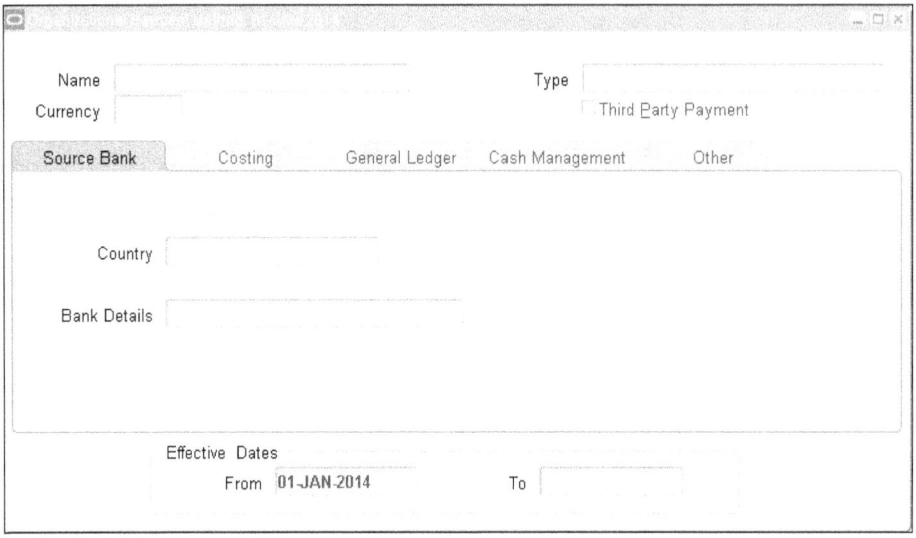

Enter the name of the payment method, enter the type such as cash, check, and so on. Enter currency, check third-party payment, if the payment is of the third-party payment type, and enter the bank details. The bank details will have information about the account from which the payments come.

Now, as we have defined the payment methods, the next step is to define a payroll. To define a payroll, navigate to **US HRMS Manager | Payroll | Description**:

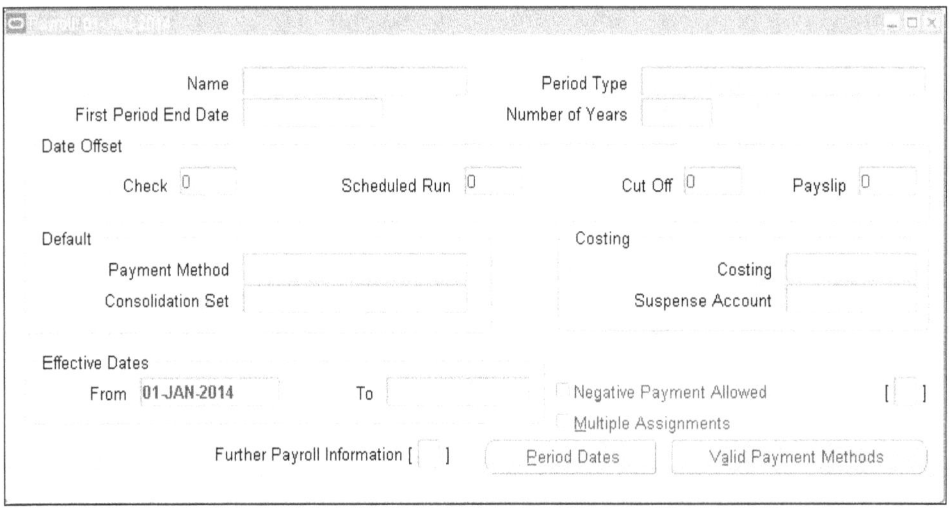

So, the payroll definition is the screen where payment dates, check dates, consolidation set, a default payment method, and so on, are assigned to a payroll.

To create a payroll, follow these steps:

1. Set the effective date from when you want to define payroll. Your effective date must be on or before the first period start date of the payroll calendar.
2. Enter the name of the payroll.
3. Select the period type. This will tell the frequency of the payroll. The **First Period End Date** field is used by the system to determine the payroll dates (start date and end date).
4. The value in **Number of Years** will indicate the number of years the payroll will be effective. If you enter the value as `100`, then the payroll will be valid for the next hundred years from the first period's end date.
5. The check date signifies the days after the end date, the checks will be cut. If you enter the value in this field as `-3` then it means that the check will be cut 3 days before the payroll end date.
6. Enter the scheduled run date, which is an offset as well, is date as of which the payroll will be run.
7. Enter the cut off date, which represents the date after which no changes should be made to the payroll data in the application.
8. Enter the pay slip date. On this date, pay slips will be available online in self service HR to the employees.
9. Enter the payment method. This will be the default payment method of the payroll. This payment method will be used if an employee has not selected any preferred payment method in his/her assignment. In most cases, it is defined as a check.
10. Enter the **Suspense Account** and **Costing** information in the **Costing** section—cost allocation KFF is used to define costing segments. If the costing of a particular payroll or element is not charged to any account, then it gets added to the defined suspended account.
11. Check the **Negative Payment Allowed** field to determine whether negative payments can be done in case the employee's deductions are higher than earnings.
12. The **Multiple Assignments** check box tells the system whether to process an employee if the employee has multiple assignments with different payrolls to each assignment.

13. The **Period Dates** button will open a new form that will show dates for each payroll cycle along with the cut off date, check date, and so on. However, these dates can be changed (overridden) in this screen, in case the dates are to be changed for a given period.
14. The valid payment methods will list payment methods that the employee can choose from.

You have now learned about defining a payroll. In the following screenshot, we have defined a new payroll:

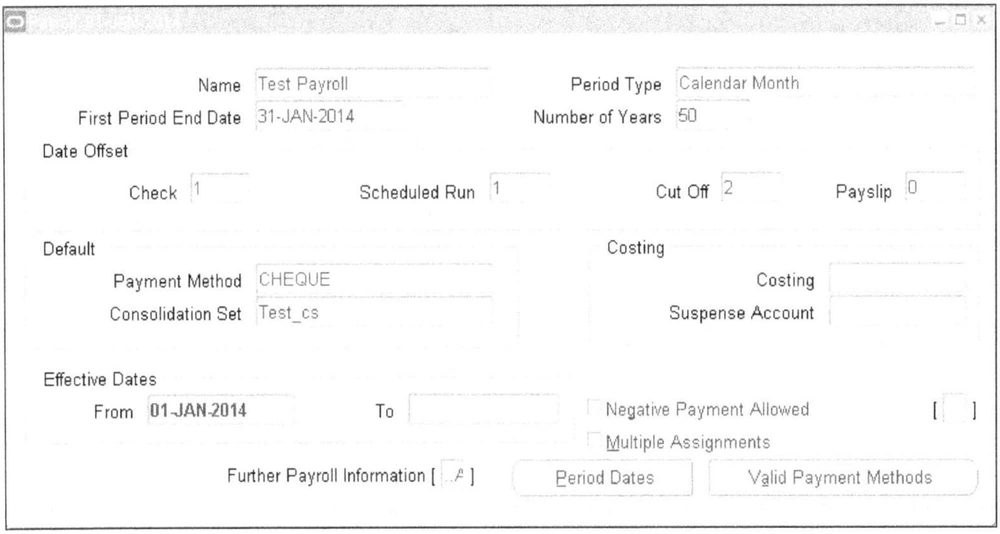

Now let's learn about salary basis in the Oracle payroll.

Salary basis is the duration for which the salary is quoted. There might be different types of employees in your organization in terms of payment. Some might be getting paid on an hourly basis, while others might be paid annually. So the salary basis defines the time span by which the salary is being defined. However, someone being on an hourly salary does not mean that the employee gets paid every hour, it means the employee gets paid per hour. If an employee is in an annual salary basis, he/she might get paid every month/week, based on the calculated salary per pay period.

To define salary basis, navigate to **US HRMS Manager** | **Total Compensation** | **Basic** | **Salary Basis**:

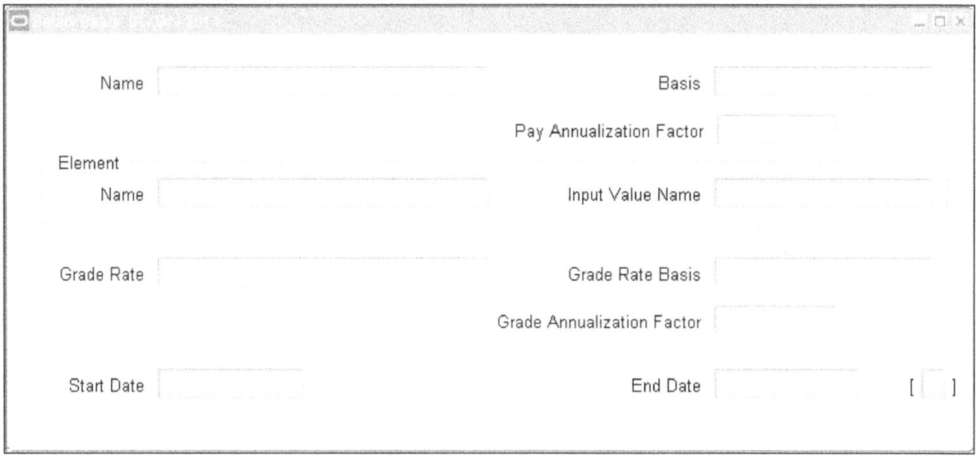

Enter the name of the salary basis. This can be one of the following options:

- **Hourly salary**: This is paid per hour
- **Monthly salary**: This is paid per month
- **Annual salary**: This is paid per annum
- **Period salary**: This is based on the pay period

Enter the pay annualization factor and enter the factor with which the salary can be converted to the annual salary. For example, if the salary is monthly, then this field will be 12, for annual it will be 1, and for hourly it will be 2,080 (52 weeks x 40 hours each week).

Leave the field blank, if you are opting for period salary basis; an application will be able to figure this out based on the pay periods.

Enter the salary element in the element name field and enter the name of the input value that stores the basis. Do not use the pay value as the input value because Oracle payroll will now be completed does not calculate on the input value, if the pay value is assigned.

The grade rate is the place holder of linking grade to the salary basis. The **Grade Rate Basis** range given in the grade rate must relate to a basis. That field gets populated here. **Grade Annualization Factor** is a factor of the grade rate based on the grade basis.

Thus, we have seen how to define a salary basis. In the following screenshot, we have created a new salary basis:

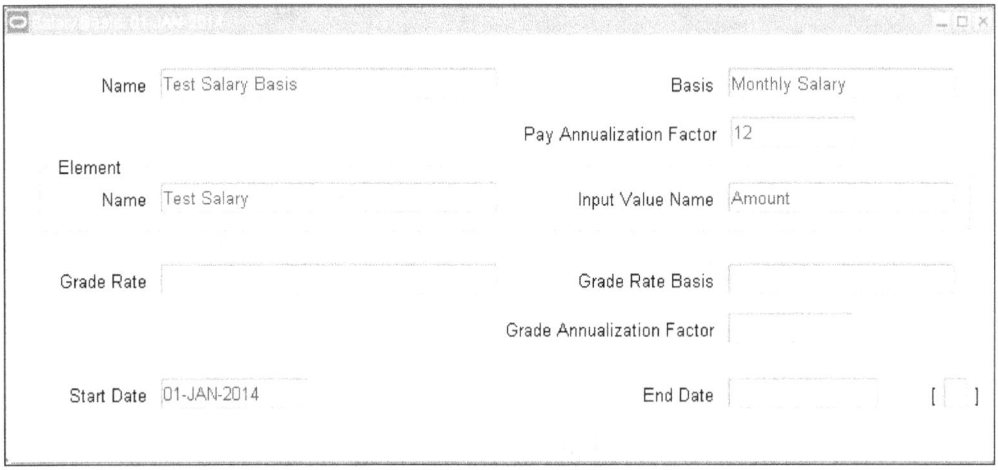

Summary

In this chapter, you learned about the concepts of jobs and positions. You learned how to define a job and position. Then we covered details about position hierarchy. We also covered the concept of People Group and came across some terminologies in payroll in which you learned about payment methods, salary basis, and payroll definition.

In the next chapter, you will learn about people management in Core HR. You will understand the hiring process and how to hire a person. Then you will learn the concept of person types in Oracle HRMS and about entering personal information in the application.

6
Entering People Information

The previous chapters were basically divided into two sections. Section one was about the basics and setup of Oracle HRMS. Section two was more on work structure in core HR. From this chapter onwards, we are going to start the third and last section, which is people management.

This is the first chapter of section three. In this chapter, we will learn about entering a person's information in Oracle HRMS. We will understand the hiring process in Oracle. This, actually, is part of the Oracle I-recruitment module in Oracle apps. Then we will see how to create an employee in Core HR. Then, we will learn the concept of person types and defining person types. We will also learn about entering information for an employee, including additional information.

Let's see how to create an employee in core HR.

Creating an employee

An employee is the most important entity in an organization. Before creating an employee, the HR officer must know the date from which the employee will be active in the organization. In Oracle terminology, you can call it the employee's hire date. Apart from this, the HR officer must know basic details of the employee such as first name, last name, date of birth, and so on.

Navigate to **US HRMS Manager** | **People** | **Enter and Maintain**.

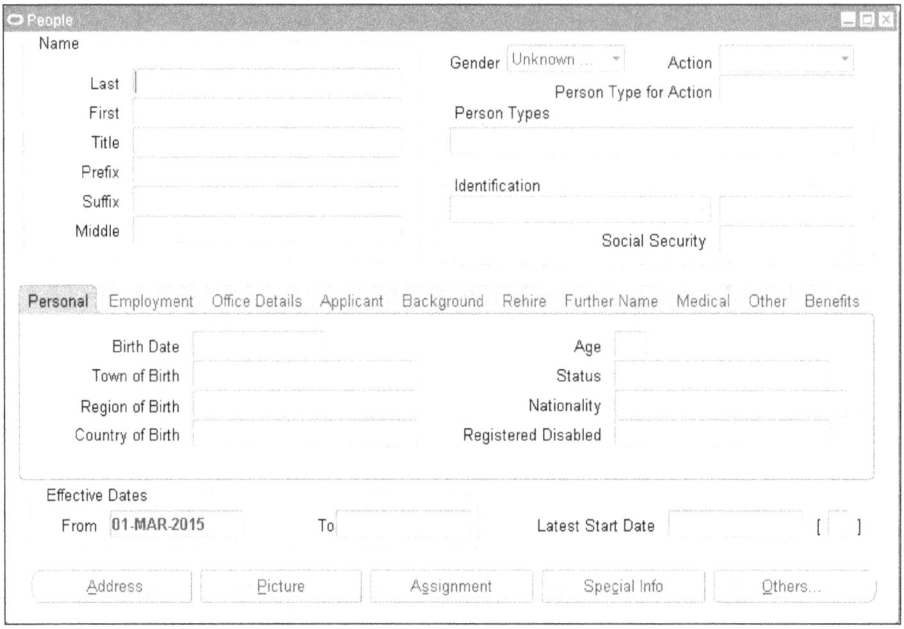

This is the basic form, called **People** in Oracle HRMS, which is used to create an employee in the application. As you can see in the form, there is a field named **Last**, which is marked in yellow. This indicates that this is mandatory to create an employee record.

First, you need to set the effective date on the form. You can set this by clicking on the icon, as shown in the following screenshot:

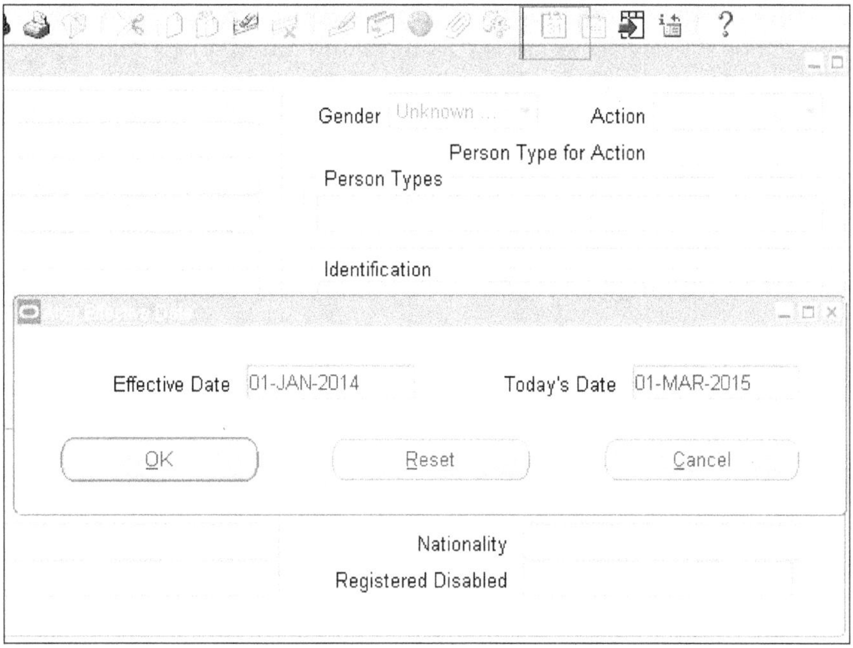

You need to enter the mandatory field data along with additional data. The following screenshot shows the data entered:

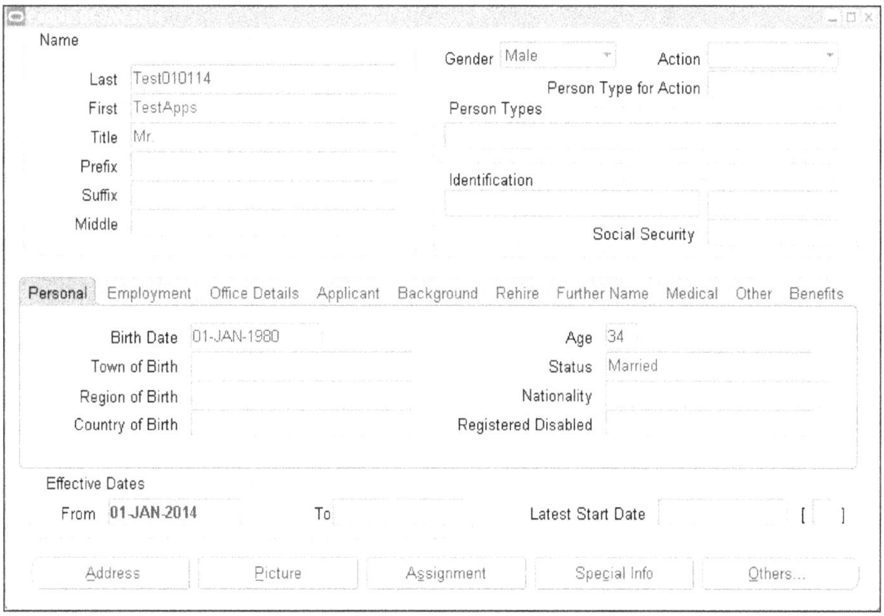

Once you enter the required data, you need to specify the action for the entered record. The action we have selected is **Create Employment**. The **Create Employment** action will create an employee in the application. There are other actions such as **Create Applicant**, which is used to create an applicant for I-Recruitment. The **Create Placement** action is used to create a contingent worker in your enterprise. Once you select this action, it will prompt you to enter the person type of this employee as in the following screenshot. Select the **Person Type** as **Employee** and save the record. We will see the concept of person type in the next section.

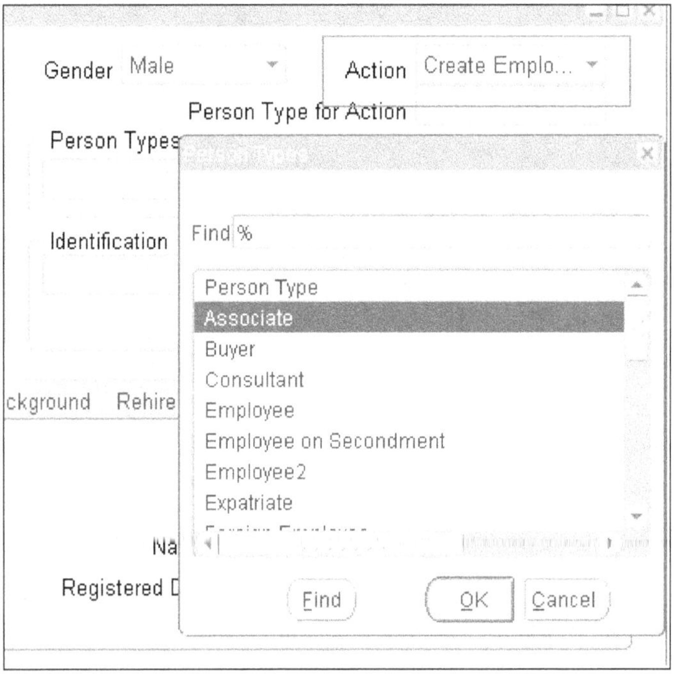

Once you select the employee person type and then save the record, the system will automatically generate the employee number for the person. In our case, the system has generated an employee number **10160**.

So now, we have created an employee in the application.

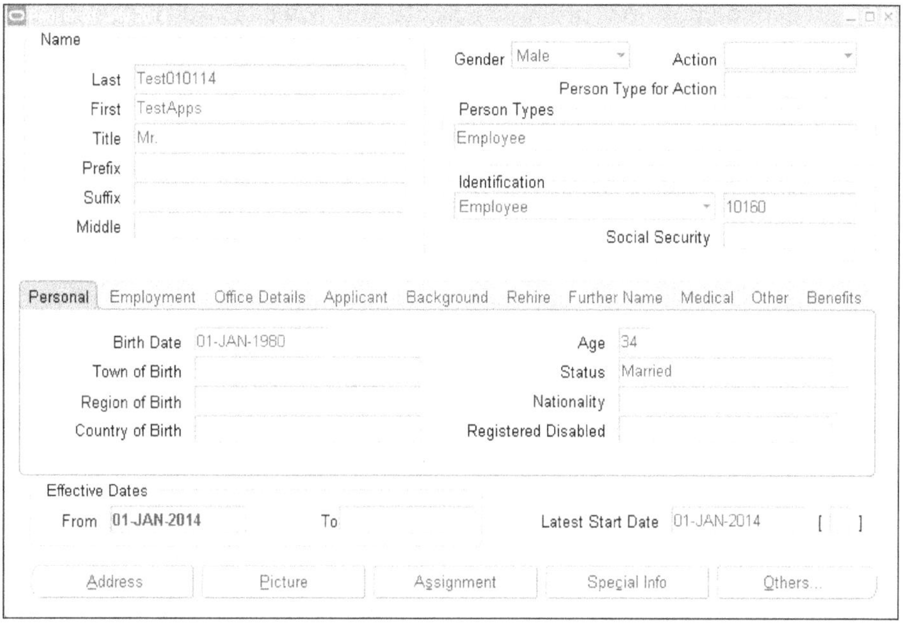

Concept of person types

In any organization, you need to identify different types of people. Here, you can say that you need to group different types of people. There are basically three types of people you capture in HRMS system. They are as follows:

- **Employees**: These include current employees and past employees. Past employees are those who were part of your enterprise earlier and are no longer active in the system. You can call them terminated or ex-employees.
- **Applicants**: If you are using I-recruitment, applicants can be created.
- **External people**: Contact is a special category of external type. Contacts are associated with an employee or an applicant. For example, there might be a need to record the name, address, and phone number of an emergency contact for each employee in your organization.

  There might also be a need to keep information on dependents of an employee for medical insurance purposes or for some payments in payroll processing.

Using person types

There are predefined person types in Oracle HRMS. You can add more person types as per your requirements. You can also change the name of existing person types when you install the system.

Let's take an example for your understanding. Your organization has employees. There might be employees of different types; you might have regular employees and employees who are contractors in your organization. Hence, you can categorize employees in your organization into two types:

- Regular employees
- Consultants

The reason for creating these categories is to easily identify the employee type and store different types of information for each category.

Similarly, if you are using I-recruitment, then you will have candidates. Hence, you can categorize candidates into two types. One will be internal candidate and the other will be external candidate.

Internal candidates will be employees within your organization who can apply for an opening within your organization. An external candidate is an applicant who does not work for your organization but is applying for a position that is open in your company.

Defining person types

In an earlier section, you learned the concept of person types, and now you will learn how to define person types in the system.

Navigate to **US HRMS Manager** | **Other Definitions** | **Person Types**.

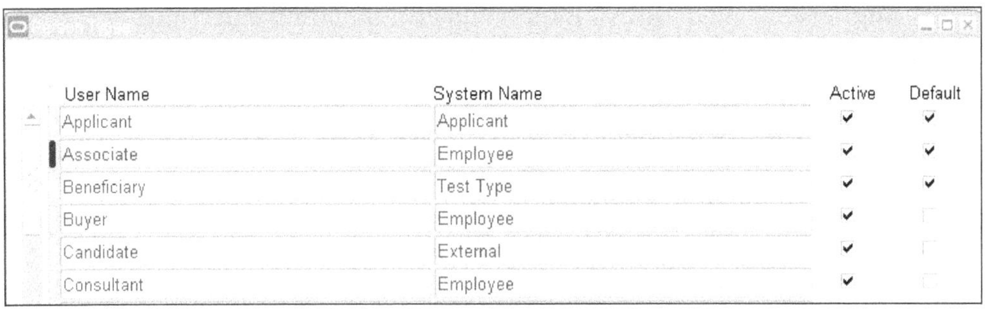

In the preceding screenshot, you can see four fields, that is, **User Name**, **System Name**, **Active**, and **Default flag**.

There are eight person types recognized by the system and identified by a system name. For each system name, there are predefined usernames. A username can be changed as per your needs. There must be one username that should be the default. While creating an employee, the person types that are marked by the default flag will come by default.

To change a username for a person type, delete the contents of the **User Name** field and type the name you'd prefer to keep.

To add a new username to a person type system name:

1. Select **New Record** from the **Edit** menu.
2. Enter a unique username and select the system name you want to use.

Deactivating person types

You cannot delete person types, but you can deactivate them by unchecking the **Active** checkbox.

Entering personal and additional information

Until now, you learned how to create an employee by entering basic details such as title, gender, and date of birth. In addition to this, you can enter some other information for an employee. As you can see on the people form, there are various tabs such as **Employment**, **Office details**, **Background**, and so on. Each tab has some fields that can store information.

For example, in our case, we have stored the e-mail address of the employee in the **Office Details** tab.

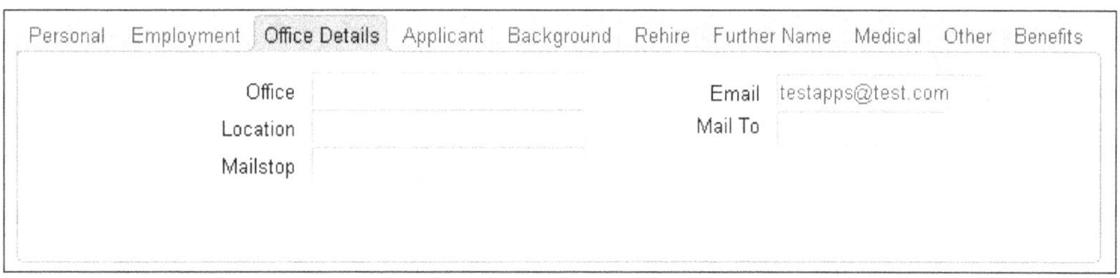

Whenever you enter any data for an employee and then click on the **Save** button, it will give you two options as shown in the following screenshot:

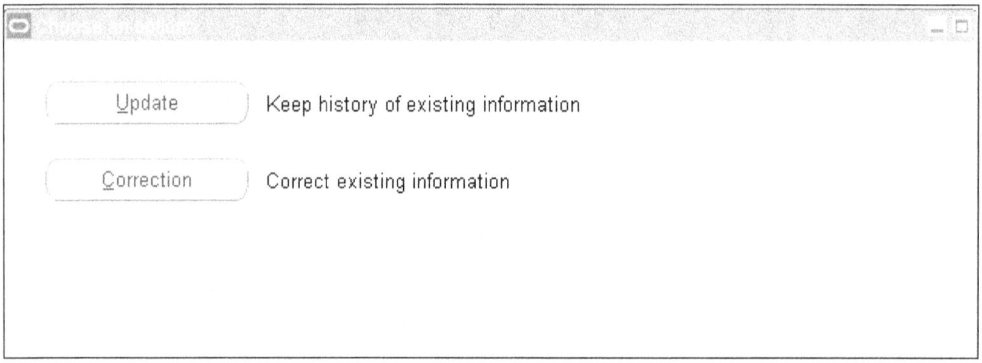

You have to select one of the options to save the data. The differences between both the options are explained with an example. Let's say you have hired a new employee as of 01-Jan-2014. Hence, a new record will be created in the application with the start date as 01-Jan-2014. This is called an effective start date of the record. There is no end date for this record, so Oracle gives it a default end date, which is 31-Dec-4712. This is called the effective end date of the record.

Now, in our case, Oracle has created a single record with the start date and end date as 01-Jan-2014 and 31-Dec-4712, respectively.

When we try to enter additional data for this record (in our case, it is phone number) then Oracle will prompt you to select the **Correction** or **Update** option. This is called the date-tracked option. If you select the correction mode, then Oracle will update an existing record in the application.

Now, if you date track to, say, 01-Aug-2014 and then enter the phone number and select the update mode, then it will end the historical data with the new date minus one and create a new record with the start date 01-Aug-2014 with the phone number that you have entered. Thus, the historical data will be preserved and a new record will be created with the start date 01-Aug-2014 and a phone number.

The following tabular representation will help you understand better in **Correction** mode:

Employee Number	LastName	Effective Start Date	Effective End Date	Phone Number
10160	Test010114	01-Jan-2014	31-Dec-4712	+0099999999

Now, if you want to change the phone number from 01-Aug-2014 in **Update** mode (date 01-Aug-2014), then the record will be as follows:

Employee Number	LastName	Effective Start Date	Effective End Date	Phone Number
10160	Test010114	01-Jan-2014	31-Jul-2014	+0099999999
10160	Test010114	01-Aug-2014	31-Jul-2014	+0088888888

Thus, in update mode, you can see that historical data is intact. If HR wants to view some historical data, then the HR employee can easily view this data.

Everything associated with Oracle HRMS is date-tracked. Every characteristic about the organization, person, position, salary, and benefits is tightly date-tracked.

This concept is very important in Oracle and is used in almost all the forms in which you store employee-related information.

Thus, you have learned about the date tracking concept in Oracle APPS.

There are some additional fields, which can be configured as per your requirements. Additional personal data can be stored in these fields. These are called as descriptive flexfields in Oracle. You learned this in *Chapter 3, Fundamentals of Flexfields / Value Sets* under the section about Descriptive Flexfields (DFF).

In *Chapter 3, Fundamentals of Flexfields / Value Sets*, we created personal DFF to store data about **Years of Industry Experience** and whether an employee is **Oracle Certified** or not.

This data can be stored in the **People** form DFF as marked in the following screenshot:

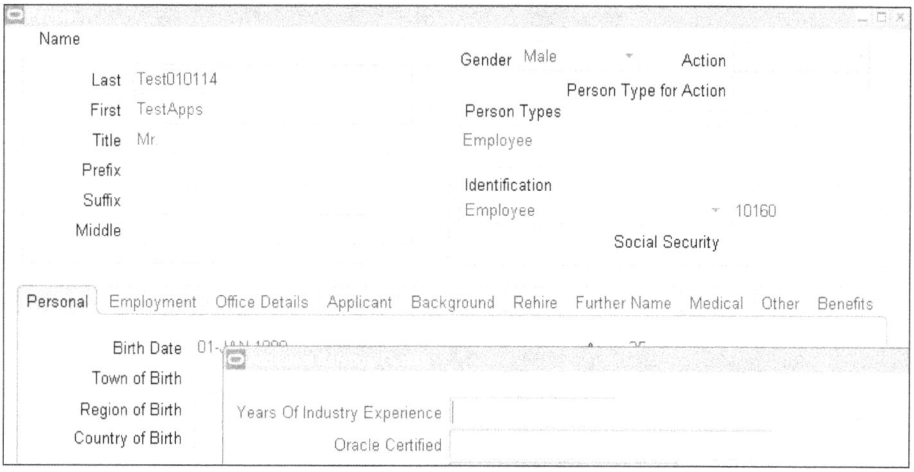

When you click on the box, it will open the new form as shown in the following screenshot. Here, you can enter the additional data. This is called Additional Personal Details DFF. It is stored in personal data; this is normally referred to as the **People** form DFF.

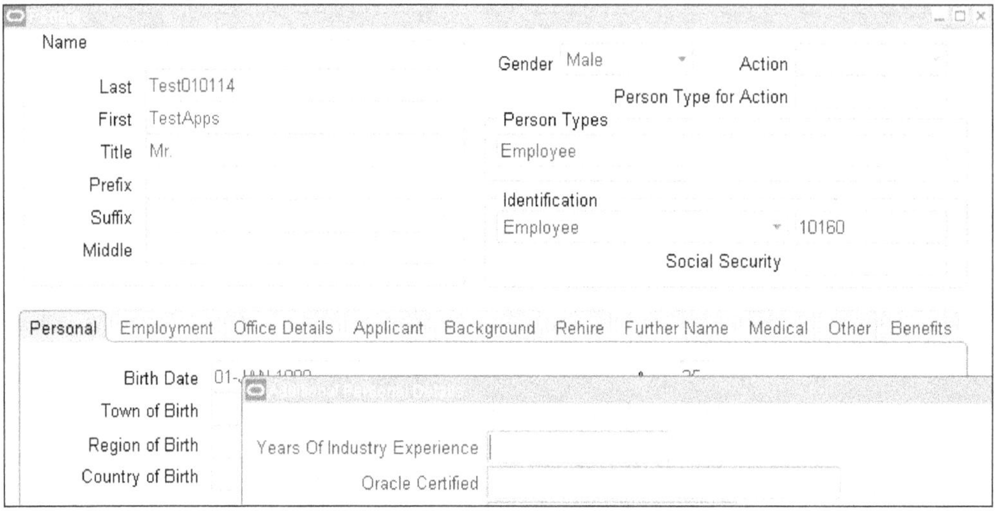

In addition to DFF, you also learned the concept of KFF in *Chapter 3*, *Fundamentals of Flexfields / Value Sets*, where we created a **Special Information Types** (**SIT**) to store information on languages known by an employee. This data will have two attributes, namely, the language known and the fluency.

This can be entered by navigating to **US HRMS Manager** | **People** | **Enter and Maintain** | **Special Info**.

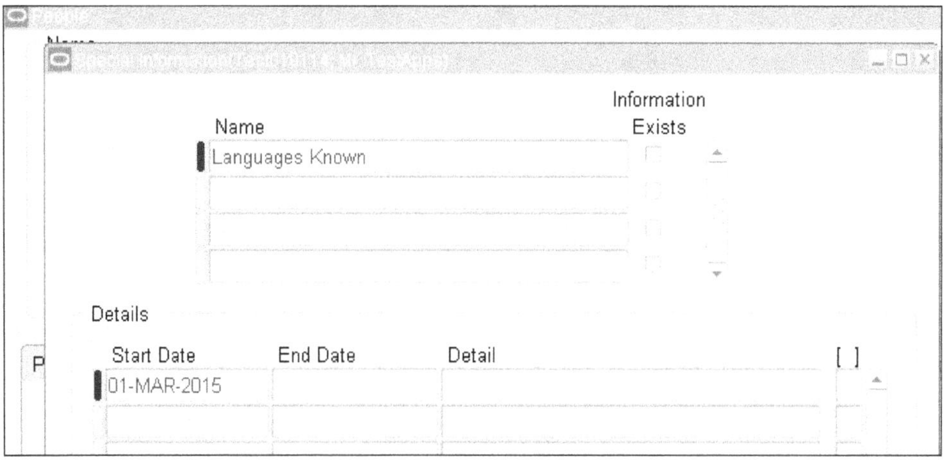

Click on the **Details** section. This will open a new form to enter the required details.

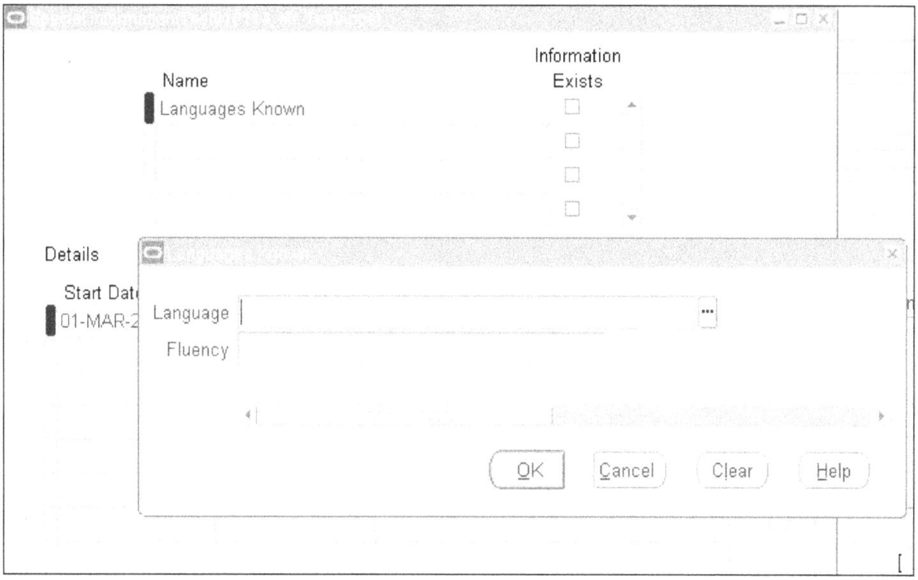

Each record in the SIT is date-tracked. You can enter the start date and the end date.

Thus, we have seen DFF in which you stored additional person data and we have seen KFF, where you enter the SIT data.

Summary

Thus we have completed this chapter. In this chapter, you learned about creating a new employee, entering employee data, and additional data using DFF and KFF. You also learned the concept of person type. In the next chapter, you will learn about entering assignment-related information.

7
Entering Assignment Information

In the previous chapter, you learned about hiring an employee and entering their personal information. In this chapter, you will learn about entering assignment-related information for an employee. When I say employee assignment, what exactly do I mean?

The assignment is a concept that links your employees to the structures (Organization, Jobs, Grade, and so on) in which they work, and the compensation and benefits for which they are eligible.

In Oracle HRMS, all activities related to HRMS such as vacancy management and budget planning are stored at assignment level and not in his/her person record.

In particular, all earnings, deductions, and other pay-related elements of the employee assignment are entered by you, rather than the employee. As payroll-related data is entered at assignment level, this makes it possible to give an employee two or more assignments, if needed.

Suppose the employee is working for more than one department and receives a salary from each department. You create two assignments for this employee and enter each department with its corresponding assignment.

An employee must have a current assignment at all times. You record things like Location, Job, Department, Grade, and so on as changes to the existing assignment. All these changes are then tracked based on the dates, that is, date tracked. In this way, you can view the history of changes that have occurred in an assignment; also, it enables you to make future-dated changes in advance.

Components of an assignment

At the basic level, an assignment tells you the following things:

- The business group for which an employee works
- The start date of the assignment
- The current status of the assignment—Active or Suspended

People Group flexfield values can be entered in an assignment form.

You can assign employees to an employment category. Employment categories include part time, regular (or full time), and temporary.

You can assign employees on a salary basis and maintain their salaries or wages using the salary administration.

Let's now see how to enter assignment-related information for an employee in the application. Navigate to **US HRMS Manager** | **People** | **Enter and Maintain** | **Assignment**.

You need to search for the employee before going to the assignment form.

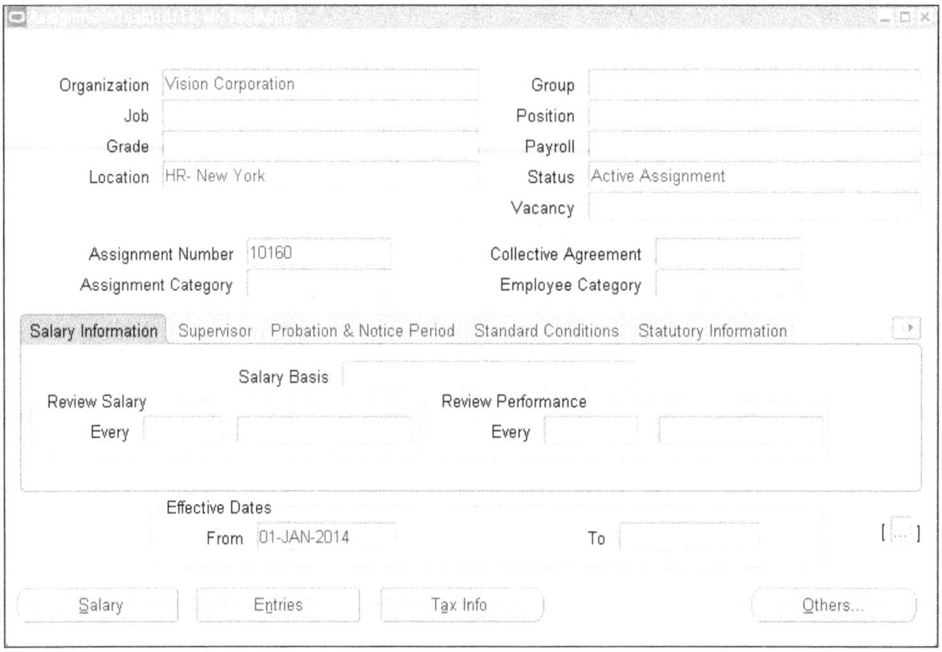

This is a form where you enter assignment-related information for an employee. Here are the steps to be followed for entering assignment information. We will use the same employee (Emp. number 10160) that we created in the previous chapter.

1. Initially, set the effective start date on the form. This will be the date for the new assignment to commence.
2. Enter the organization to which you want to assign the employee. If you do not enter this value, by default, the employee will be assigned to the business group organization. If you have defined a location for the business group or another organization, it will show by default in the location field. When you override these defaults, a window appears asking if the change is an update or a correction. Select the appropriate mode.
3. Enter a payroll for an employee.
4. Enter an appropriate grade.
5. Enter Job and Position.
6. Select an assignment status for the assignment. The default assignment status for an employee is **Active Assignment**. The assignment status will primarily tell you if an employee is active or not. There are various assignment statuses which you can define. If an employee is suspended, then you can select assignment status **Suspended**. If an employee goes on maternity, then you can select assignment status **Maternity**. Assignment statuses also have an impact on Oracle payroll. While creating assignment statuses in the application, you can specify whether you want to process payroll or not for a particular assignment status. Defining assignment statuses will be covered in the next section.
7. Enter an **Assignment Number** to uniquely identify the assignment. By default, this number is the same as the employee number, for the employee's first assignment.
8. Save the record.

In the following screenshot, we have entered the assignment information for our employee:

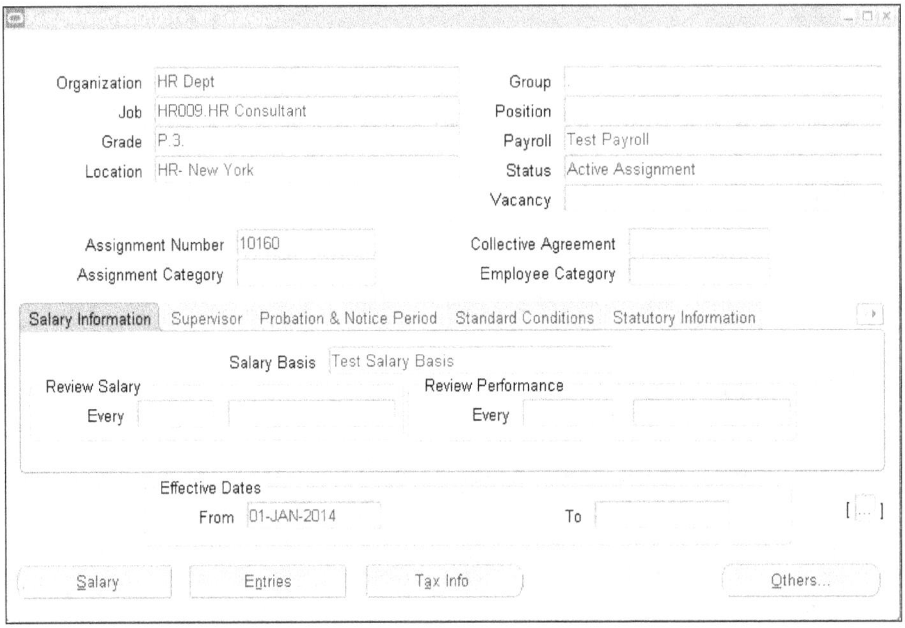

In the **Supervisor** tab, you enter the supervisor (manager) for an employee. You can also enter the **Name** or **Worker Number**, which is the employee number of the supervisor.

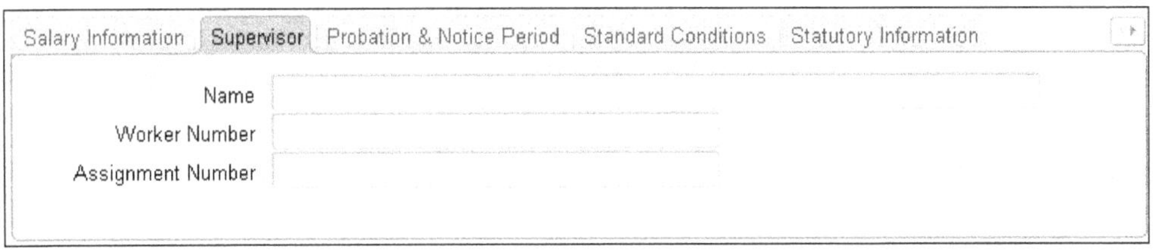

In the **Probation & Notice Period** tab, you can enter probation and notice period data about the employee.

In the **Standard Conditions** tab, values defaulted at the employee's organization or business group are populated. However, you can override them as per your requirements.

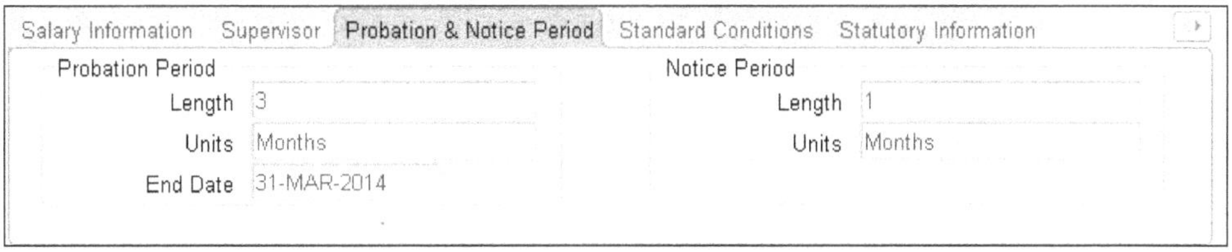

In **Salary Information**, you assign a **Salary Basis** for an employee.

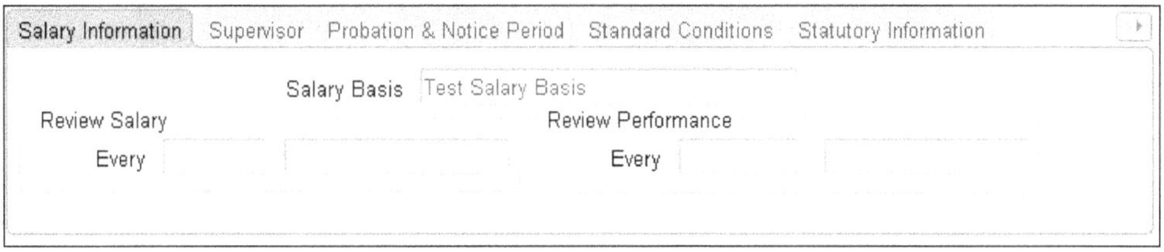

Assignment statuses

The use of assignment statuses is to define an employees current status in an organization. It discloses whether an employee is working in the organization or has been inactive. It will help track temporary or permanent departures of employees from your enterprise. An example of temporary departure is Paid or Unpaid absence.

An example of a long paid assignment status is maternity leave. An example of a permanent departure assignment status is resigned.

Assignment statuses are classified into two types:

- Primary
- Secondary

Primary assignment statuses

All primary statuses can be classified into four system statuses, as follows:

- Active assignment is used when an employee is currently working.
- Suspend assignment is used when an employee is on leave of absence, but remains an employee of your enterprise.

- Terminate assignment is used when an employee is no longer employed in the organization. It is still possible to make payments through Oracle Payroll for the assignments at the terminate assignment status.
- End means that all payrolls processing for the assignment are completed and the assignment is a historical record now. This status is not recorded in the assignment, as it causes the assignment to end.

You can have multiple user statuses for each system status. For example, an employee may have a suspended assignment, but you may not know the real reason for the suspension. In this case, you can create a user status type with names such as maternity leave, military leave, and so on and tag them to the system status suspend assignment.

Secondary assignment statuses

Secondary assignment statuses can be set up and used for analysis and reporting purposes. These statuses, however, have no effect on the assignment processing.

Defining assignment statuses

Both primary and secondary user statuses can be defined by you for your enterprise in the assignment statuses. Navigate to **US HRMS Manager** | **Work Structures** | **Status**.

User Status	External Status	System Status Human Resources	Payroll	Type	Active	Default
Active Assignment	Active Assignment	Active Assignment	Process	Primary	✔	✔
Maternity Leave		Active Assignment	Process	Primary	✔	
Promotion		Active Assignment	Process	Primary	✔	
Reorganization		Active Assignment	Process	Primary	✔	
Transfer		Active Assignment	Process	Primary	✔	
Reduced Hours		Active Assignment	Process	Primary	✔	
Involuntary Separation		Active Assignment	Process	Primary	✔	
Voluntary Separation		Active Assignment	Process	Primary	✔	

Follow these steps to create a primary assignment status:

1. Select **New Record** from the **Edit** menu.
2. Enter your **User Status**, and select **System Status**.

3. Select a Payroll System Status. It will have values **Process** and **Do not Process**. It controls whether Oracle payroll processes the assignment in a payroll run.
4. Save the new status.

In the following screenshot, we have created `Maternity Leave` as a new primary assignment status:

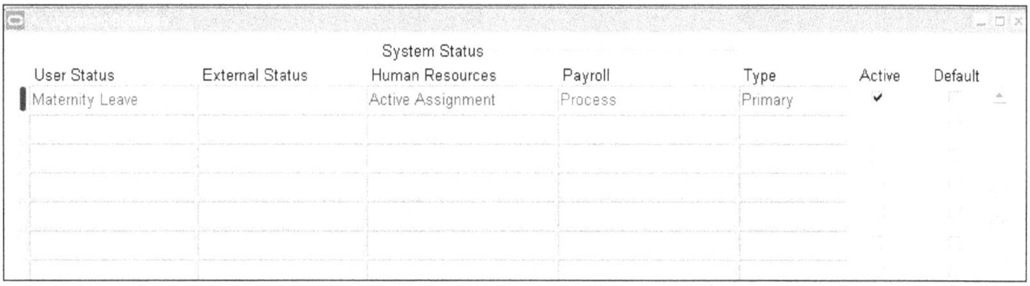

Follow these steps to create a secondary assignment status:

1. Select **New Record** from the **Edit** menu.
2. Type in a user status and do not select a system status.

The **Type** field displays **Secondary** automatically.

In the following screenshot, we have created `Maternity New birth` as the new secondary assignment status.

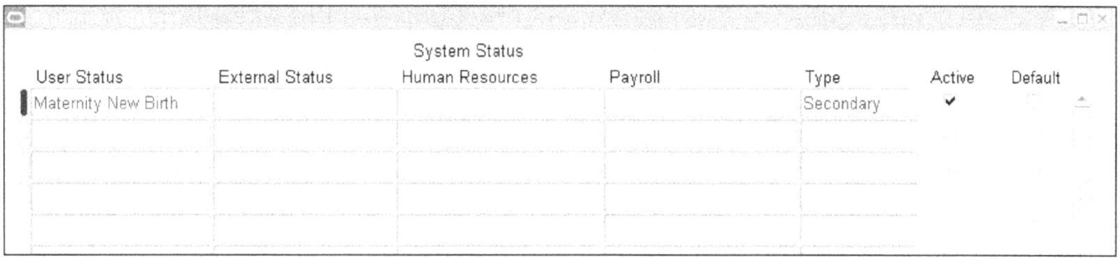

Changing assignment information

During the tenure of an employee in an organization, there can be many changes in assignment-related information. An employee might receive a promotion in which his/her grade might change. An employee may opt for transfer in which his/her work location might change. These changes happen from a particular date. This will again involve the concept of date tracking.

When you change the effective date on the form, you can see data as of that date. Whenever there is a change in assignment, it might also impact other areas. For example, a change in grade might result in a change in salary; a change in location might result in some additional location allowance. This implies that the assignment is the most basic entity in Oracle payroll. Without an assignment, you cannot run Oracle payroll in your application.

There might be a scenario in which an employee has more than one assignment. In that case, one assignment will always be the primary assignment. The other will be the secondary assignment. At any given point, the employee must have one primary assignment.

There might be a requirement in which the employee's secondary assignment has to be elevated to the primary assignment. In order to change the primary assignment to the secondary assignment or vice versa, you need to update the **Primary** flag in the **Miscellaneous** tab of the assignment form as shown in the following screenshot:

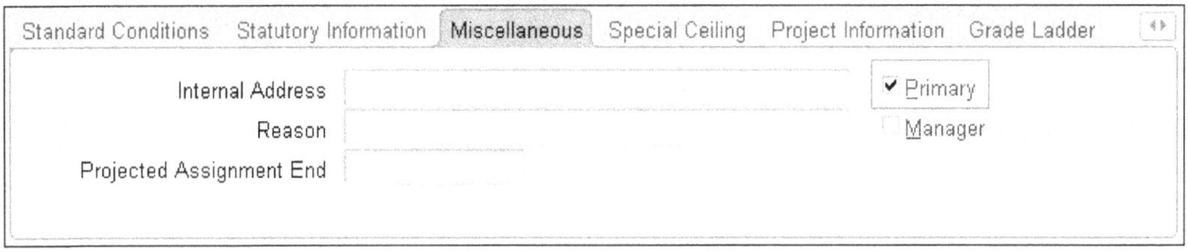

Salary-related information

Once you have created an employee's assignment, you are eligible to enter salary information for an employee. An assignment must have a valid payroll and salary basis assigned to it.

Navigate to **US HRMS Manager** | **People** | **Enter and Maintain** | **Assignment** | **Salary**.

This will open a self-service page rather than a professional form, as in the following screenshot:

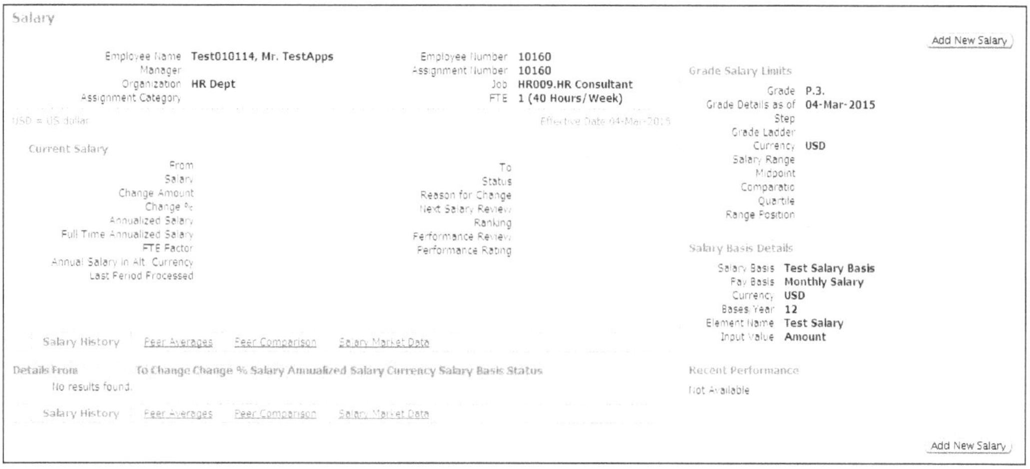

Use the **Add New Salary** option to add the salary. Enter the amount you want to pay.

The salary basis determines the duration for which their salaries are valid. It might be hourly or monthly. For new employees, when you enter the starting salary, it will be approved automatically.

For current employees, you enter the proposed salary changes, expressed either as a new amount, a changed amount, or a percentage. The proposals proposed also changes the proposals; although, they will not take effect until they receive an approval.

In the following screenshot, we have added the salary for an employee:

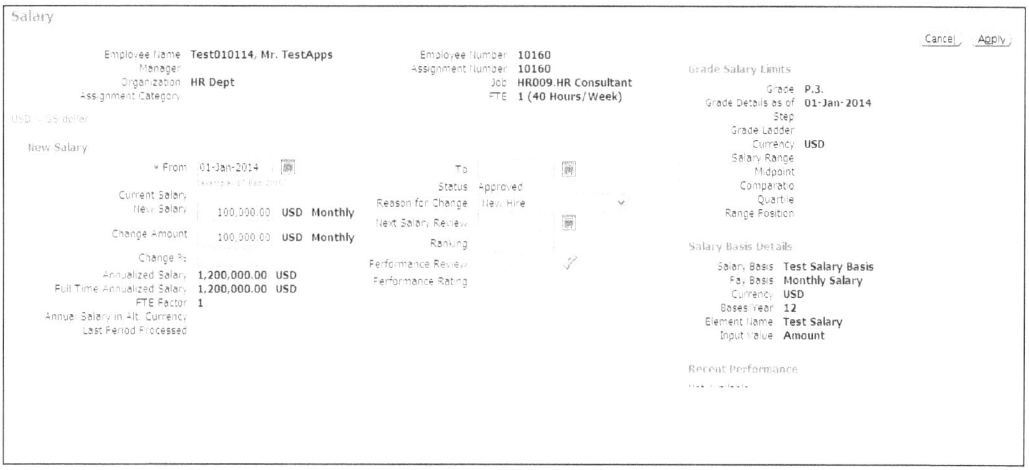

Click on the **Apply** button to apply the Salary for the employee.

Summary

In this chapter, you learned how to enter assignment information, in which you studied various components of assignment. You also learned about entering assignment-related information.

Then, you learned assignment statuses in Oracle HRMS and entering salary for employees.

In the next chapter, you will learn the concept of termination in Oracle HRMS.

8

Terminations

In the previous chapter, you learned about entering assignment information for an employee. Once an employee assignment is created, the employee becomes an integral part of the system. Once an employee becomes fully active in the system, the next step is the termination process.

In this chapter, we will cover termination in Oracle apps. When we say termination, it can fall into the following categories:

- Termination of employment
- Termination of assignment

Termination of employment

First, we will cover termination of employment. You terminate an employment when an employee leaves the company. It means all of his/her assignments will end on that date and the person type will change from employee to ex-employee. The record of ex-employee remains in the system so that you can later rehire or reinstate the person.

When you terminate an employee, it ends all the assignments too, by applying an end date value to each of their assignments which is equal to their last day with the company.

So if there is any future-dated assignment created for an employee, then the system will not allow the termination of that employee.

To terminate an employee navigate to **US HRMS Manager** | **People** | **Enter and Maintain** | **Others** | **End Employment**.

This will open a new form as shown in the following screenshot:

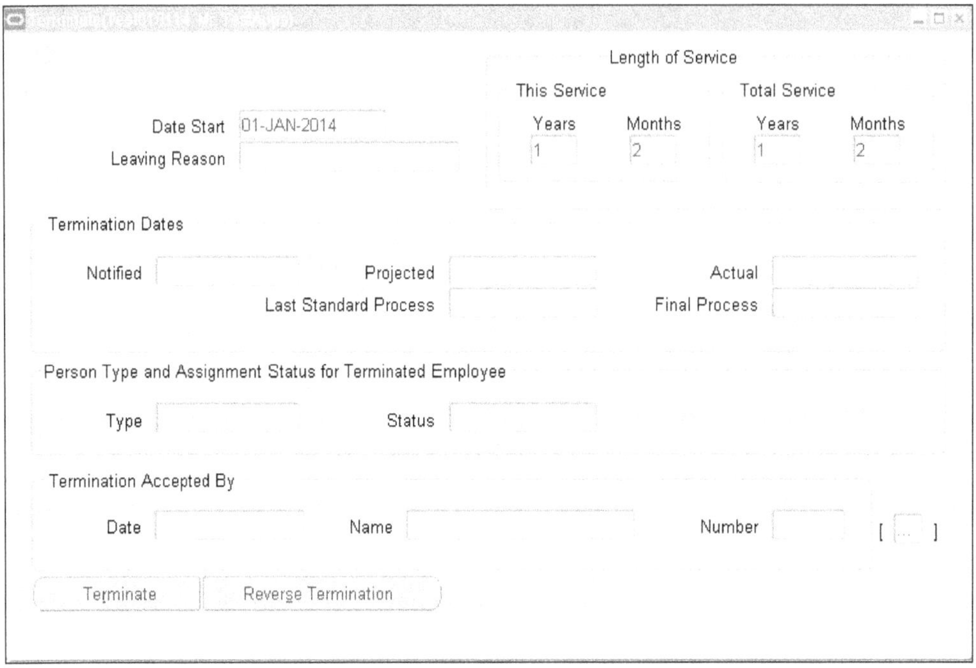

The **Date Start** field is the hire date of the employee in the company and the **Length of Service** section will show the total years of service as of the date set on the form.

The following are the steps to terminate an employee:

1. Enter the reason for the termination. This is an optional field. The list of values for leaving reasons comes from looking up **LEAV_REAS**. You can add additional values in this lookup as per your needs. To add lookup values, navigate to **US HRMS Manager** | **Other Definitions** | **Lookup Tables**.

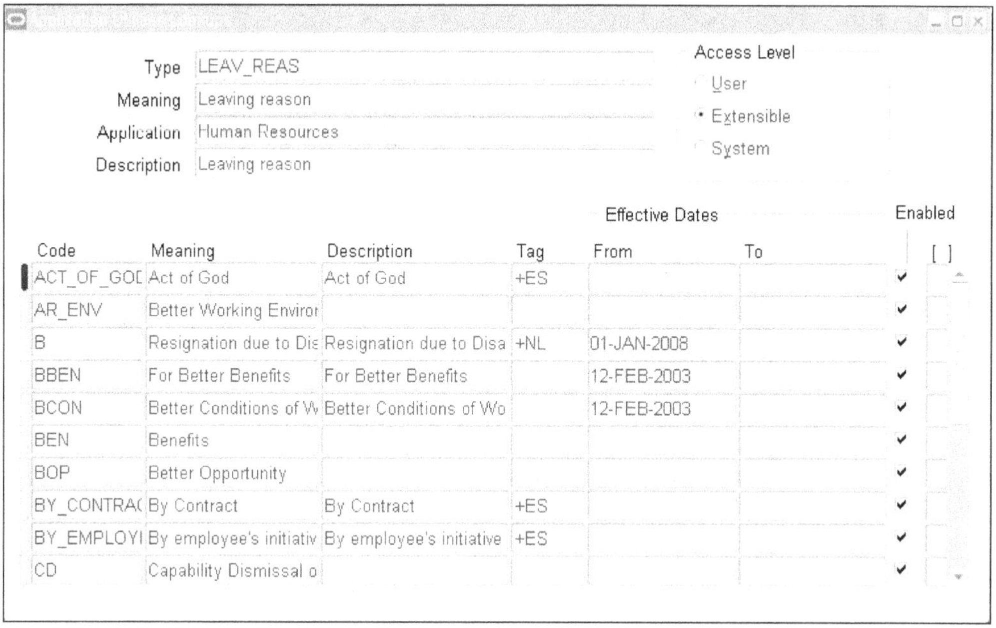

Each Lookup value will have **Code**, **Meaning**, **Description**, **Tag**, **From**, and **To** and **Enable** flag, **Code** and **Meaning** should be unique for each record and are mandatory fields. **Description** is not mandatory.

The **Tag** field will have legislation codes for a country. As we can see in the screenshot, lookup code **B** with the meaning **Resignation due to Disability** is valid only for the Netherlands, that is `+NL`. If this field is kept blank, then the lookup value is valid for all countries. If the value is set to minus such as `-US`, then that value is valid for all except United States.

2. Now enter the termination dates. There are five dates to be entered. The **Notified** and **Projected** dates are for information only. The actual termination date is the date when the employee's person type changes to **Ex-employee**.

   If you are using Oracle Payroll, then the **Final Process** date is a date after which no further payroll processing for the employee can occur.

For the **Final Process** date:

- There might be a need to process payroll for an employee even after the employee leaves the company. An example of this is full and final settlement payments. In this case, either we have to leave the **Final Process** date blank or put some future date.
- If you do not need to continue payroll processing, set the **Final Process** date to the **Actual** date.
- If you are an Oracle Payroll user, you must also enter a **Last Standard Process** date. This is the last date for normal processing, while the **Final Process** date is the last date for full and final settlement payments. Element entries are closed down on **Last Standard Process**, the **Actual** date, or the **Final Process** date, depending on how you have defined the elements.

3. When the information is complete, click on the **Terminate** button to complete the termination.

In the following screenshot, we have entered the termination details:

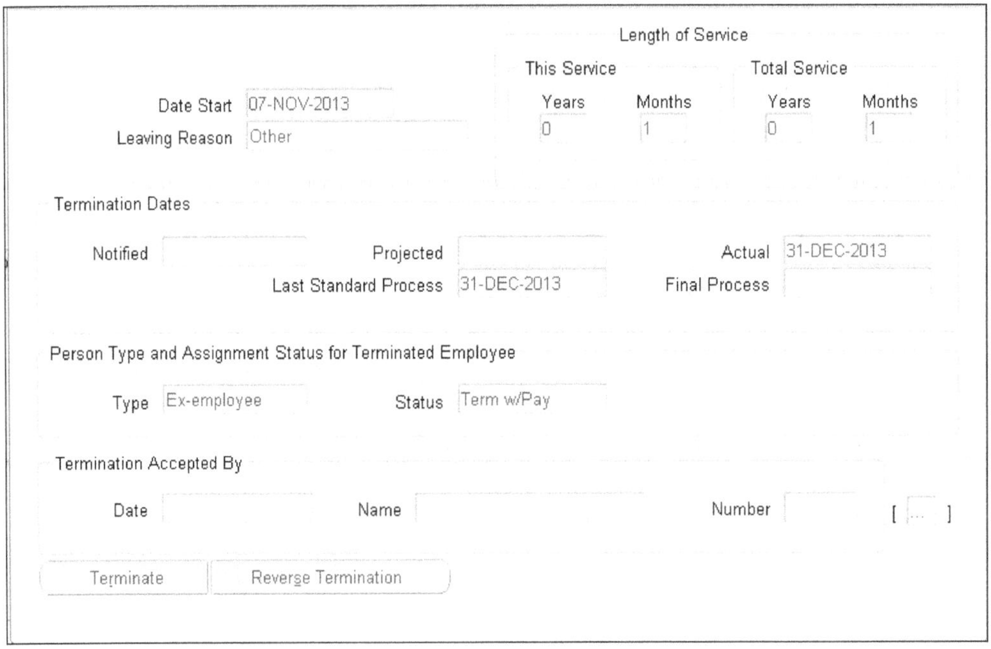

We have kept the actual termination date as **31-DEC-2013**. This will be the last active date for the employee in the company. Automatically, from 01-JAN-2014, the employee assignment status and person type will change to Terminate Assignment and Ex-Employee, respectively.

The following screenshot is of the people form in which you can see the person type as **Ex-employee** from 01-JAN-2014.

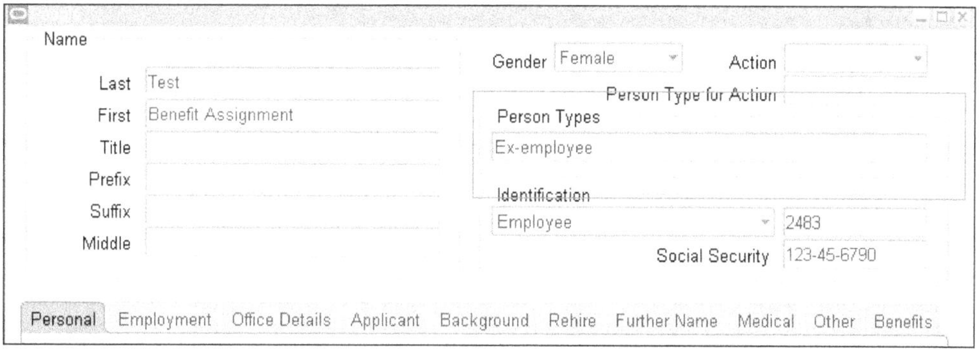

Similarly, you can see the assignment status changed to terminate W/Pay, as you have selected in the termination form.

Cancelling termination

You can cancel a termination if the employee decides to stay in the company or the date of leaving changes.

Oracle HRMS reopens the assignments previously closed and brings an assignment to a state as it was exactly before the employee termination happened. It will also restore other information to its state before termination. For example, it will take out the end date put on recurring element entries for the assignment.

There might be some nonrecurring (one time) entries, which might get deleted during termination. These nonrecurring entries must be entered manually again, if you reverse terminate an employee.

To cancel a termination, click on the **Reverse Termination** button in the **Terminate** form.

To change the termination date, click on the **Reverse Termination** button, which will cancel the termination. Then, enter a new **Actual** date and click on the **Terminate** button.

Terminating an assignment

As previously mentioned, a person will not exist in Oracle HRMS as an employee until an Active assignment has been created for that person. This means that an employee must always have at least one active assignment at any point in time. So if an employee has only one active assignment, the only way to end the assignment is to terminate the employee, using the **Terminate** window, which we have seen already.

If an employee has more than one active assignment, then you can end all except one assignment. This can be done by selecting the assignment status as **End** or **Terminate** in an assignment form.

Follow these steps to end an assignment:

1. Set your **Effective Date** on the form to a date that you want to terminate the assignment on.
2. Update the assignment status to **End** or **Terminate Process Assignment** (or the equivalent user status on your system):
    - Use **Terminate Process Assignment** (with a payroll system status of **Process**) if further payroll processing of the assignment is required after the date the assignment ends.
    - Use **End** (with a payroll system status of **Do Not Process**) if all pay processing for the assignment is finished.

In the following screenshot, you can see that an employee has an additional assignment existing to active assignment. The assignment number of the secondary assignment is **10160-2**.

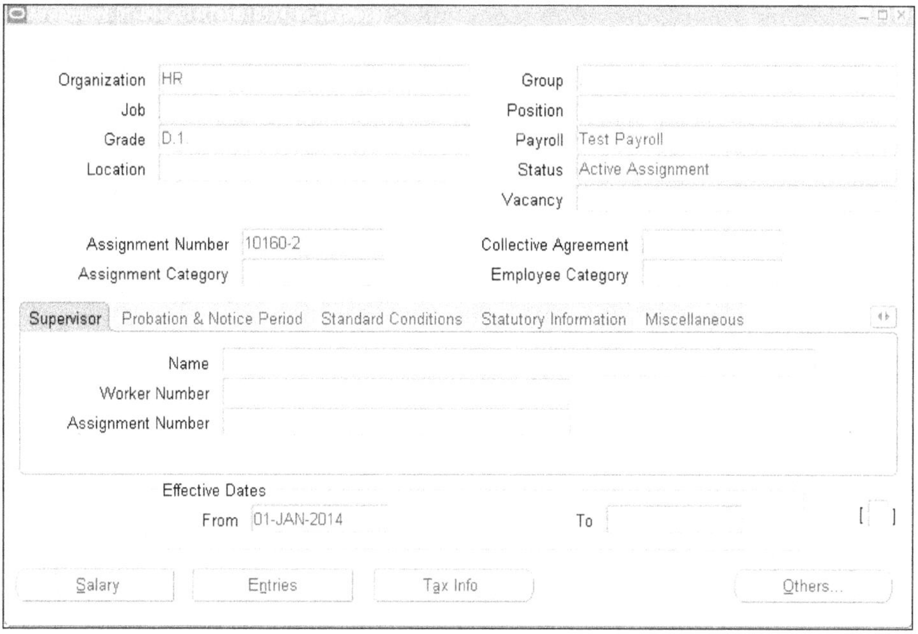

We will change the status to **End** as of 01-AUG-2014, as shown in the following screenshot, and save the details.

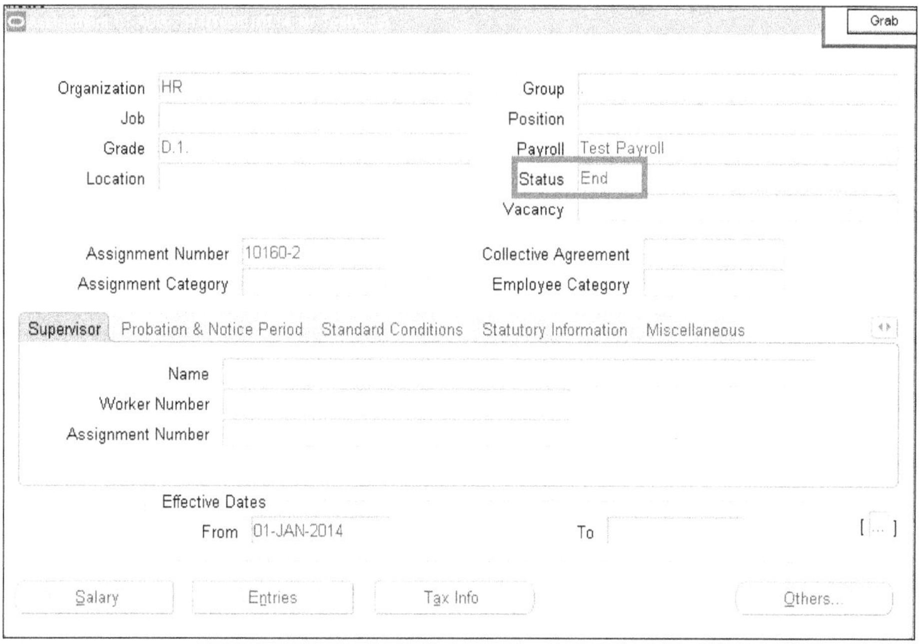

Once you save the record, the assignment will be ended on **01-AUG-2014** as in the following screenshot. The assignment will no longer be visible after **01-AUG-2014**.

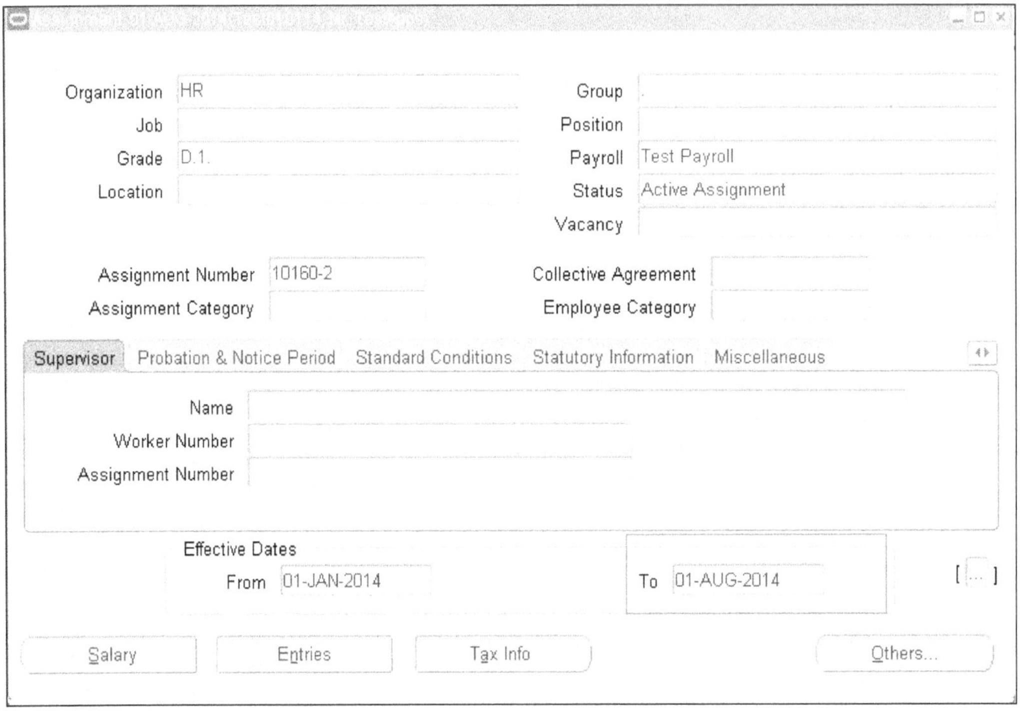

So we have seen how to terminate an assignment.

Summary

In this chapter, you learned about terminating an employee. You also learned how to reverse terminate an employee. We also saw how to terminate an assignment rather than an employee.

In the next chapter, you will learn about absence management and the concept of **Paid Time Off** (PTO) accrual plans.

9
Absence Management

In the previous chapter, you learned about the termination of an employee and assignment in Oracle HRMS. Thus, we have covered the people management concept in Oracle Apps HRMS.

In this chapter, you will learn about absence management, which is an important module of Oracle HRMS.

In this we will see in detail the concept of absence management and accruals in the absence module.

Getting started

Let's understand some basics before diving deep into absence management.

Absence

An employee can take a leave of absence from work for various reasons such as illness, vacation, injury, medical appointments, professional duties, and so on. In each case, absence can either be paid or unpaid. An employee on vacation will mostly be on paid absence, whereas, if an employee is on a long term study leave, then the employee will mostly be on unpaid leave. This means the employee will not be paid for the duration he/she is on leave.

Maintaining information on employee absences for reporting and analysis is an important aspect of Oracle HRMS. Here, accruals come into the picture (about which you will learn in the next section).

Accrual plans

Let's say you are working for an organization that allows you 12 days of sick leave per year. Therefore, the organization has laid out a rule for your sick leave.

When I say 12 days per year, then various question arise, such as which year needs to be considered? Shall we consider the financial year, that is, 1st Jan to 31st Dec? Or should we consider the year starting from the employees joining date?

Another question that will arise is how to allocate these 12 days per year? Do you want to allocate all the leave at one time or do you want to allocate one day per month?

There might be some other questions regarding carried-over leaves. What if the employee did not utilize all 12 leave days, then what is done about these left-over days?

When you get answers to these questions, then you can build a plan in Oracle HRMS. This plan is called Accrual Plans in Absence Management in Oracle HRMS. Thus, leaves that do not have such rules and regulations then we do not need to create an accrual plan in absence management (for example, military leave) where an employee can apply leave any time the employee wishes to.

Before moving on to the setup part of absence, we first need to understand certain concepts such as absence type, absence category, and absence reason.

Absence type is the type of absences in your organization, for example, illness, injury, medical appointment, vacation leave, maternity leave, and paternity leave. These are types of leave in an organization.

An absence category is a group of related absence types, for example, you can categorize illness, injury, and medical appointment as the medical leave category.

You can add reasons for each absence type. For example, Leg Injury is a reason for an injury absence type. You can have multiple reasons for each absence type. However, this is not mandatory.

The following table will help you understand this concept in a better way:

Absence Category	Absence Type	Absence Reason
Medical leave	Illness	Fever
	Injury	Leg injury, ankle pain, and so on
	Medical appointment	
Personal leave	Vacation	
	Personal business	
Family leave	Dependent care	Child care
		Elder care
		Disabled care

Setting up absence management

Let's now see how to set up absence management in Oracle HRMS.

The following are the steps to set up absence in HRMS:

1. Create the Absence element.
2. Create the Element Link.
3. Create the Absence type (steps 1 and 2 are mandatory for step 3).

These are the three basic steps required to create an absence setup. An additional setup, as follows, will be required if you are creating an accrual plan:

1. Create an accrual plan.
2. Attach an accrual formula to the accrual plan.
3. Attach a plan to the employees to make them eligible for the plan.

In our case, we will create an absence type of Illness for regular absence. For absence based on accruals, we will create an accrual plan with certain rules, taking an example of vacation leave types.

Absence setup

So let's start by setting up regular absences. First, we are going to create an element named Illness. To create an element, navigate to **US HRMS Manager** | **Total Compensation** | **Basic** | **Element Description**.

The following form is used to create any element in the application:

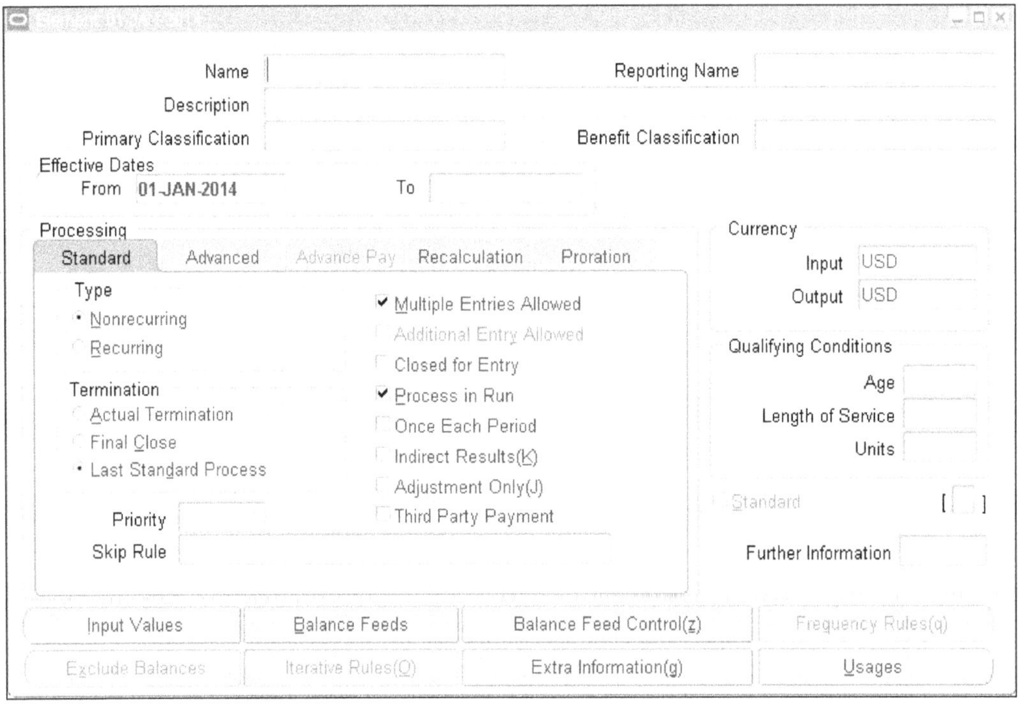

Element **Name**, **Classification**, and **Priority** are mandatory fields in the form. We have entered the details in the form. The classification will be information. This element will only store the duration of the absence. The duration can be in days or hours, depending on your requirement. In our case, we will keep all the absences in days rather than hours.

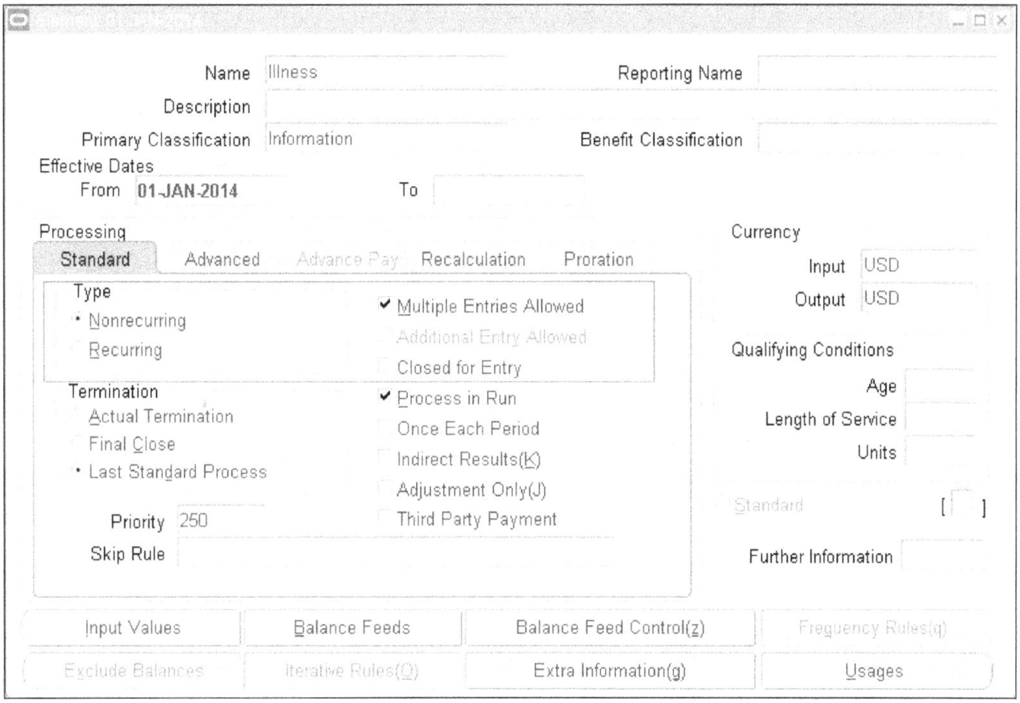

In the preceding screenshot, we have kept the processing type as **Nonrecurring**. It implies that this absence will only be applicable for the payroll period in which it is applied.

In the second flag, multiple entries are allowed. It means you can have multiple absence entries in the same payroll period. You can, for example, apply for illness from 3rd January to 8th January, and again from 21st January to 25th January in the same month. If this flag was not set, then you would not have been able to apply for leave for more than once in your payroll period, considering your payroll period to be a month. So ideally, all the absence elements must have these two values set to **Nonrecurring** and **Multiple Entries Allowed**.

The **Qualifying Condition** region's fields will be used if we want to restrict employees from applying for absence based on their age or the number of years completed in an organization.

After saving the record, we need to create an input value for the element. Click on the **Input Values** button to create an input value for an element. As mentioned earlier, we need to capture the duration of absence, and input value is the placeholder for this. It will hold the amount of time taken for an absence. Select **Day** as the value of **Units**, as we will store absence in days.

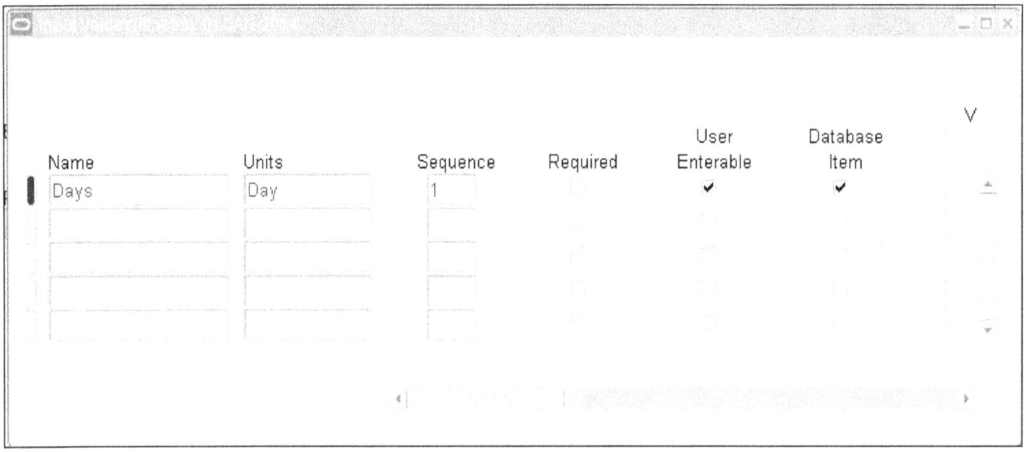

You can set minimum and maximum days that can be entered in an absence by an employee. If you set this, then we also need to select what will happen if these limits are crossed:

- Select **Warning** if you just want to warn users but allow them to breach the limits
- Selecting **Error** will issue an error message and thus it will not allow employees to save an entry that breaches the limits

This can be set at an input value level only by scrolling to the right of the form as shown in the following screenshot.

In our case, we have set the minimum as `0` and maximum as `10`. If the employee tries to apply for leave for a duration of more than 10 or less than 0, then the system will display an appropriate error and not a warning.

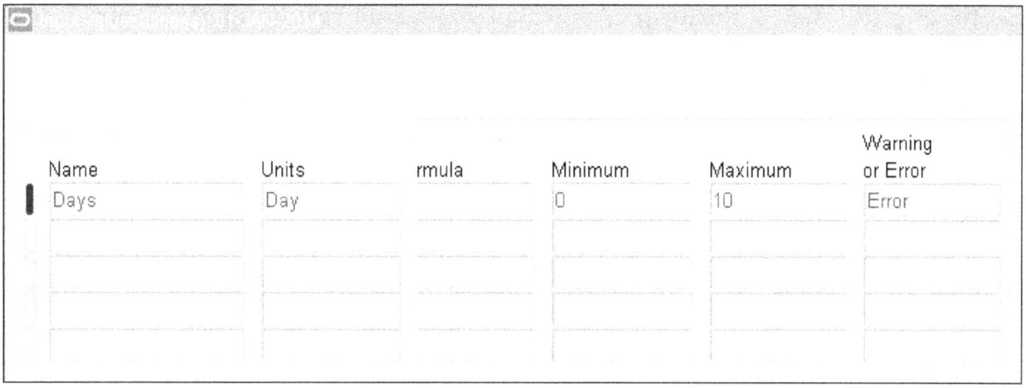

The next step is to create a link for the absence element `Illness`. The link will define eligibility for an absence by certain criteria.

To create a link ID, navigate to **US HRMS Manager** | **Total Compensation** | **Basic** | **Link**.

The following form is used to create a link for an element:

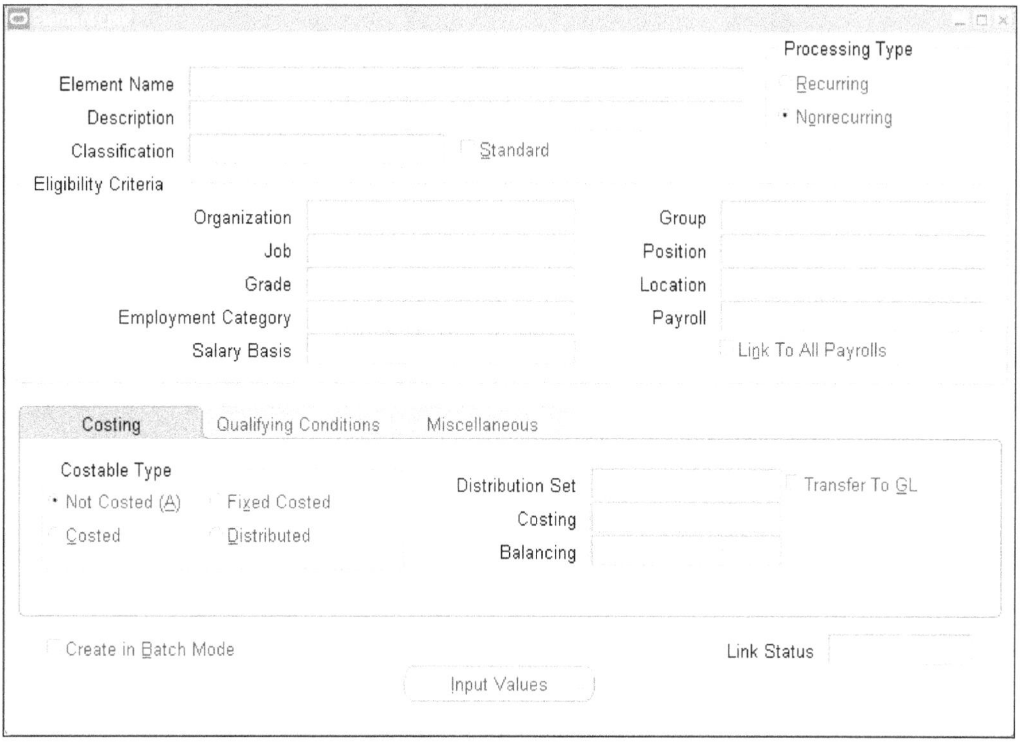

Set the effective date of the form from which you want to create a link. In our case, we will create the link from the same date we created an absence. The date is **01-JAN-2014**.

Select the element name for which you want to create the link. **Eligibility Criteria** must be set for the absence element. Do not select any criteria if you want that element to be available for all the employees.

If you want that this absence will be applicable for only those employees that are on payroll, then select the **Link To All Payrolls** checkbox. Save the link.

We have defined the link for the element as follows:

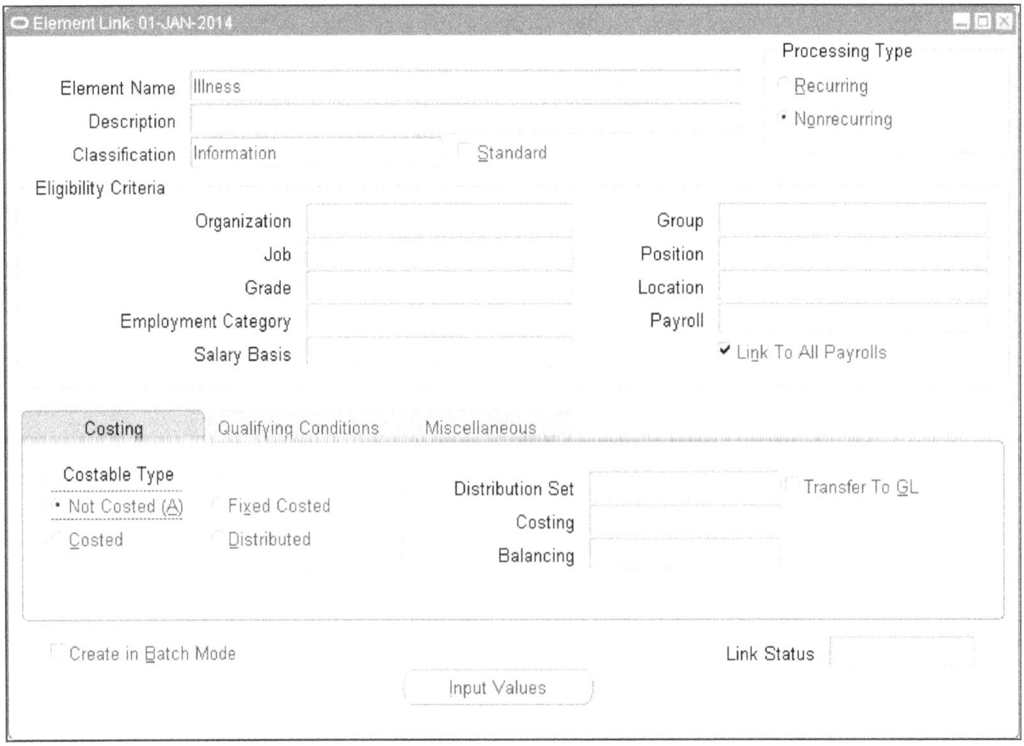

Once we have defined the link, the next step is to create the absence element. To create the absence element, navigate to **US HRMS Manager** | **Total Compensation** | **Basic** | **Absence Types**.

The following form is used to create an absence type:

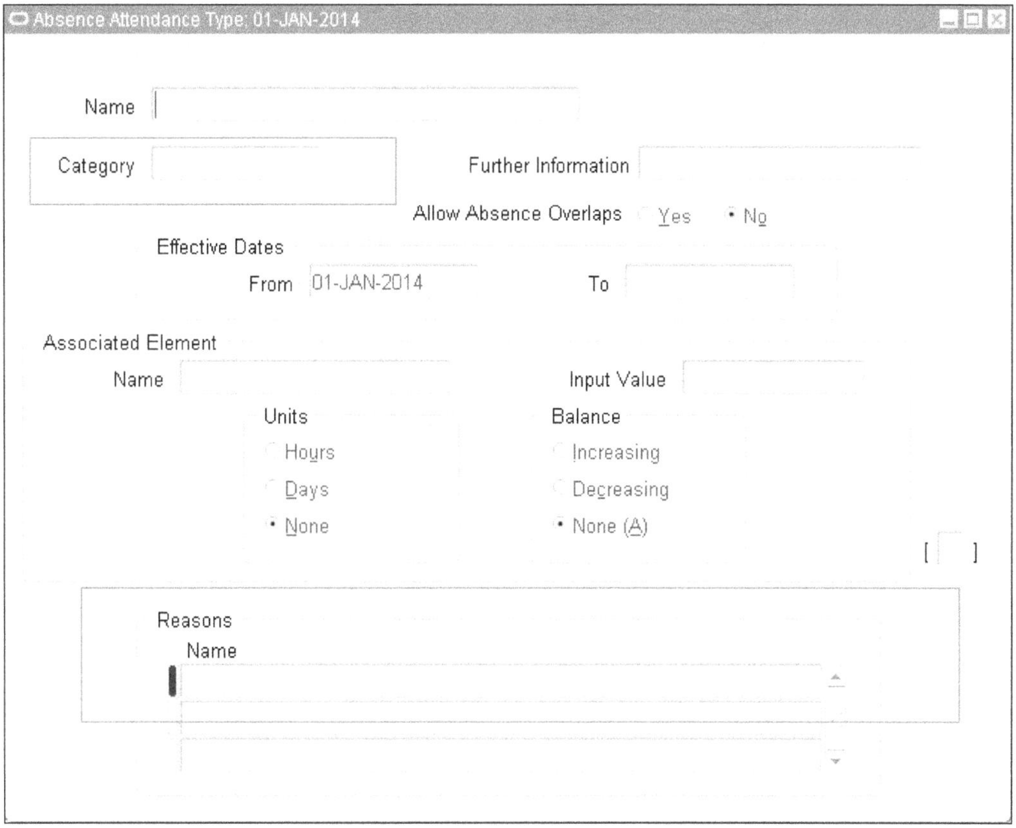

In the following form, you can see what we discussed earlier, that is, absence category and absence reason. In our case, absence type is 'Illness' and we will keep the category as Sickness and reason as Back Problems, Cold, and Other.

You can add an absence category and absence reason in Lookup `ABSENCE_CATEGORY` and `ABSENCE_REASON` respectively.

Let's now create an absence type. Please follow these steps:

1. Enter the name of the absence type. It is best practice to keep the element name the same as the absence type or vice versa. In our case, the absence name and element name is the same, which is `Illness`.
2. Enter the absence category. In our case, it is `Sickness` leave.
3. Select the **Allow Absence Overlaps** value, which is **Yes** or **No** if absences of this type can overlap other absences, which you might define. If you choose the value as **No** then the system will issue a warning if you enter an absence that overlaps another defined absence of any type.
4. Select the element name that we created in the **Associated Element** region.
5. The **Input Value** field will have the input value name of the element that we defined as `Illness`, and the unit of measure for the input value appears in the **Units** region, which is **Days** in our case.
6. In the **Balance** region, select **Increasing** if you want the balance of leave to increase each time leave is taken. It is basically a balance that will store the leave taken. In the case of increasing balance, this balance will keep on accumulating for an employee as employees apply for leave. Initially, this balance will have zero value. If for the first time, the employee applies for illness leave for 4 days, then this balance will have the value 4. Again, if the employee applies for the same leave for some other dates with a duration of 2, then the total balance will come to 6.
7. Select **Decreasing**, for absence types that have a set maximum amount of days allowed. In this case, you first initialize a balance for this leave. Initialization of balance is an entirely different concept. This will not be in the purview of this chapter. You can initialize a balance at, say, 20. Then, this balance will keep on decreasing for the employee each time the employee applies for leave. Decreasing balances require more maintenance.
8. Select the appropriate reasons.
9. Save the record.

Thus, we have created the absence type `Illness` as shown in the following screenshot:

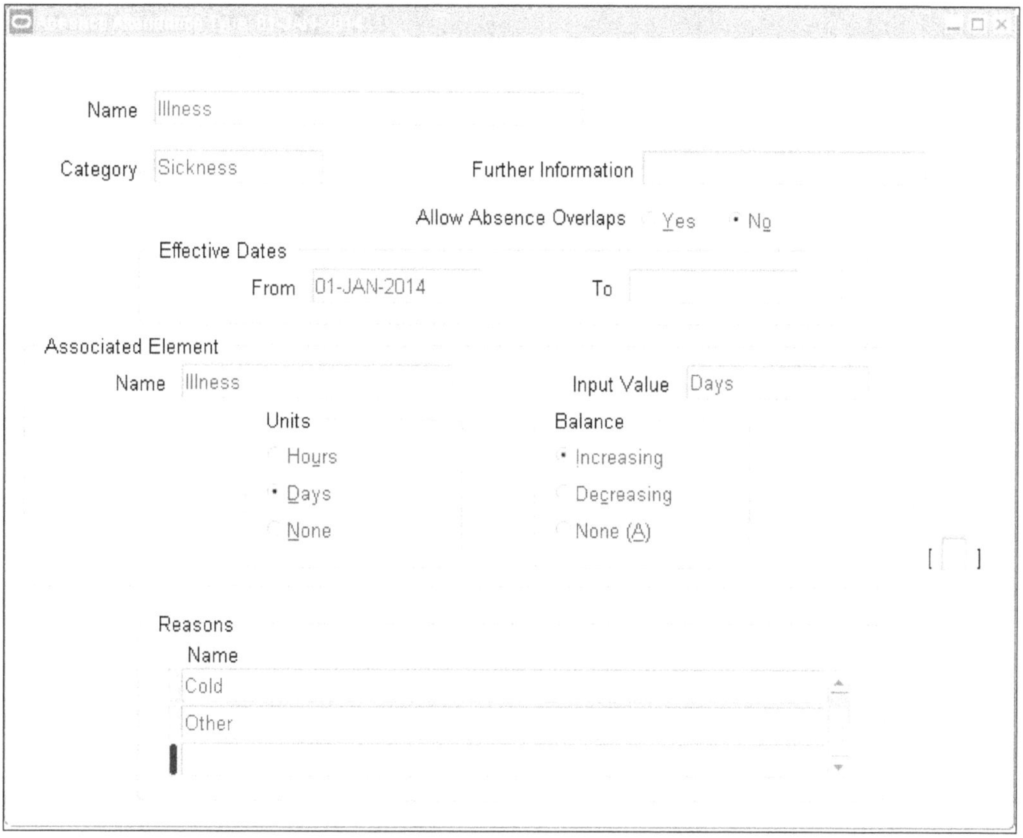

The setup part is now completed for the basic absence management. Thus, the task of configuration is completed.

The next part is actually applying for an absence. This now involves the employee because it is the employee, or someone on his/her behalf, who will apply for an absence. When I say someone on the employee's behalf, it can be the HR manager or the employee's immediate supervisor, who can have access to apply for leave on the employee's behalf if the employee himself/herself cannot apply for leave in the system.

The employee usually applies for leave using self-service. In Oracle HRMS, we refer to it as employee self-service. The HR manager usually applies for leave on behalf of an employee using the Profession forms, which are also referred to as Oracle forms.

We will first see how an HR manager can apply for leave for the employee. There are a couple of navigations used. You can follow either of them, **US HRMS Manager | People | Enter and Maintain | Other | Absence** or **US HRMS Manager | FastPath | Absence**.

We will consider employee number 10160 in our example.

The following is the absence form that is used to apply for leave of an employee:

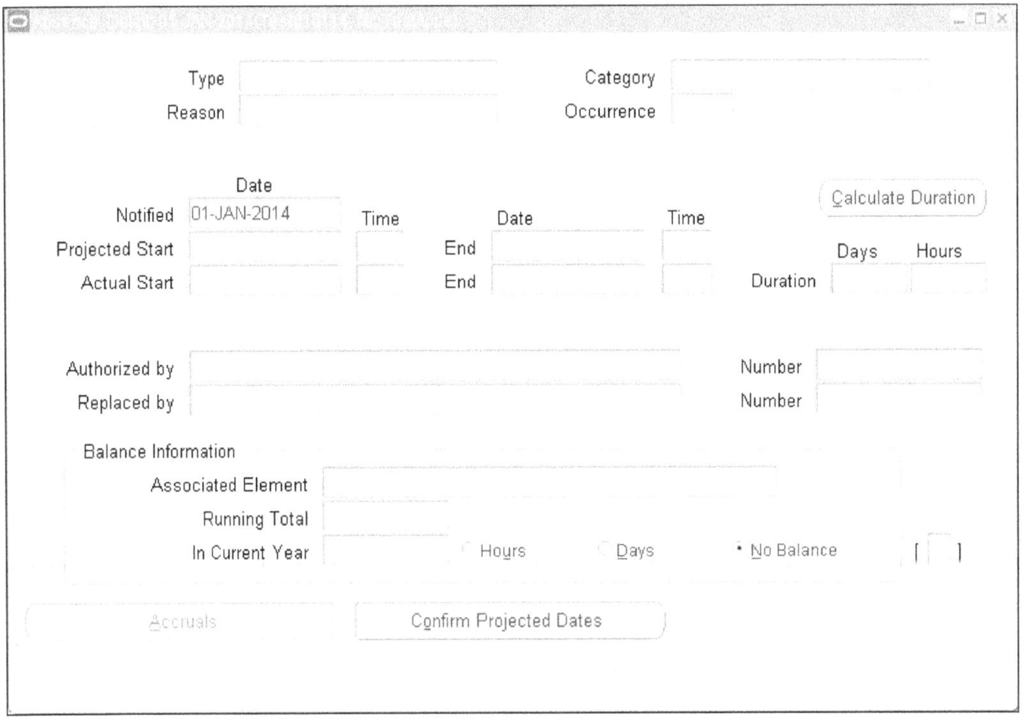

To enter absences for an employee, follow these steps:

1. Enter the absence type. In our case, it is `Illness`. The following information will appear automatically:
    - The category of the type. In our case, it is `Sickness`.
    - The occurrence of the new absence record you are entering. For example, if the employee has already taken five absences of this type before, the occurrence of the new absence that you are entering will have the value 6.

- The running total will show leaves taken or remaining. For absence types that are defined as increasing balances, this is the number of days absent or when leave was taken (in the past or future). For types defined as decreasing balances, this is or the number of hours or days remaining to be taken.
- The number of days the employee has taken this leave in current calendar year will be shown in the **In Current Year** field.
- Associated element in the **Balance Information** region will populate the element defined for the absence.

2. Do one of the following:
    - Enter projected dates for the absence you want to take. You can later copy them to the **Actual Date** fields by choosing the **Confirm Projected Dates** button.
    - Enter actual dates and duration as days or hours. For duration in hours, you must enter start and end times along with start and end dates.
    - It is not mandatory to enter the duration manually each time you apply for leave. Once you enter the start and the end date, the application automatically calculates the duration based on the dates entered.
    - The application used logic written in fast formula `BG_ABSENCE_DURATION` to calculate duration for each absence. We will see further details about this formula later in the chapter.
3. You can also select:
    - Reasons for the absence
    - The employee who is authorizing the absence
    - Replacement for the absent employee for the duration of the absence

4. Save your work. Thus, we have applied an absence of our employee and can see it in the following screenshot.

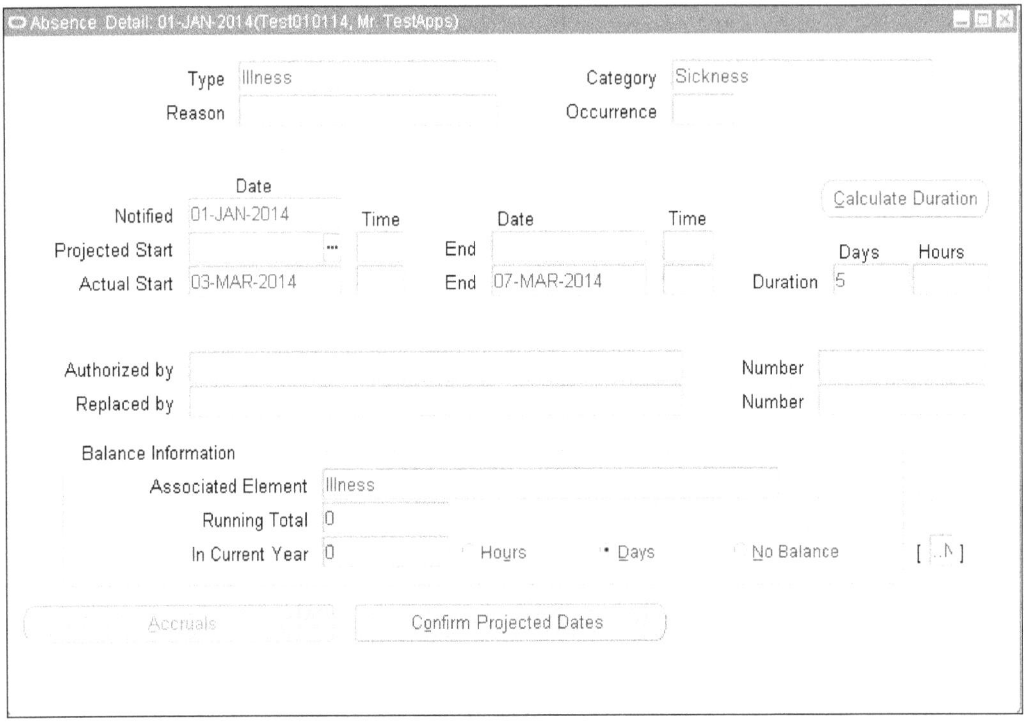

In our case, we have entered the actual start and end date as 03-MAR-2014 and 07-MAR-2014 respectively. It comes to 5 working days, that is, 03-MAR-2014, Monday, 04-MAR-2014, Tuesday, 05-MAR-2014, Wednesday, 06-MAR-2014, Thursday, and 07-MAR-2014, Friday.

Hence, the absence duration calculated by the system is 5 days.

Thus, we have seen how the HR manager can apply for absence on behalf of employees.

The employee uses the employee self-service responsibility to apply for his/her absence. We will now see how the employee can apply for his/her absence in the application. For this, we will need the username of the employee to access the application, and we also need to assign him/her the employee self-service responsibility to his/her login. We will use the same employee number 10160 for this example. I have already created the username `TEST-10160` and have assigned the required responsibility.

Once you login using the username you will be able to view the home page with the **Employee Self-Service** responsibility as shown in the screenshot:

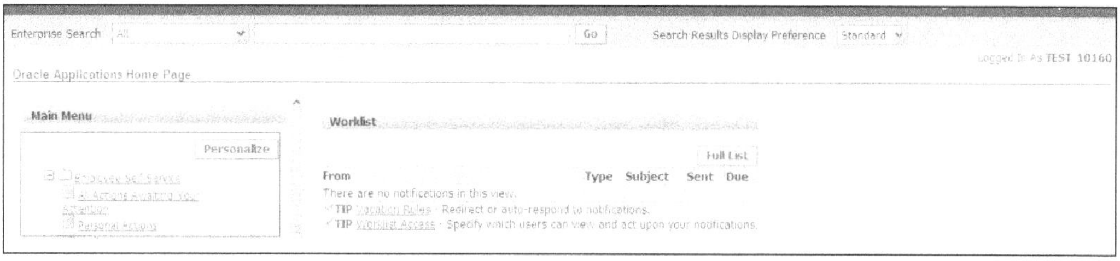

To apply for leave, navigate to **Employee Self-Service | Personal Actions | Absence Management**. You can see it in the following screenshot. Select the **Absence Management** option and **Section Action** as **Start**:

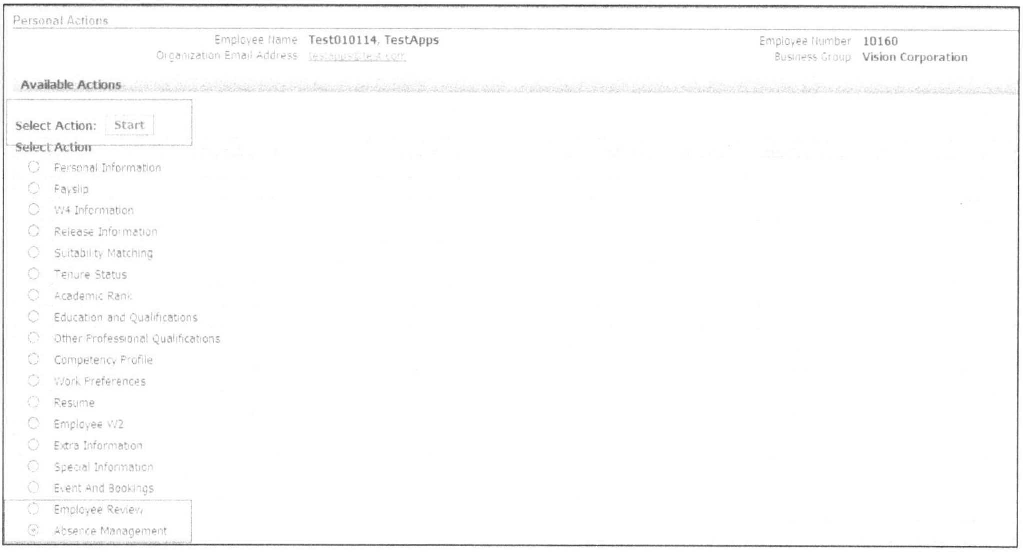

Once you click on **Start** you will see a new page that will have the details of all days of absence of the employee. Here, in the following screenshot, we can see an absence dated **03-Mar-2014** to **07-Mar-2014** already applied for and approved by the HR manager:

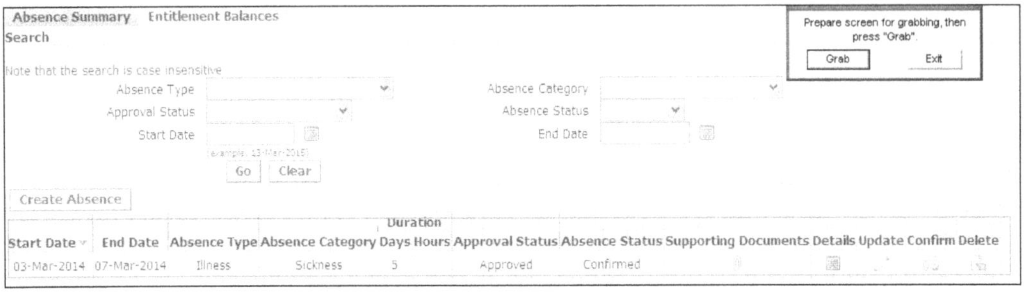

Click on the **Create Absence** button to enter a new absence. The following is the page used to create the absence for an employee:

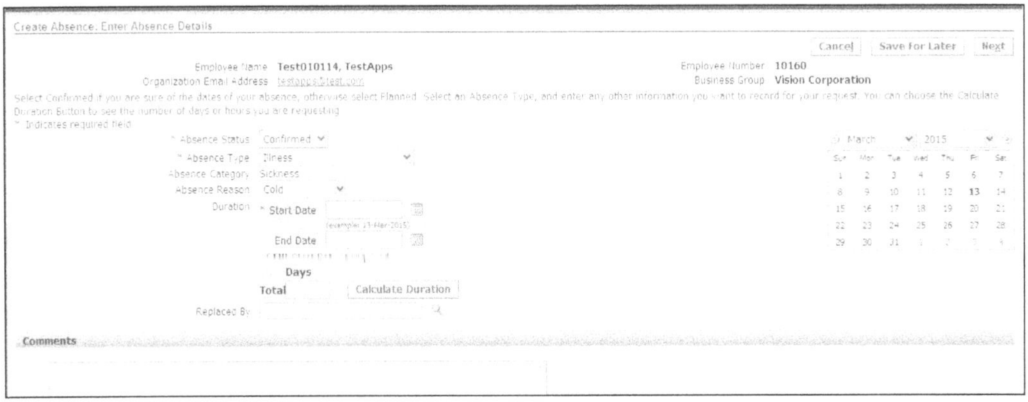

Enter the following details in the preceding form:

1. Enter **Absence Status**. It can be either **Planned** or **Confirmed** leave.
2. Enter the absence type. In our case, it will be **Illness**.
3. Absence category will be populated automatically.
4. Enter the appropriate absence reason. You can keep it blank if not required.
5. Enter the start and end date of the absence. We have entered it as **15-Apr-2014** and **16-Apr-2014** respectively.
6. Click on **Calculate Duration**. The system will automatically calculate the duration as 2 days.

7. Enter the person who will be replaced during the leave period. This is just for information.
8. You can either enter the comments or leave it blank.

   These values entered can be seen in the following screenshot:

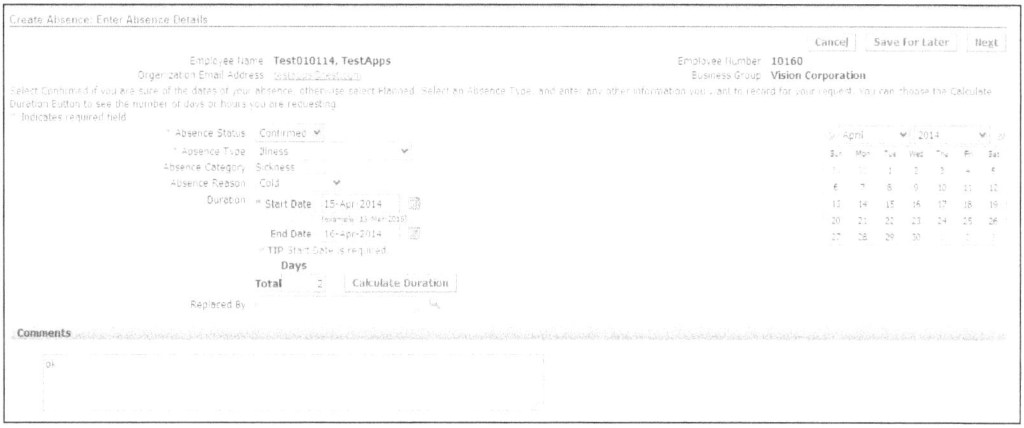

9. Click on the **Next** button. It will take you to the review page and display. You can see the details that you have entered on the previous page. Once you verify these details, then you can click on the **Submit** button to submit the leave application as in the following screenshot:

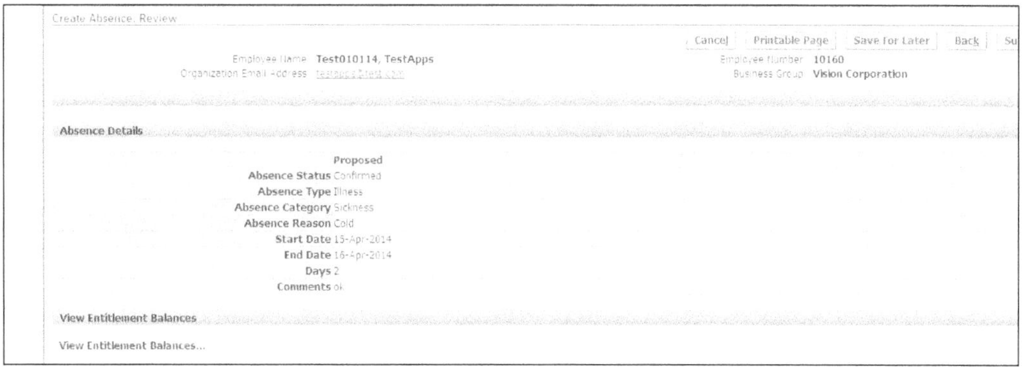

10. Once you have submitted, the leave will be created in the application and it will be displayed on the home page of the employee:

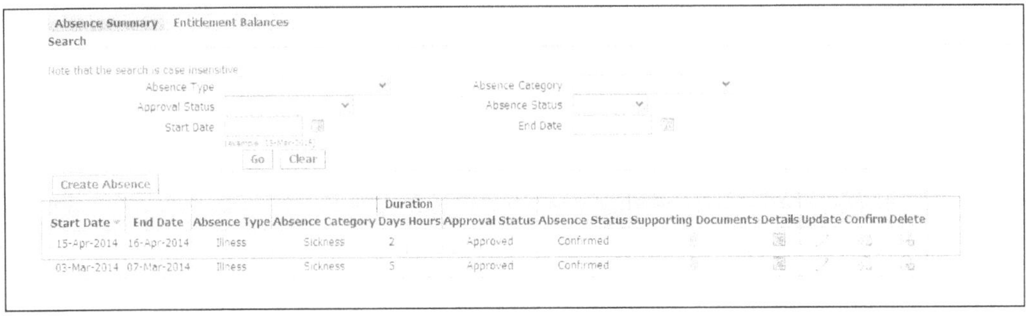

Note that we have not set created any approval mechanism for this leave application process. You can set various approvals for the leave application process. You can place an approver for each type of absence based on various conditions. For example, you can create an approval rule for absence type `Illness`. The rule will state that if an employee applies for absence of type illness, then it will go for immediate supervisor approval as well as HR approval. Once both of these approve this request, then a **For Your Information** (**FYI**) notification must be sent to the payroll department. This setup can be done in Oracle Apps using the concept of **Approval Management Engine** (**AME**). However, this concept is not taken up in this book.

As absence is applied for by the employee, the same absence can be viewed by HR in the professional form window by navigating to **US HRMS Manager** | **FastPath** | **Absence**.

The following screenshot shows the applied for absence:

In the preceding screenshot, you can see the value of the **Occurrence** field. It has the value **2** because we have already applied the same leave type before. The previous leave records can be viewed by clicking on the down arrow of the keyboard as shown in the following screenshot:

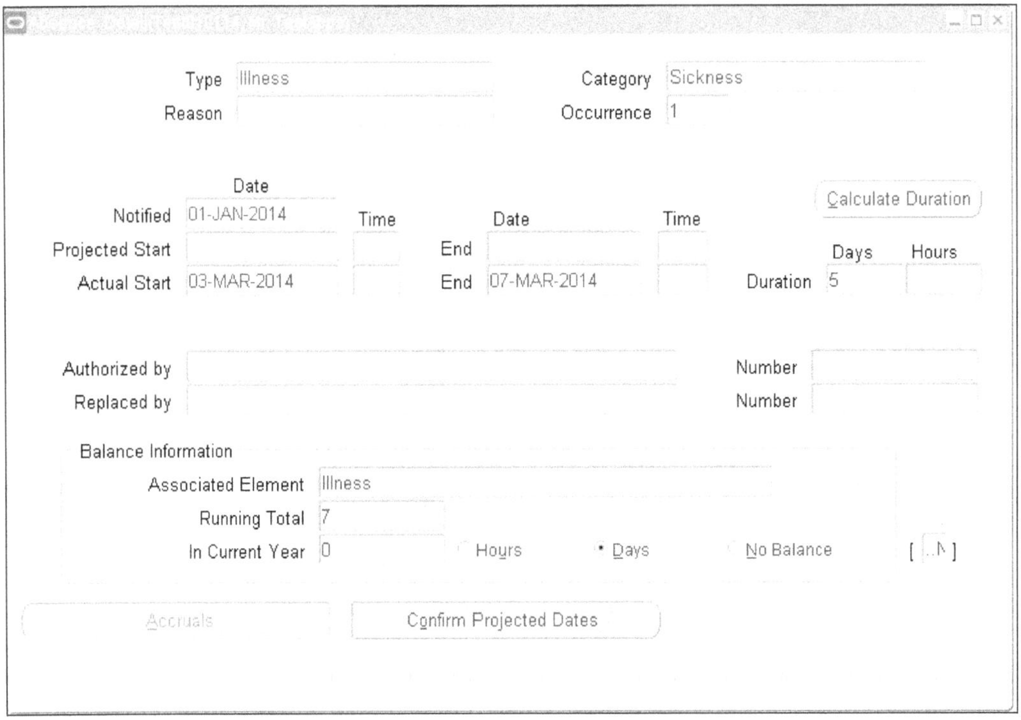

Thus, you have learned how absence is recorded in the system by the employee as well as the HR manager.

Let's now look at the reporting and enquiries part. Since absence data is at the employee level, application users such as HR managers and various stakeholders in the company might need to report to analyze certain data.

Oracle has provided some basic reports to cater to these needs. One of the queries is the View history of employee absence. In this, you can view each absence of only one employee.

Navigate to **US HRMS Manager** | **View** | **Histories** | **Absence**. It will open a form that will have the parameter to enter the employee name or employee number. Enter either of these and click on **Find**. You will get details of the employee's absences. Let's check for our employee with the employee number 10160. In the following screenshot, we can see the details of our employee's leave.

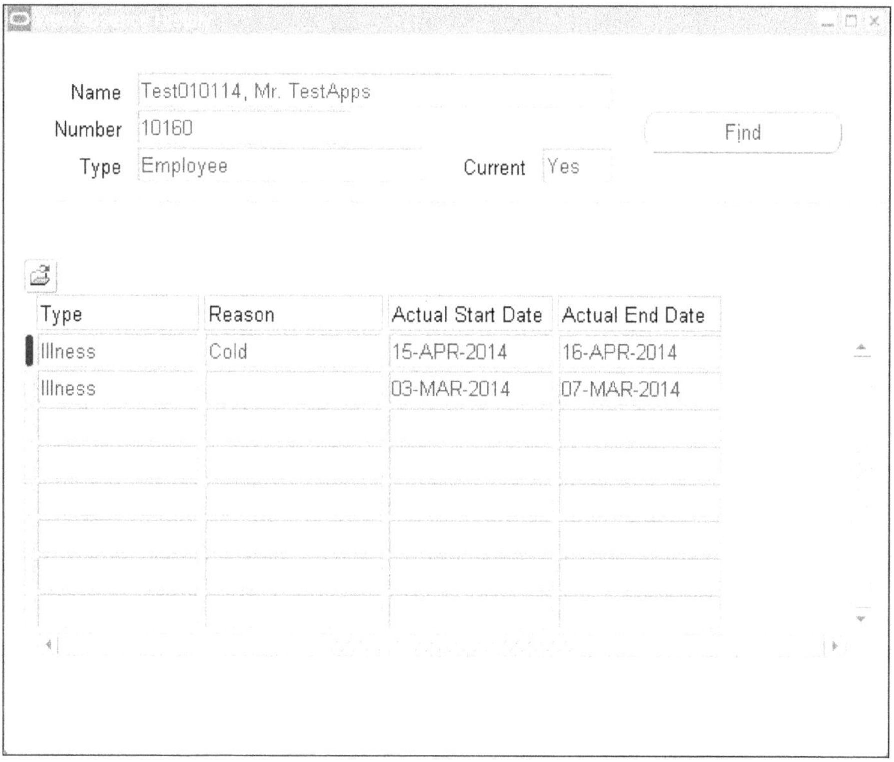

Similarly, you can find an employee based on the absence type. For example, if you want to find all employees who have taken illness leave, you can navigate to **US HRMS Manager | View | Lists | Employees by Absence Types**. This will open the following form with the basic parameters:

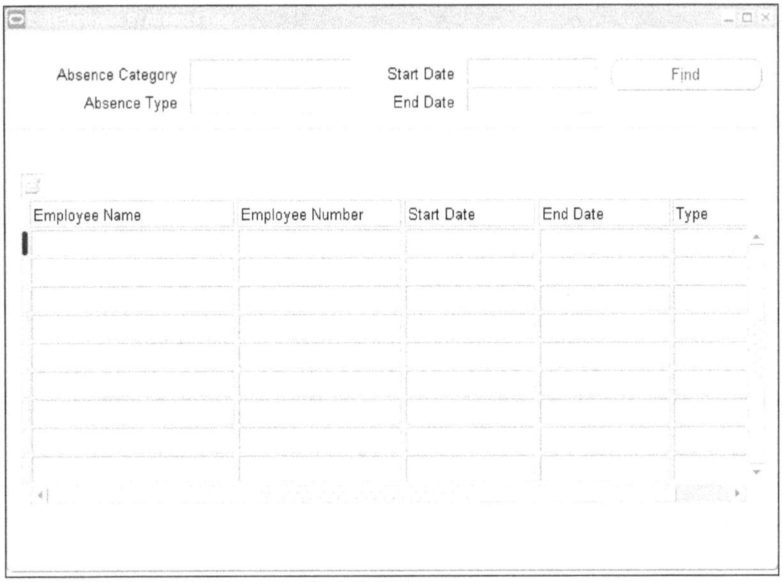

Enter absence type as Illness and click on the **Find** button. It will give you list of all the employees who have taken the illness leave type:

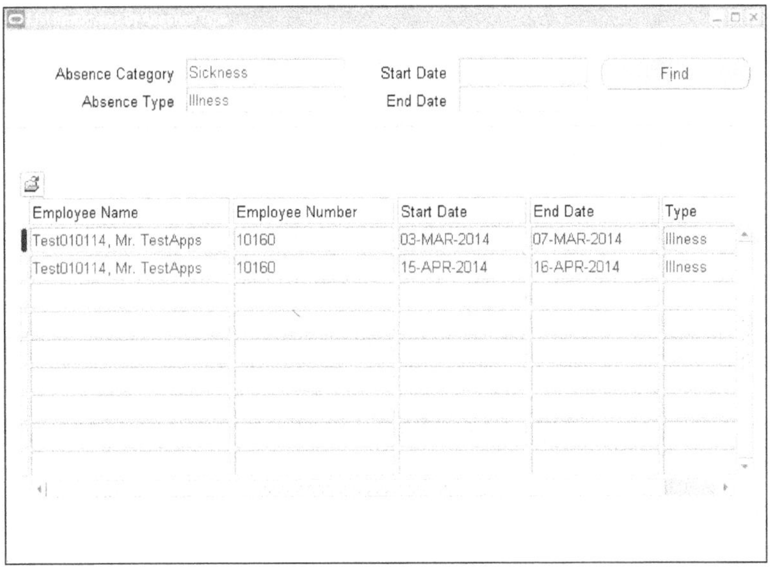

As of now, only employee number 10160 has applied for this type of leave in the application. Hence, you can see only employee number 10160 recorded in the system. There is one more report that is a concurrent program named `Absences Report`. In this report, you can view the absence for one employee for a particular period. However, the only advantage of using this report is that you can view up to 10 absence types for an employee. In the previous query, you could either view by employee or by absence type. In this report, you can view one employee for 10 absence types. You can see the program and the parameter in the following screenshot:

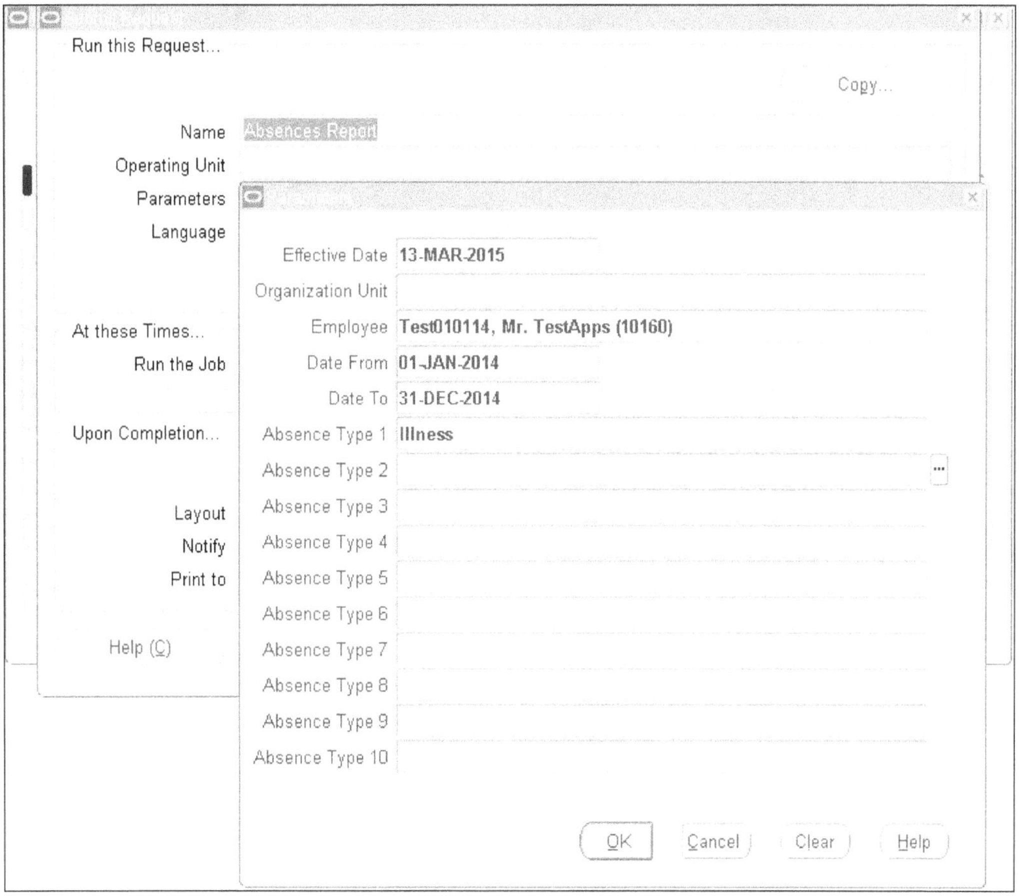

Click on **OK** and then on the **Submit** button to view the output of the program.

The output of the program will be as follows:

```
Absence Types:  Illness
    Date From:  01-JAN-2014
      Date To:  31-DEC-2014
 Organization:

Employee:  Test010114, Mr. TestApps [10160]

                                                                                                    -Length of Absence-
Type                           Reason                          Start Date            End Date                    Days     Hours
------------------------------ ------------------------------- --------------------- --------------------- ---------- ---------
Illness                                                        Monday    03-MAR-2014 Friday    07-MAR-2014          5
Illness                        Cold                            Tuesday   15-APR-2014 Wednesday 16-APR-2014          2


Summary Totals
--------------

                              ---Total Amount---              -----------------------Balance Details-----------------------
Type                              Days     Hours Occurrences Element Name        Input Value         Type       Current
----------------------------- --------- --------- ----------- ------------------- ------------------- ---------- -----------
Illness                               7                     2 Illness             Days                Increasing           7
```

So these are basic enquiries and reports that are part of absences.

Let's now see an interesting part of the absence module, which is referred to as the `BG_ABSENCE_DURATION` formula. This formula is used to calculate the duration of the absence that the employee applies for. The question that arises here is what we can do using this formula? When we configure this formula in our business group, then you can calculate the duration of absence based on the requirement of the company. Let's say there are a couple of requirements; there might be a requirement that the employee cannot have more than 5 days of Illness leave. So, if the employee tries to submit leave for more than 5 days, the system will raise an error and the employee will not be able to apply for more than 5 days. There is one further requirement that states that only male employees can take the illness leave type. If any female employee tries to apply this leave, it must show an appropriate error.

The solution for both the preceding requirements can be to use the `BG_ABSENCE_DURATION` formula. You can write your own logic in this formula to cater to these requirements. This formula is triggered by the application whenever an employee clicks on the **Calculate Duration** button on the basic absence form or from the employees self service page.

Oracle does provide a standard template for this formula named `TEMPLATE_ABSENCE_DURATION` and the type of the formula is `QuickPaint`.

To find the formula, navigate to **US HRMS Manager** | **Total Compensation** | **Basic** | **Fast Formula** | **Write Formula**. The following screenshot shows the formula provided by Oracle:

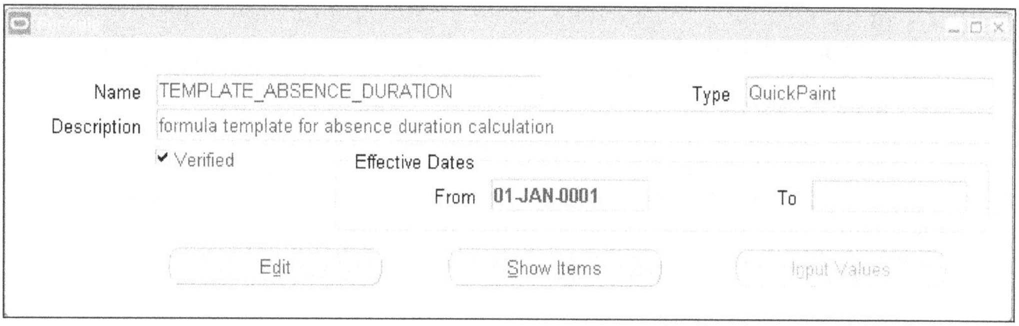

You will need to copy the code of this formula, create a new formula named `BG_ABSENCE_DURATION`, and write the logic for it in this formula.

I have copied the code from the formula `TEMPLATE_ABSENCE_DURATION` and created a new fast formula named `BG_ABSENCE_DURATION` of the same type that is `QuickPaint`.

Use the following steps to create a new formula:

1. Set the effective date from which you want to create the formula.
2. Enter the formula name.
3. Enter the formula type.
4. Click on **Edit** and paste the code from `TEMPLATE_ABSENCE_DURATION`.
5. Save the formula.

The following screenshot shows the newly created formula:

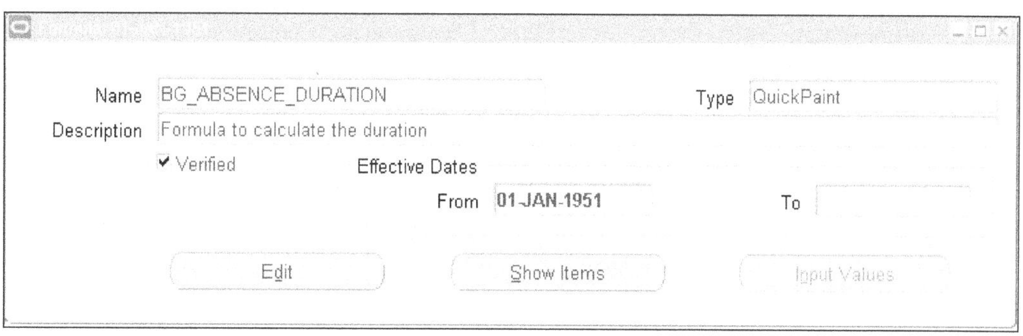

As discussed earlier, there were a couple of requirements; one was that only male employees can take leaves of type Illness and the other was that you cannot have more than 5 days of illness leave at a given point.

You can edit the formula `BG_ABSENCE_DURATION` and add the following lines of code at the end of the formula:

```
if to_num(duration) > 5 then
  (
    duration = 'FAILED'
    invalid_msg = 'Not allowed more than 5 days in this leave
    type'
  )

if PER_SEX = 'Female' then
  (
    duration = 'FAILED'
    invalid_msg = 'Only Male are allowed to take leave type'
  )
```

When I try to apply for leave for more than 5 days, then an error message will appear as in the following screenshot:

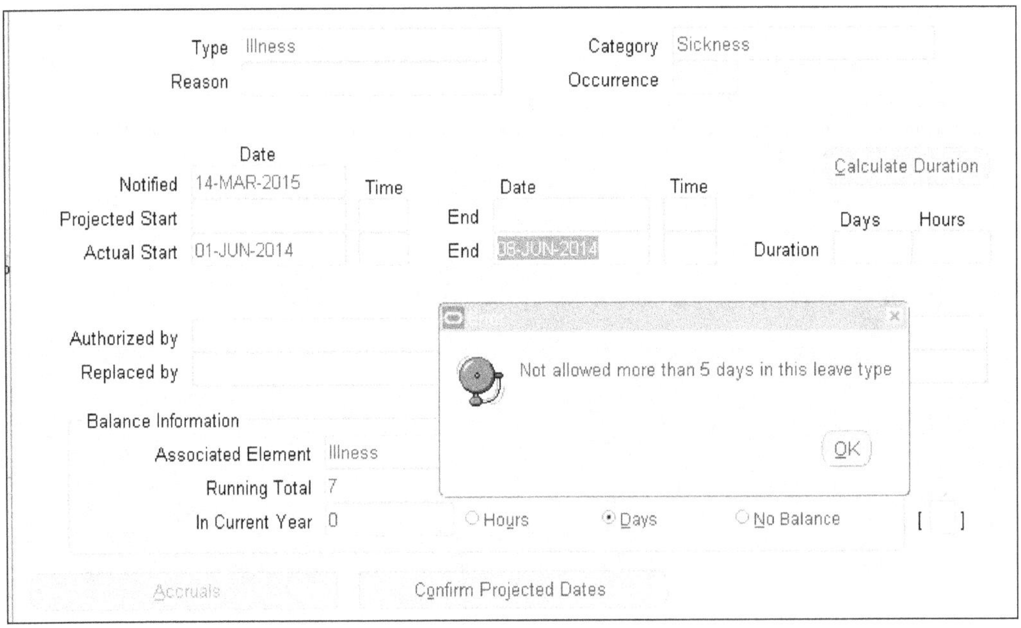

For the next case, if any female employee tries to apply for illness leave, then the following error message will appear:

Please note, the condition that we added is a generic condition and is not only for a particular leave type. Hence, this error will be fired for all absence types. You can, however, restrict this for particular absence types based on your requirements.

Summary

So, in this chapter, you have learned the basics of absence management in Oracle. You studied the configuration of absences in which you learned defining absence types, elements, and so on.

You also learned about entering absences by HR and employees. You also learned an important concept of calculation of absence duration.

Index

[PACKT] enterprise
PUBLISHING
professional expertise distilled

Oracle E-Business Suite Financials R12: A Functionality Guide

ISBN: 978-1-84968-062-2 Paperback: 336 pages

Know what Oracle E-Business Suite can do before you implement it

1. Take a deep dive into the key elements of Oracle EBS financial transaction processing.
2. Understand the functionality and critical configuration steps.
3. Master Oracle EBS product highlights and their effective usage.

Oracle CRM On Demand Administration Essentials

ISBN: 978-1-84968-500-9 Paperback: 304 pages

A one-stop implementation reference guide to Oracle CRM On Demand, the world's best-selling of CRM technology

1. Full of illustrations, diagrams, and tips with clear step-by-step instructions and real-time examples.
2. Master Application Customization by learning custom page layouts, homepage layouts, search result layouts, and dynamic layouts.
3. Understand User Management and Access Control.

Please check **www.PacktPub.com** for information on our titles

www.ingramcontent.com/pod-product-compliance
Lightning Source LLC
LaVergne TN
LVHW080047210926
848481LV00011B/3294
9781782177388